CULTURES
IN CONFLICT
THE VIET NAM
WAR

Recent Titles in
The Greenwood Press Cultures in Conflict Series

Cultures in Conflict—The American Civil War
Steven E. Woodworth

Cultures in Conflict—The Arab-Israeli Conflict
Calvin Goldscheider

CULTURES
IN CONFLICT
THE VIET NAM
WAR

Robert E. Vadas

The Greenwood Press Cultures in Conflict Series

GREENWOOD PRESS
Westport, Connecticut • London

Library of Congress Cataloging-in-Publication Data

Vadas, Robert E., 1952–
    Cultures in conflict—the Viet Nam War / Robert E. Vadas.
      p. cm.—(The Greenwood Press cultures in conflict series, ISSN 1526–0690)
    Includes bibliographical references and index.
    ISBN 0–313–31616–3 (alk. paper)
    1. Vietnamese Conflict, 1961–1975—Personal narratives. 2. Vietnamese Conflict,
  1961–1975—Sources. 3. Culture conflict. I. Title: Viet Nam War. II. Title.
  III. Series.
  DS557.7.V29 2002
  959.704'3—dc21   2001054716

British Library Cataloguing in Publication Data is available.

Library of Congress Catalog Card Number: 2001054716
ISBN: 0–313–31616–3
ISSN: 1526–0690

First published in 2002

Greenwood Press, 88 Post Road West, Westport, CT 06881
An imprint of Greenwood Publishing Group, Inc.
www.greenwood.com

Printed in the United States of America

The paper used in this book complies with the
Permanent Paper Standard issued by the National
Information Standards Organization (Z39.48–1984).

10 9 8 7 6 5 4 3 2 1

Copyright Acknowledgments

Letter excerpts from Allen Paul, John Dabonka, Marion Lee Kempner, Robert Salerni, Jack Swender, Stephen Pickett, George Ewing, William Kalwas, Bernard Robinson, Ed Vick, Howard Goldberg, and Mike Rush originally appeared in *Dear America: Letters Home from Vietnam*, ed. Bernard Edelman for the New York Vietnam Veterans Memorial Commission, published by W.W. Norton & Co. (1985) and subsequently by Pocket Books (1986).

Excerpts from Frank Denton's, "Some Effects of Military Operations on Viet Cong Attitudes" (Memorandum); David W.P. and Elliot Mai's, "Documents on Elite Viet Cong Delta Unit" (Memorandum); L. Goure, A.J. Russo, and D. Scott's, "Some Findings of the Viet Cong Motivation and Moral Study" (Memorandum); and Melvin Gurtov's, "The War in Delta: Views from Three Viet Cong Battalions" (Memorandum) are all reprinted with permission courtesy of the RAND Corporation.

Every reasonable effort has been made to trace the owners of copyright materials in this book, but in some instances this has proven impossible. The author and publisher will be glad to receive information leading to more complete acknowledgments in subsequent printings of the book and in the meantime extend their apologies for any omissions.

To those from all of the lands touched by the horror of the conflict in Viet Nam. Especially those who have dedicated their lives to understanding, reconciliation, and forgiveness in the collective dream to realize: never again.

A special thanks to my wife, Hanh, and sons, Julian and Nicholas, for their patience and support.

To those who made a special effort to assist this project: Huang Van My, Steve Hassna, Alan Canfora, John Lancaster, Martin Bolha, and my patient editor, Dr. Anjali Misra.

Contents

Preface

Perhaps there are parallel ways to truth.
Perhaps each perspective provides a special insight which is
indispensable to the complete picture.
—Ishwar C. Sharma[1]

Not since the American Civil War in the 1860s has an event caused
such division within the American people as did the war in Viet Nam.
Merely mentioning Viet Nam can still illicit strong emotions from
those who endured the painful legacies of that era. Viet Nam has
occupied a part of the American psyche that resides somewhat dor-
mant but still precariously near the surface of the collective memory
of a nation still struggling to define its meaning—a memory still ach-
ing, although not nearly as profound as in the past, a memory in the
early stages of healing, but a haunted memory created and molded
more by confused imagery than by comprehensive understanding.

These images inspire a cautious approach to the topic as many recall
a more passionate time when the wrong word could illicit an angry
or even violent response. These same cautions, however, have also
left Americans with a certainty that their perspectives and the imagery
that helped develop them are, in fact, the correct ones and that contrary views are from those who simply do not understand.

Profound cultural differences exist between Vietnamese and Americans that contributed to the horror of the war, differences that exist today and remain obstacles to reconciliation. These differences continue to alienate and have seriously prevented the nation from developing a collective understanding of the war. Most who lived through the war years have been left with a powerful melding of intense emotions and the "certainty" of the facts as they have come to be "known." This fusion has been the foundation for struggles to fit Viet Nam into its proper place in American history. As a result, the "truth" about Viet Nam has remained elusive.

Yet, within this clash of cultures lie secrets to understanding the complexities of the war as they, like all human diversity, possess hidden similarities as well. As Ishwar Sharma's words imply, in the opening quotation, perhaps there are parallel paths to finding a common truth about Viet Nam, paths that truly require mutual understanding of perspectives that still rage silently within a nation grasping for a consensus on the war. This book attempts to clarify the many perspectives and images of the war, to give these views their due, to help direct the reader along new and perhaps parallel paths of understanding, while at the same time providing an accurate and untethered exploration of the facts about a war that seems to defy understanding.

As the Viet Nam generation has aged and struggled with which "truth" to agree upon, a whole new generation, born after the war's end, quietly came of age. The enigma of the Viet Nam War lies not so much in the divisions that the war once wrought but rather in the persistent battles since the war's end over which imagery will ultimately prevail. This war of images has represented a rationale to continue the fighting of a war that appears never to end.

> "The great enemy of the truth is very often not the lie—deliberate, contrived, and dishonest—but the myth—persistent, persuasive, and unrealistic."
>
> JFK, 1960[2]

Those old enough to have lived the war were left with powerful images impressed deeply in their minds, images that seem to have grown over the years to become "truths." Most who lived the war will clearly recognize these "truths": Viet Nam was the first war America ever lost; Viet Nam veterans are lost souls who shoot people in flashback rampages; America fought the war to stop North Viet Nam from invading the South; the Viet Cong were godless Communists who preyed on their own people while sending babies to drop hand grenades on Americans; it was a war we could have won because America fought only a "limited" war; President John F. Kennedy started the war and Richard M. Nixon ended it; America lost because of the media; and so on.

These images, strongly tied to the war in Viet Nam, have one common thread: None are true. The facts on the Viet Nam War reveal data contrary to many common beliefs: Most Viet Nam veterans have led successful lives comparable with those of non-veterans their age; many "Viet Cong" were actually Buddhists and strongly believed that they were fighting for their country's independence; ex-Secretary of Defense Robert McNamara has disclosed that he knew back in 1964 that America could never have "won" the war in any realistic sense; it was President Harry S Truman who first sent U.S. troops to Viet Nam in 1950; it was President Gerald R. Ford who was in office when the war ended in 1975.

Viet Nam is not a war; it is a country, and understanding that country and its millions of inhabitants is also a major goal of this book. I spent many years traveling throughout Viet Nam and the United States, gathering stories from Vietnamese and Americans. I have attempted to address the many important concepts, issues, and themes about the war, and the stories told in this book are representative of those themes. After the war, Americans went into deep denial. Other than a few isolated teachers, the nation's schools omitted Viet Nam from its core curricula with the sad consequence that an entire generation matured with only vague ideas and misinformed images to guide them through their many questions.

> "Those who do not know history will have history created for them."
>
> George Orwell

Orwell's prophetic words describe an entire generation who have had history "created" for them by Hollywood, the press, and numerous interest groups or individuals wishing to promote their own myths and "truths." Movies like *Rambo, Hamburger Hill*, and *Platoon* helped create or perpetuate images of the war, and though many of the images might be rooted in reality, they are still limiting— limiting in that they offered no explanation and usually treated the Vietnamese as mere shadows or casual participants in the "pain" that Americans went through. In them, Viet Nam became a purely "American" ordeal that Americans "suffered." Vietnamese trauma, even though they suffered the loss of nearly 3 million people, has seldom been noted and generally is seen as irrelevant.

While teaching at SUNY Potsdam, I have had students enroll in my Viet Nam courses who bring an intense curiosity along with strong opinions, ironically, with little or no knowledge of basic facts. It is this irony that has come to symbolize the need to reconstruct Viet Nam's myth-laden legacies into a confident understanding of the war. To accomplish this, I have presented dozens of primary documents in somewhat of a chronological order in chapters 3 through 6, divided into two basic categories: documents from all sides of the conflict, such as letters and prison documents, and stories of ordinary participants (or perhaps "less famous" should be used, as their stories are anything but ordinary) that weave into discussions of the major controversies and issues of the war. In this way, major sides of the conflict are addressed. It has been my goal to address major perspectives associated with Viet Nam, and I apologize to the many people whose stories I was unable to integrate into this book for lack of space. I understand that a thorough understanding of Viet Nam is strongly tied to the multitude of stories borne of the war, and until these untold stories are heard, the final "truth" about Viet Nam patiently waits to be discovered.

NOTES

1. St. Elmo Nauman, Jr. *Dictionary of Asian Philosophies.* "Introduction" by Ishmar C. Sharma (Secaucus, NJ: Citadel Press, Philosophical Library, 1978), xi.

2. John F. Kennedy. Public campaign speech, September 1960.

A Note on Terms

News accounts, documentaries, and specials on Viet Nam continue to refer to "Communist forces" or simply the "Communists." The term "Viet Cong" was, and continues to be, used in almost all references. American GIs fighting the war used a wide range of adjectives to describe their enemy and the people of Viet Nam in general, including gook, slant, slope, momma san, and Charley or, when respect was given, Mr. Charles. The Vietnamese in turn also had their own terminology for the Americans and their allies. Americans were called crooked noses or monkeys, both derogatory in Vietnamese, and *de quoâc My* (aggressive imperialist Americans). They referred to the Army of the Republic of Viet Nam (ARVN) as "puppet" forces and to the South government as the "puppet" regime.

The terminology used in this book reflects historical accuracy for both sides unless the context, or personal text or quotes, allows for the use of the more common slang. Americans are referred to as U.S. forces or the U.S. Army, Navy, Marines, or Air Force. Soldiers fighting for the South government are referred to as ARVN. Soldiers fighting for Ho Chi Minh's Democratic Republic of Viet Nam are called People's Army of Viet Nam (PAVN), and those fighting for the military wing of the National Liberation Front in the South are People's Liberation Army (PLA). The PLA fighters referred to themselves as *boí doí giai phoøng* (liberation front soldiers), thus the many references in personal letters to the simplified "front."

VIETNAMESE LANGUAGE

Linguists are not certain of the origins of Vietnamese, but most agree that it is a mixture of Thai, Mon-Khmer, and Muong languages interspersed with a healthy dose of Chinese. Early documents were written in Chu Nho, although spoken Vietnamese sounded different. Thirteenth-century Vietnamese scholars altered this form into a Vietnamese variation called Chu Nom. In the sixteenth century, however, Catholic missionaries introduced a romanized system of writing called Quoc Ngu. As a result, Vietnamese is written in a script familiar to most Westerners. Vietnamese is a tonal language, and voice inflections can dramatically change the meaning of most words.

Acronyms

ARVN Army of the Republic of Viet Nam. The army of the "South Viet Nam" government, trained and equipped by the U.S. government and military.

CIA Central Intelligence Agency. U.S. intelligence-gathering organization developed during the "Cold War." Used mainly to wage war on communism throughout the world, the CIA was deeply involved in Viet Nam from the 1940s until 1975.

COINTELPRO Counter Intelligence Program. This was set up during Richard Nixon's presidency to engage the Federal Bureau of Investigation in efforts to disrupt, spy on, and discredit antiwar activists including Viet Nam veterans.

DRV Democratic Republic of Viet Nam. What Ho Chi Minh's Northern "regroupment area" was called from 1946 to 1975.

HUAC Begun in 1938, the U.S. House of Representatives Un-American Activities Committee pursued Americans who were vocal in their dissent against American policies or engaged in activities deemed un-American. HUAC was at center stage of the so-called McCarthy hearings during the 1950s, led by Senator Joseph McCarthy, and the efforts to root out Communists in the motion picture industry.

NLF National Liberation Front. Coalition organization created in 1959 to unify resistance to Ngo Dinh Diem's South Viet Nam government.

NVA North Vietnamese Army. Reference to PAVN forces by Americans.

OSS Office of Strategic Services. Commando and intelligence-gathering organization of the United States during World War II.

PAVN   People's Army of Viet Nam. The armed forces of the DRV, usually
            referred to as "NVA" by Americans.

PLA   People's Liberation Army. The military wing of the NLF. The PLA
            were called "Viet Cong" by Diem and later by Americans.

ROTC   Reserve Officers' Training Corps. Many American universities
            worked with the U.S. military in providing educational oppor-
            tunities for young men and women training to be officers in the
            various branches of service. During the height of the Viet Nam
            War, these ROTCs became the focus of antimilitary and war pro-
            tests on campuses.

SEATO   South East Asia Treaty Organization. Started by the United States
            in 1954 as an anti-Communist organization, SEATO was unable
            to achieve unity of all its eight partners. Because of political dif-
            ferences, SEATO was disbanded in 1977. Some U.S. officials
            used SEATO as justification for U.S. intervention in Viet Nam.
            Viet Nam, however, never was a member, and U.S. intervention
            began before SEATO.

SRV   Socialist Republic of Viet Nam. Title proclaimed on July 2, 1976,
            for the reunified nation of Viet Nam.

A Viet Nam Timeline of Key Events

931	Battle of Bach Dang: Using guerrilla tactics, Vietnamese general Ngo Quyen defeats a Chinese invasion, ending 1,000 years of Chinese rule.
1803	U.S. Captain John Briggs is the first American to set foot on Viet Nam soil.
1845	The U.S.S. *Constitution* shells Da Nang to free French missionaries.
1858	French conquest begins.
1925	The Communist party gains credibility with Vietnamese as an alternative to French rule.
1941	Japan solidifies control over Viet Nam.
1941	Nguyen Ai Quoc and others form the Viet Nam Doc Lap Dong Minh, called the "Viet Minh."
1945	Viet Minh forces fight guerrilla war against Japanese. U.S. bombers and then of the Office of Strategic Services officers assist Ho Chi Minh.
August 1945	Japanese forces surrender.
September 2, 1945	Ho Chi Minh claims Viet Nam's independence from French.
September 23, 1945	French and British forces regain control of Viet Nam.
September 26, 1945	U.S. Lieutenant Colonel A. Peter Dewey is killed

	by guerrillas in Saigon, the first American to die in Viet Nam.
August 2, 1950	Ten American soldiers arrive in Viet Nam as advisors.
June 18, 1954	French defeat at Dien Bien Phu leads to cease-fire.
July 22, 1954	The Geneva Accords call for a two-year truce between Ho's Northern parts of Viet Nam and the French-created South Viet Nam.
1955	President Ngo Dinh Diem's regime in the South prohibits elections and wages a war against political opposition.
May 1959	At the Fifteenth Plenum of the Central Committee in the North, a call is made for "helping the Southerners overthrow Diem and expel the United States."
December 1960	The National Liberation Front is formed in the South as a united front dedicated to overthrowing Diem.
November 1963	President Diem is assassinated.
November 23, 1963	President John F. Kennedy is assassinated.
August 5, 1964	The Gulf of Tonkin Resolution is passed by the U.S. Senate. This gives President Lyndon B. Johnson authority "to prevent the defeat of South Viet Nam."
March 8, 1965	U.S. Marines, first combat troops, land at Da Nang.
November 1965	First major ground engagement between U.S. and Vietnamese forces occurs in the Ia Drang Valley.
May 1966	Buddhists throughout South Viet Nam rise up in protest against government policies and the American presence in Viet Nam.
July 15, 1966	U.S. Marines launch Operation "Hastings."
January 8, 1967	U.S. forces launch massive drive to sweep People's Liberation Army (PLA) forces from Cu Chi and "Iron Triangle" Districts in Operation Cedar Falls.
October 21, 1967	Fifty thousand antiwar protesters march to the Pentagon in Washington, D.C., in the first major U.S. protest against the war in Viet Nam.

November 23, 1967	Units of the 173rd Airborne Brigade capture Hill 875 after several days of brutal fighting.
January 31, 1968	Coinciding with Tet Nguyen Dan, PAVN and PLA forces launch major attacks throughout South Viet Nam.
March 16, 1968	U.S. soldiers slaughter 504 villagers in My Lai hamlet.
March 31, 1968	President Johnson removes himself from the presidential race and commits to Paris Peace Talks and ending the war.
July 1968	For the first time ever, a majority of Americans favor pulling out of Viet Nam.
November 1968	Richard M. Nixon, promising a "secret" plan to end the war, wins a narrow victory in a three-way U.S. presidential race.
January 25, 1969	The first session of the four-way Paris Peace Talks begins.
February 1969	Nixon begins secret bombings of Cambodia.
April 30, 1969	U.S. troop levels peak at 543,400.
May 8, 1969	Nixon orders the first American troops home.
May 11, 1969	The battle for Dong Ap Bia (Hamburger Hill) begins as U.S. troops assault a fortified ridge in the Highlands.
September 2, 1969	Ho Chi Minh dies in Hanoi. Vietnamese leaders pledge to fight on.
April 30, 1970	U.S. forces invade Cambodia to destroy PLA sanctuaries.
May 4, 1970	Four students are killed at Kent State University by National Guardsmen during protests of the Cambodian invasion. Two more die at Jackson State University in Mississippi a few days later.
June 24, 1970	The U.S. Senate, by a vote of eighty-one to ten, repeals the Gulf of Tonkin Resolution. President Nixon ignores this as irrelevant.
January 1971	Viet Nam veterans testify at the Winter Soldier Investigation Hearings in Detroit, Michigan.
March 6, 1971	Army of the Republic of Viet Nam forces, with U.S. troops in a minor supporting role, invade Laos to cut Ho Chi Minh Trail.

May 1971	Viet Nam War veterans toss their medals over the White House gates to protest the war.
June 13, 1971	The *New York Times* begins publication of classified government documents on Viet Nam called the "Pentagon Papers." These papers contradicted many statements to the American public.
March 1972	Offensive by PAVN forces involves conventional warfare for the first time during what is called the "Easter Offensive."
May 8, 1972	Nixon orders the mining of all North Vietnamese ports as a result of the Easter Offensive.
August 1972	Nixon is nominated for a second term as thousands protest outside the convention hall in Miami, Florida.
November 1972	Nixon wins in a landslide over Democratic candidate George McGovern.
December 1972	Nixon orders "Christmas" bombings of Hanoi in an attempt to force Hanoi into signing the peace accords.
January 1973	The United States signs a peace accord with the North. Last U.S. combat forces are scheduled to depart Viet Nam. Prisoners of War (POWs) are to be returned.
January 27, 1973	The draft ends. America turns to an all-volunteer service.
January 27, 1973	The Paris Peace Accords are signed to end American involvement in Viet Nam.
February to March 1973	Operation "Homecoming" involves the release of U.S. POWs.
November 7, 1973	Over Nixon's veto, Congress enacts the War Powers Act.
August 9, 1974	President Nixon resigns in disgrace. Vice President Gerald R. Ford takes over.
March 24, 1975	PAVN and PLA forces launch their "Ho Chi Minh" campaign to end the war with a major push toward Saigon.
April 29 to 30, 1975	U.S. troops evacuate thousands of American and Vietnamese personnel as PAVN forces ring Saigon.

April 30, 1975   PAVN and PLA forces take Saigon, ending the war.

February 1979   To "punish" Viet Nam for its military assault on the Khmer Rouge in Kampuchea (Cambodia), China invades Viet Nam.

November 23, 1982   The Viet Nam Memorial, since referred to as the "Wall," is dedicated in Washington, D.C., as thousands of Viet Nam veterans march.

1978 to 1984   An estimated 1 million Vietnamese flee intense poverty, the war with Kampuchea, and government policies in Viet Nam.

1988   Viet Nam announces "Doi Moi," or renovation, to begin an "open door" policy of economic expansion and trade.

November 1992   William J. Clinton is elected president of the United States and reexamines U.S. policies toward Viet Nam.

February 1994   President Clinton lifts the U.S. economic embargo on Viet Nam.

July 11, 1995   President Clinton officially extends diplomatic recognition to Viet Nam. American businesses begin economic investment there.

May 9, 1997   Pete Peterson, an ex-POW in Hanoi, becomes U.S. ambassador to Viet Nam.

March 8, 2000   U.S. Secretary of Defense William Cohen travels to Viet Nam and discusses future military cooperation between the two nations.

November 2000   President Clinton visits Viet Nam, the first U.S. president since the end of the war, the first president ever to visit Hanoi.

PART I

CULTURAL AND HISTORICAL PERSPECTIVES

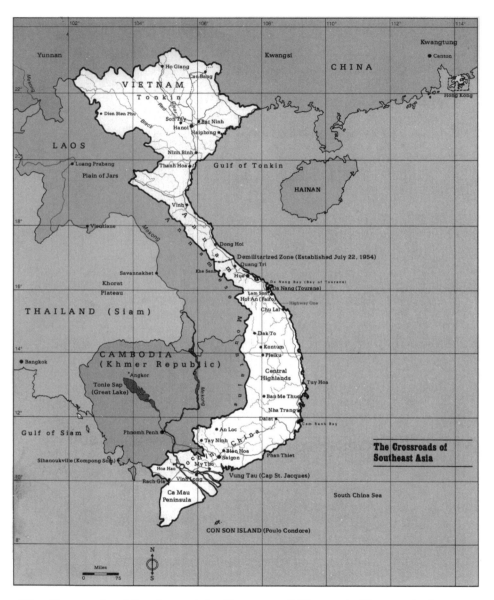

The Crossroads of Southeast Asia. Courtesy of *Newsweek*, Newsweek, Inc. All rights reserved. Reprinted by permission.

Chapter 1

A Historical Review of the Viet Nam War

HISTORICAL BACKGROUND

The American involvement in Viet Nam has its roots in the institution of European colonialism, more specifically, French efforts to colonize Southeast Asia in the late 1800s. After centuries of internal conflict and domination from China, Viet Nam entered the nineteenth century with hope for their elusive independence. The Nguyen dynasty, begun in 1802, witnessed a rise in anti-Catholic sentiment. Reacting to the growing interference in village affairs from French Catholic missionaries, Vietnamese officials introduced antimissionary policies that gave France the excuse to intervene directly into the affairs of Viet Nam.

Arriving in 1858, as part of an effort to force China into a satisfactory trade agreement and to stabilize Indochina for the exploitation of Viet Nam's resources, French troops landed in Tourane Bay (Da Nang) and later sailed south and captured the city of Saigon. Like many French, Japanese, and American forces who would later follow, initial French military efforts were plagued with high losses from disease in the tropical climate, supply problems, and guerrilla warfare from a Vietnamese populace that refused to quietly accept domination under a French rule whose cruelty continuously spawned numerous rebellions. As Viet Nam entered the twentieth century, the tone of the revolts took on the revolutionary ideals that were sweeping the continents, exemplified by the revolution in Russia in 1917.

Each uprising escalated the violence, with brutal reprisal from the French. After every defeat, surviving Vietnamese urged their children to continue their ancient struggle for independence (tranh dau) and avenge the death or imprisonment of their fathers. One, twenty-nine-year-old, Nguyen Ai Quoc, audaciously petitioned the Versailles Peace Conference, then deciding the fate of postwar Europe, for Vietnamese independence. The petition was quickly denied, but the tone was set for a revolutionary movement to oust the French. This led to the development of the first Communist organization in Viet Nam in 1925. This movement appealed to the many fledgling peasant anticolonial organizations that had aligned themselves against French rule and included several dynamic young leaders. Along with Nguyen Ai Quoc, Vo Nguyen Giap and Pham Van Dong organized "people's soviets," or ruling committees made up of farmers, in two provinces and redistributed land to desperate peasant farmers. The French reacted with brutal efficiency and nearly destroyed the revolution. Estimates run as high as 10,000 Vietnamese killed by the French with tens of thousands more sent to prisons throughout Indochina. The surviving party members withdrew to remote regions and set about planning future rebellions.

The fall of France in 1940 left a pro-German government in southern France that still controlled colonies in Indochina. Japan's aggressive expansion in the Pacific led to the signing of the Franco–Japanese joint defense treaty for Indochina. On March 9, 1945, nearly ninety years of French rule came to an end when Japanese troops took over Viet Nam and arrested the French Governor Admiral Jean Decoux.

The Vietnamese resistance leaders met in the remote village of Pac Bo on May 10, 1941, and organized an inclusive party platform to defeat both the French and the Japanese invaders. There, the Viet Nam Doc Lap Dong Minh (Viet Nam Independence League) was formed for a unified effort to create an independent Viet Nam. This party, "Viet Minh" for short, recognized Nguyen Ai Quoc as its leader and began strengthening political and military organizations throughout Viet Nam.

THE UNITED STATES GETS INVOLVED: THE FIRST INDOCHINA WAR

While revolutionary storms gathered in Viet Nam, political upheaval developed throughout the region, including China, Viet Nam's northern neighbor. China's civil war saw Mao Zedong's revolution vying for control against the Kuomintang (Chinese Nationalists). In early 1942, these nationalists arrested Nguyen Ai Quoc and forced the Viet Minh underground. After nearly a year in China, he was released and arrived in the Viet Minh base camp in Cao Bang with a new name, Ho Chi Minh (One Who Enlightens). China finally recognized the Viet Minh to lead Viet Nam against the Japanese, and the decision received instant support from the United States.

During World War II, Japan had used Viet Nam's ports to ship natural resources back to Japan and the country as a staging area for assaults in the Pacific theater. For these reasons, the United States viewed Ho Chi Minh and the Viet Minh as useful to the Allied war effort. Cutting these supply lines from Southeast Asia to Japan became a major goal of General Claire Lee Chennault's "Flying Tiger" forces fighting in China, and soon U.S. forces began to bomb Viet Nam's port facilities as the Viet Minh tied down Japanese troops, provided intelligence, and returned downed pilots to China.

In January of 1945, with Germany and Japan losing the war, President Franklin D. Roosevelt worked out a tacit agreement with England after Winston Churchill became angered by Roosevelt's anticolonialist rhetoric. Roosevelt was sensitive to his European allies but regarding Indochina he was less so, writing to his Secretary of State Cordell Hull that "France has had the country . . . for nearly one hundred years and the people are far worse off than they were at the start."[1] The Americans began working collaboratively with Ho Chi Minh as medicine and military hardware were parachuted to Viet Minh forces in remote mountain enclaves along with American Office of Strategic Services (OSS) members.

In August 1945, Japan surrendered to the Viet Minh, giving Ho's forces a sizable military prize of weapons. Ho announced on September 2, 1945, to a large and ecstatic crowd assembled in Hanoi, that Viet Nam was a free and independent nation. At that ceremony, Ho read the new Declaration of Independence, which, ironically, was written with a heavy influence of the American Declaration of Independence from 1776 (Appendix A).

Within days, the last emperor of Viet Nam, Bao Dai, abdicated. Viet Nam was finally free. Ho lost little time in establishing a new government, and on September 8, 1945, he signed a decree calling for the election of a national assembly for the new nation, now called the Democratic Republic of Viet Nam (DRV). Campaigns were waged to rebuild the shattered economy, and land reform swept the nation. The most significant policy that the Viet Minh enacted was the redistribution of land to the peasants, giving the DRV a solid foundation of support with the Vietnamese people.

The major powers of the United States, Soviet Union, England, and France met to discuss the new world order at Potsdam, Germany, on July 16, 1945. Little attention was paid to the legitimacy of the Viet Minh to rule in Viet Nam. The United States agreed to allow British, Chinese, and French forces to occupy Viet Nam when the Japanese surrendered on August 13, 1945.

The task for organizing postwar Viet Nam was given to Lord Louis Mountbatten, supreme commander of all British forces in Asia, who passed on the responsibility to General Douglas Gracey. Gracey was given clear orders not to "reestablish" French rule, but Gracey was strongly attached to British colonialism and felt it appropriate to assist the French in regaining their former colonies.

Reacting to Gracey's neo-colonial attitude, the Viet Minh organized a series of strikes against British authorities in Saigon. In response, Gracey declared martial law on September 17, 1945. He then set about arming former French prisoners and ironically, Japanese troops, who proceeded to move throughout Saigon and into the surrounding villages. On September 23, French troops under Colonel Jean Cedile stormed the city hall, arrested members of the ruling Viet Minh, and raised the French tricolor flag over Saigon. The Viet Minh responded by organizing guerrilla resistance. The British and French formed a new government in Saigon as their troops attacked Viet Minh forces. On October 16, 1945, the Viet Minh were forced out of Saigon, not returning until April 1975. The First Indochina War was on.

The end of World War II shifted the balance of world power to the United States and the Soviet Union. Perceiving the United States as a nation he could turn to, Ho Chi Minh sent a message to President Harry S Truman, requesting that the United States pressure the British to cease their efforts at recolonization (Appendix B). Truman ignored this and seven more communiqués sent between September and December 1945. The Viet Minh felt betrayed by this change in policy, a change traced to President Roosevelt's sudden death in Georgia in April 1945. Harry S Truman, bringing an entirely different philosophy to the presidency, saw a Communist conspiracy in the growing power of the Soviet Union and the many postwar rebellions around the globe. With Communist movements in China, Greece, Turkey, Poland, North Korea, Yugoslavia, and other nations, Truman was not concerned with independence movements in Indochina. Most Americans were unaware of the growing political turmoil that would eventually catapult the United States into a costly war in Viet Nam, though some, such as General of the Army Douglas MacArthur, did openly oppose U.S. involvement, stating: "If there is anything that makes my blood boil, it is to see our allies in Indochina . . . deploying Japanese troops to reconquer the people we promised to liberate. It is the most ignoble kind of betrayal."[2]

OSS Lieutenant Colonel Peter Dewey, who became the first American casualty of the new war when he was accidentally shot in a Viet Minh ambush in Saigon, also opposed the policy, writing to his command just before his death that "CochinChina is burning, the French and British are finished here, we ought to clear out of Southeast Asia."[3]

Major Archimedes Patti, an OSS agent, met with Ho Chi Minh and explained why Truman would not assist the Viet Minh. Patti told Ho that Washington saw him as Moscow's puppet. Ho responded that he was a "free agent" and nobody's stooge and that his sole mission in life was to gain independence for his beloved Viet Nam. Though a U.S. State Department investigation in July 1948 concluded that Ho had no direct ties to Russia or China, Americans were in no frame of mind to see Ho as anything but a puppet of Russia and China. Ho's allegiance was the center of a growing Cold War debate among officials in Washington and London, and President Truman took the stance that given the situation in postwar China, the United States could ill afford a Viet Minh victory in Indochina.

The United States allied with the French, and in 1947 Truman granted $160 million in credit to give military assistance to the French. Russian leader Joseph Stalin ignored this American venture, and Ho stated, in response, that "we apparently stand quite alone."[4]

To facilitate the delivery of military hardware to the French, the United States sent, on August 2, 1950, the first troops, ten U.S. Army officers, to set up the Military Assistance Advisory Group in Viet Nam. By the end of 1951, the total strength in Viet Nam rose to 128 military advisors with an additional 200 air force technicians arriving in January of 1953. The situation in Korea, in which North Korea troops, armed with Russian weapons, charged across the 38th Parallel to destroy the South Korean government, intensified Truman's resolve to fight and contain "Communist aggression" wherever, and as a result, Truman pushed U.S. involvement in Viet

Nam even deeper. By 1954 the United States was financing 81 percent of the French war effort as trucks, planes, tanks, and guns were
delivered to Indochina.

The French were never able to pacify the rebellion. Using tactics
closely resembling those later employed by the Americans, French
troops were vulnerable to ambush, and support in France waned as
the war dragged on. French morale sagged as casualties mounted.
The French, like the Americans in the 1960s, attempted their own
Vietnamization policy, but for the most part, the majority of Vietnamese peasants either sided with the Viet Minh or remained neutral.
As defeats mounted, a new French leader, General Henri Navarre,
took the war to the remote regions of northern Viet Nam. Building
an "undefeatable" series of forts around the small hamlet of Dien
Bien Phu, Navarre believed that he could root out the enemy from
their remote hideouts and cut them off from supplies. It was the
French, however, that were cut off as thousands of Viet Minh eventually encircled the besieged forts, and on March 13, 1954, the Viet
Minh launched an intense artillery bombardment on the French with
guns that the French believed could not be made available in the
rugged mountain terrain. The French surrendered on May 8, 1954.
An uneasy truce settled over Indochina as a conference was organized
in Geneva, Switzerland. Nearly 100,000 people died in the nine years
of war, with hundreds of thousands more wounded or made homeless. Three Americans died, two from combat. In the summer of
1954, representatives from France, the Viet Minh, the United States,
China, the Soviet Union, and Britain met to peacefully end the conflict in Indochina. The Geneva Accords that resulted on July 21,
1954, however, did little to resolve the overall situation in Viet Nam
and laid the groundwork for continued hostilities. The accords called
for a cease-fire, a temporary partition of Viet Nam into two "regroupment" areas—north and south of the seventeenth parallel, withdrawal
of the French within two years, and an election in 1956 after the
French withdrawal in all of Viet Nam to determine the nation's future. The French had reinstated Bao Dai as a leader in the southern
parts of Viet Nam during the war, and neither Bao Dai nor Ho was
happy about a divided nation. Both sides agreed to compromise, but
for differing reasons. The Viet Minh, in a position of power capable
of defeating French forces, were urged to compromise by China and
the Soviet Union. Ho was also very reluctant to continue a bloody
war when he felt confident that he could easily win an election in two

years; as a result, the Viet Minh agreed to the accords. Bao Dai, on the other hand, had little authority other than the French to assist his position and sought a truce in order to build a new nation, one that was favorable to the West and therefore could rely upon U.S. support, with Vietnamese Catholics being used as a political base. The Americans wanted a chance to build a non-Communist nation and favored a truce. They feared an election that could result in complete control by the Viet Minh because of Ho Chi Minh's popularity.

The United States refused to sign the accords but did, however, agree in principle that it would "refrain from the threat or use of force" to disrupt the accords. With a wary eye on Communist China after Mao's victory over the nationalists in 1949, the United States stated that it would "view any renewal of aggression with grave concern and as seriously threatening international peace and security."[5]

By October of 1954, the French withdrew from Hanoi, and thousands of Viet Minh soldiers once again entered their capital as a victorious army. Many Vietnamese took advantage of the 300 days of free movement provided for by the Geneva Accords. Hundreds of thousands of Catholics, many of whom were anti-Communist and fearful of retribution from the Viet Minh for assisting the French, headed toward the areas around Saigon. Many loyalists from the south were sent north for further training within Viet Minh political or military organizations. This unexpected influx of humanity stretched the already thin and fragile logistical system in place at the time, and this well-publicized human drama brought Viet Nam into the American news front at a national level for the very first time.

In February 1954, U.S. pilots, in a highly classified operation called "Paul Revere," began flying cargo planes in support of the French war effort. By May 1954, at the time of the fall of Dien Bien Phu, there were 462 U.S. military personnel inside Viet Nam, of which 5 became the first U.S. prisoners of war (POWs) on June 14, 1954, when Viet Minh soldiers took them into custody. They were later released on August 31, 1954, after the Geneva Accords were put into place.[6]

The reports of thousands of Vietnamese fleeing "Communist aggression" fanned the flames of the growing anti-Communist sentiment in the United States. Coming at the peak of the McCarthy–Army hearings, in which now even members of the U.S. military were accused of being Communists by Senator Joseph McCarthy and the House of Un-American Activities, it was now evident that America's fight against communism might well be in a small country in Southeast Asia. The American people were little disposed to question the growing commitment in Viet Nam.

In 1954, then-U.S. Secretary of State John Foster Dulles sent Colonel Edward Lansdale of the Central Intelligence Agency (CIA) to Saigon to provide information on the growing chaos in Viet Nam. Dwight D. Eisenhower had replaced Truman as president and was persuaded by his advisors to continue the American presence there. Lansdale ordered a CIA team to the Hanoi area to begin psychological operations or "psywar," designed to promote anticommunism and sabotage Viet Minh efforts to develop a government in Hanoi.

THE SECOND INDOCHINA WAR

> "Americans do not like long, protracted wars with many casualties. I intend to give America such a war."
>
> Ho Chi Minh, 1956[7]

Ho Chi Minh, confident of victory in the projected elections, set about consolidating Viet Minh power and building the new DRV. While never losing sight of their ultimate goal—a unified Viet Nam free of foreign influence, the worker cadres and peasants that had assisted Ho in his struggle against the Japanese and French toiled endlessly to rebuild the war-torn nation. Cutting deals with Russia and China, Ho was able to bring a steady flow of goods, currency, and technicians into Viet Nam. While rebuilding the agricultural and industrial bases on the Red River, Hanoi, and Haiphong areas, the DRV was able, by 1957, to claim an economic success that rivaled any in Asia. The success was not without controversy, however, as Ho's collectivization of many farms coincided with a sometimes brutal purging of landlords deemed "enemies of the people." This purging sent tens of thousand to prison, with perhaps hundreds being executed.

The DRV, by 1959, had become a relatively strong economic force in Southeast Asia, with Ho ruling with a stable, albeit harsh, government that most Vietnamese accepted as improving their general standard of living.

The Geneva Accords did not mention a "North" or "South" Viet Nam, instead referring to a temporary separation of Viet Nam into two "regroupment zones." But when the Geneva Conference was convened in 1954, the United States and France turned to a strongly anti-Communist Catholic named Ngo Dinh Diem. Diem was perceived by U.S. officials as perfect for developing a new nation: He was Catholic and pro-West, had an anticolonial reputation, and, after visiting the United States and meeting with Eisenhower's approval, appeared competent. While Diem seemed perfect to the Americans, he was equally imperfect to most Vietnamese. Being Catholic in a predominantly Buddhist nation did not bode well with most peasants, and he was perceived as a "foreign puppet."

The United States began pouring millions of dollars into Diem's effort at nation building, betting on the idea that a successful economy in the South might entice the masses of pro–Ho Chi Minh peasants throughout Viet Nam into rejecting Ho's call for a unified socialist nation. Diem's difficulties were severe in that he lacked a well trained and highly motivated army. The Viet Minh, now called the "People's Army of Viet Nam" (PAVN), gave Ho power to establish firm rule in the North, a stabilizing influence that was lacking in the political chaos found in the South. In an October coup in which General Nguyen Van Hinh was to take power for Bao Dai, Diem was rescued by the CIA chief of operations in Saigon Colonel Lansdale. Using bribery when necessary or outright force, Diem surprised his staunchest foes, managing to break up several religious sects such as the Cao Dai and the Hoa Hao, which offered powerful military resistance to the new Diem regime not far from Saigon itself.

Flush with victory, Diem organized an assembly and a constitution giving himself great powers. In the United States, officials waved a sigh of relief as they now felt confident that Diem could lead the anti-Communist fight that Washington, D.C., desired (see Appendix B). Diem now turned his attention to eliminating revolutionary sentiment entrenched throughout the Vietnamese countryside where the Viet Minh controlled nearly two-thirds of the South's villages and nearly half of the country. In 1955 Diem initiated his "Anti-Communist Denunciation Campaign" and began to seek and destroy the many Viet Minh cadres that existed everywhere in South Viet Nam. By 1956 a decree allowing for the arrest of anyone suspected of being dangerous to the state resulted in the closing down of newspapers, the arrest and execution of many former Viet Minh, and the general persecution of all political dissidents. By the summer of 1956, the loosely connected plethora of revolutionary organizations were severely diminished, with the survivors fleeing to the North or to the more remote areas of the South. Nguyen Van Linh, one of the few cadre leaders of that time to survive, in an interview, told how Diem's

Denunciation Campaign in 1955 was the worst time that the resistance experienced in all the years of fighting and looked back on those years as a "ferocious time."[8]

Though these moves assured Diem of American support, they did nothing to align the majority of farmers and workers with the new government. In 1956 Diem proceeded to his most controversial move yet: the refusal to honor the Geneva Accords elections that were coming due.

The defeat of the French at Dien Bien Phu in 1954 left Ho's forces in a position of power. The French were defeated yet still held sizable portions of Viet Nam. Ho was willing to gamble that the French would leave and that the Geneva compromises he made would pay off in a bloodless reunification of a free and independent Viet Nam— a policy that angered many Viet Minh such as Le Duan, Ho's future successor, who felt Ho was foolish to believe that either the French or the United States would allow open elections. Ho declared during his Tet speech in 1955 that "we shall work closely and broadly from the north to south and support our southern compatriots in their struggle for freedom and democracy in conformity with the Geneva Agreement. . . . All this work must be done to prepare the ground for free general elections for national reunification."[9]

As the deadline approached, Ho realized that his gamble had failed. Diem's successes in the South left no indication that any elections would be held at all. By July of 1956, the deadline for elections had passed and Diem refused to participate, stating that he could not be guaranteed the elections in the North would be free and open. Ho responded with tirades against the United States, claiming on July 6, 1954, that "U.S. imperialists and the pro-American authorities in South Viet Nam have been plotting to partition our country permanently and prevent the holding of free general elections as provided for by the Geneva Agreements."[10]

Diem responded by denouncing the "communist regime in the north,"[11] while the press in the United States fanned anti-Communist fervor against Ho's anti-American statements. The stage was now set for the renewal of fighting in Viet Nam.

The Geneva Accords did not, and probably could not, stop a perhaps inevitable clash between a revolutionary movement determined to unify Viet Nam and a new world superpower, a United States convinced that Viet Nam was the place to stop the spread of communism. Ho Chi Minh violated the accords by keeping organized

Viet Minh in the South regroupment zone, Diem violated the accords by denying free elections, and the United States violated the accords by increasing its military presence above the Geneva Accords limit of 342 men. The United States claimed that it never signed the accords, although it did violate its promise not to intervene by engaging in nation building in South Viet Nam.

By 1960 nearly 700 U.S. military personnel, mostly advisors attempting to train Diem's forces, were in place in Viet Nam. By January 1961, when John F. Kennedy (JFK) took office, over 3,000 Americans were in South Viet Nam. Although the American effort in Viet Nam had become extensive by 1960, the conflict there was still a predominantly Vietnamese affair as fewer than fifteen American soldiers had been killed in action supporting Diem's forces.

Various organizations tied to former Viet Minh began fighting back at Diem's ruthless persecution. By late 1956, Le Duan wired Ho and reported the dire situation that Diem's policies had created. He implored Ho to take action lest the movement in the South should quickly vanish. China and the Soviet Union, allied in principle with the DRV, cautioned against going to war too soon. In July of 1957, Mao Zedong recommended that the Vietnamese people wait much longer in "ambush" for the correct time to reunify Viet Nam.

The Southern cadres, meanwhile, continued to resist Diem until late 1958. By then, Le Duan again implored Ho to intervene, and this time, going against the recommendations of China, Ho agreed. In May 1959 at the Fifteenth Plenum of the Central Committee of the DRV Communist party, a call was made to help Southern cadres overthrow Diem and oust the United States. The first order of business was for PAVN General Vo Bam to be ordered, on May 19, 1959, to expand a series of jungle trails running through the Truong Son Mountains into a passable road in which the Southern rebels could be supplied by Hanoi. This road, to be known as the Ho Chi Minh Trail, soon became the lifeline of the revolution. By November of 1959, People's Liberation Army (PLA) units in the South began to raid isolated South Vietnamese government outposts. Terrorist activities were begun, and several local leaders and government agents were killed by execution squads. This policy of executing Vietnamese tax collectors, government officials, police agents, and others working for Diem would become an effective means of inciting terror in those Vietnamese willing to collaborate with the Americans or the South Vietnamese government. It also was used by the American press to incite American public opinion against the "Viet Cong," as the PLA came to be known. As the kidnappings and killings increased, many government officials resigned from their posts out of fear.

Diem intensified his persecution of those associated with the revolution, Communist or not, and initiated several policies to keep the rural peasants from assisting the movement, including the "strategic hamlet" and "agroville" programs. These were designed to separate villagers from revolutionary influence and to promote the South government's stature. Both failed as the farmers, strongly alienated by Diem's repressive regime and land reform, would not cooperate.

On December 20, 1959, a number of organizations opposed to Diem joined to form the National Liberation Front (NLF). One month later, the PLA, the military wing of the NLF, was organized with an initial strength of nearly 10,000 trained guerrilla fighters. Diem had referred to his opposition as Viet Nam Cong San (Vietnamese Communists) since 1956 and applied the name to the newly formed NLF in an attempt to associate the broad-ranged political organization with communism. The phrase was shortened to "Viet Cong," derogatory to many in the PLA who were not, in fact, Communists.

The NLF cadres were ordered to "eat with, live with, and work with" the peasants and villagers throughout Viet Nam in an effort both to win their hearts and minds as well as to provide intelligence for the revolution on South Vietnamese government policies, informers, and troop locations. Southern Vietnamese disassociated themselves from the Diem regime for three primary reasons: Diem's political repression coinciding with favoritism for the Catholic minority; Diem's land reforms and the abolishment of village elections, which violated traditional Vietnamese village authority; and Diem's ties to the United States, whose mere presence inflamed ancient Vietnamese animosities. As a result, the NLF's effort to recruit members and fighters from rural areas was very successful in the early 1960s, and it was not long before the PLA strengthened their influence throughout the South.

As the PLA increased pressure, the United States responded in kind by increasing its support for Diem. President Kennedy, now the third American president to have to deal with conflict in Indochina, wavered about what direction to take. Kennedy was anti-Communist but, unlike Truman and Eisenhower, saw the roots of communism in poverty and despair and less in international conspiracy. Viet Nam, initially, was less of a problem to Kennedy as his attention was turned to Laos by Eisenhower, who briefed Kennedy before leaving office. Kennedy began building troop strength in Viet Nam while keeping his doubts about U.S. involvement in the growing political chaos of Viet Nam private. The Kennedy-approved troop augmentations resulted in an increase to roughly 16,000 by November of 1963, most of which, however, were limited to advising and training.

That training was tested on January 2, 1963, in Ap Bac, about forty-five miles southwest of Saigon. Army of the Republic of Viet Nam (ARVN) troops planned, with their American advisors, a three-pronged attack around the PLA 514th Battalion, which was augmented with some local militia. The ARVN forces were defeated by inferior PLA forces and suffered heavy casualties. The PLA stood and fought with a determined resolve that was lacking in the ARVN assault. Colonel John Paul Vann, the chief advisor on the scene, watched in amazement as the attack faltered. The battle was a complete rout for the American-trained troops, setting a pattern of military incompetence that would continue, with some notable exceptions, throughout the war. The PLA, suffering just eighteen dead, were elated with their success, giving them confidence that led to higher recruitments and support from the local peasants.

Despite nearly nine years of training by American advisors, the well-armed ARVN troops performed miserably. After Ap Bac, most residents in the delta region were now either openly supportive of the NLF or took a neutral stance. Few could be called upon by Diem's officials to resist the revolutionary movement sweeping the South.

President Kennedy had also increased American efforts in Laos, fighting a "secret" war with extensive undercover and special forces. There was a flurry of secret meetings, memos, and investigations concerning Viet Nam, indicating that the Kennedy administration was uncertain about what policy ultimately to adopt in Indochina. In December 1962, Senator Mike Mansfield led a fact-finding mission to Viet Nam and returned with strong warnings to Kennedy that the U.S. support of Diem was creating political instability. Mansfield suggested that the U.S. policy was flawed and that the United States should get out of Viet Nam. Kennedy ignored Mansfield in his bid not to be seen as "soft" on communism and continued America's slide toward open war in Viet Nam. Kennedy's concern grew out of America's deep involvement in a potentially explosive Cold War. Russian Premier Nikita Khrushchev had recently tested the young president and had taken Kennedy to the brink of nuclear war in the Cuban missile crisis while rebellions and revolts were spreading

Quang Duc, a Buddhist monk, burns himself to death on a Saigon street on June 11, 1963, to protest alleged persecution of Buddhists by the South Vietnamese government. AP photo: Malcolm Browne

across the globe. Kennedy feared, as Eisenhower had predicted with his domino analogy in 1956, that Viet Nam's fall would be disastrous.

JFK thought that Diem's treatment of the peasants was a barrier to effectively fighting a Communist movement. CIA and U.S. officials began sending implicit messages to opposition leaders that the United States was now backing off in its support for Diem, and it was not long before several officers and generals in the army, bolstered by the new message stemming from the United States, began conspiring to oust Diem once and for all.

The beginning of the end arrived on May 8, 1963, when Diem's troops fired on a peaceful Buddhist demonstration in the old imperial capital of Hue, touching off more protests to which Diem responded by jailing many leaders. On June 11, a Buddhist monk, Thich Quang Duc, shocked the world by setting himself on fire on a street corner in Saigon to protest Diem's policies. The Buddhist rebellion exploded on the night of August 21 when Diem's guards, with the help of local police, raided Buddhist pagodas in various cities, arresting over 1,400 monks, ransacking the temples, and killing dozens in a night of terror reminiscent of Nazi assaults on Jewish synagogues on "Krystal Nacht" in 1938. President Kennedy was outraged at this latest act of brutality. Opposition leaders began plotting Diem's end.

The night of November 1, 1963, ARVN forces stormed the presidential palace in Saigon. Diem and his brother, Nhu, escaped but were later found in Cholon, the Chinese district of Saigon. On the way through the streets of Saigon in an American APC (Armoured Personnel Carrier), Diem and his brother were both shot in the back of the head. As word of the deaths spread, Vietnamese poured into the streets in wild celebration. Though American officials denied any knowledge, Kennedy and other U.S. officials were well aware of the impending coup and had resigned themselves to its inevitability.[12]

On November 21, 1963, John F. Kennedy was assassinated as he traveled in a motorcade in Dallas, Texas. The killing of the president shocked the nation and was a turning point in the war. Lyndon B. Johnson (LBJ) inherited a political nightmare as Diem's death was followed by several more coups over the next sixteen months by various generals. Ultimately, by early 1965, the commander of the ARVN Fifth Division, Nguyen Van Thieu, and Air Marshal Nguyen Cao Ky consolidated power and were accepted by U.S. officials as the right leaders to fight the NLF-led insurgency. LBJ responded to the coup by angrily shouting, "I don't want to hear any more of this coup [expletive]! I've had enough of it, and we've got to find a way to stabilize those people out there."[13]

By mid-1964, the NLF was clearly winning the war. As Johnson considered his options, the political situation in the South went from bad to worse. The strategic hamlet program was in disarray; Montagnard's troops, representing various ethnic minorities in the central highlands organized into civilian irregular defense groups by the CIA to oppose the PLA, were on the verge of open revolt against the south government; and NLF influence was spreading in nearly every province. For the third time since 1945, the anticolonial and pro-Communist movement in Viet Nam was close to victory.

Secretary of Defense Robert McNamara went to Viet Nam to assess the situation and on his return told how the NLF controlled over half the population, of how village defense teams refused to fight, many even deserting and joining the PLA, and of a growing antiwar sentiment among the Vietnamese, especially the Buddhists. McNamara had serious doubts about the U.S. mission in Viet Nam but reported to Johnson only that the United States should enlarge the ARVN forces, augment economic aid, and plan to expand the war to the North. Johnson, passing on the opportunity to get out of the

National Liberation Front leaders urge local villagers outside of Cu Chi Village to join the revolution against Diem and the Americans. Courtesy of Duong Thanh Phong.

conflict, announced a troop level increase to 21,000 on July 28, 1964, and increased aid to the beleaguered Southern government. The U.S. Army Joint Chiefs of Staff began to plan for an air and land campaign designed as a gradual and limited effort with the intent to persuade Hanoi to stop assisting the NLF. This plan grew from an American belief that a small but deadly effort would be more than enough to scare Hanoi. They were to be proved wrong.

President Johnson's military buildup from 1964 to 1967 began with Operation "Plan 34-Alpha" (OPLAN 34-A), a mystery-shrouded code name for operations rooted in covert activities. Johnson authorized air and naval surveillance of the DRV and commando raids against radar and other military installations along the coast. U.S. pilots bombed Pathet Lao positions in Laos, and LBJ sent a warning to the DRV leadership that unless they stopped assisting the NLF in the South, the United States would inflict devastating damage in the North. Premier Pham Van Dong defiantly responded to the American threat by saying that they would continue the war of liberation until victory and prophesied that the United States had two choices: Get involved in a war it could not win, or withdraw.

LBJ was running for reelection and wanted to appear as a peace candidate against conservative Republican candidate Barry Goldwater. His initial unwillingness to initiate war against Viet Nam changed dramatically when, on the night of July 31, 1964, CIA-directed raids by South Vietnamese patrol boats were spotted and fired upon by PAVN boats. The battles carried on until August 2, when PAVN PT boats (high-speed motorboats) fired on the U.S. destroyer *Maddox* engaged in surveillance missions along the coast. According to the Pentagon Papers, the PT boats had mistaken the U.S. ship for a South Vietnamese ship escorting the raiding South Vietnamese PT boats. The next night, the *Maddox* reported more incidents and being fired upon by torpedoes, although no evidence of the second attack has ever been substantiated. This incident, to be known as the Gulf of Tonkin incident, was what LBJ needed to sway public support, and a resolution was sent through Congress in rapid order, passing the House by a vote of 416 to 0 and the Senate by a vote of 88 to 2 on August 5, 1964. The resolution gave LBJ legal authority to "take all necessary measures to repel any armed attacks against the forces of the United States and to prevent further aggression."[14] The air war had begun before the resolution had passed as jets began bombing targets "in retaliation" for an incident that, most likely, never occurred.

The American press supported LBJ's message and helped inflame war fervor throughout the country. Public opinion polls showed that 85 percent of Americans approved of the air strikes and that LBJ's popularity in the United States rose from 42 to 72 percent in a matter of days. LBJ carried that popularity through the November elections, defeating Barry Goldwater by one of the largest margins in American history.

The immediate response from the DRV was to tell the United States they would go to war if the United States continued to intervene in the internal affairs of Viet Nam, and three regiments of regular PAVN troops were ordered south along the Ho Chi Minh Trail to assist the NLF. These were the first of many PAVN troops to make the four- to six-month trip down the jungle trail to fight in the South. PLA forces, meanwhile, planned retaliatory raids of their own and, on November 1, rained mortar and rockets onto the Bien Hoa Air

Base, killing four Americans and wounding seventy-two while destroying or damaging thirteen U.S. warplanes. It was the first time in the war that PLA forces directly attacked U.S. troops. In Binh Dinh Province, long an area of revolutionary sentiment, PLA forces occupied nearly the entire area, resulting in the decision by LBJ and his advisors that only by directly bombing the North could they stop the impending NLF victory. Most civilian advisors sought a controlled policy, while most military advisors wanted a massive bombing campaign. Only one major advisor, George Ball, the under secretary of state, opposed any bombing at all. Ball had studied air campaigns in World War II and had first-hand knowledge of the situation in Viet Nam. He advised LBJ, who ignored him, to begin negotiating a political settlement in Viet Nam. LBJ took the road advocated by McNamara and the other civilian advisors.

Operation "Rolling Thunder" set in motion a massive escalation of the war. Planes, personnel, ships, supplies, construction equipment, and all things associated with a modern military presence, begun as a trickle in 1950, now were flooding into the ports of South Viet Nam. The PLA also increased its guerrilla activity against the American-backed South Viet Nam government. By the end of 1964, PLA troop strength doubled to 175,000 as volunteers from the villages and towns flooded to the "cause." Now organized into dozens of battalions throughout the South, the PLA was ready for a final assault on the weakened Southern government.

On February 7, 1965, the PLA launched attacks against a U.S. base near Pleiku in the Central Highlands. LBJ implemented Operation "Flaming Dart" against selected sites in North Viet Nam in retaliation. The PLA retaliated to that by bombing sleeping quarters of U.S. Air Force personnel at Qui Nhon on the coast on February 10. Twenty-three Americans were killed and another twenty-one were wounded. LBJ retaliated again with even heavier strikes against military targets in the North, determined to "convince" the Vietnamese leadership in the DRV that the United States meant to punish the North for each act of violence perpetuated against the South. The PLA and the DRV remained defiant to these latest acts and kept the pressure on the reeling Southern government. On March 2, 1965, the United States began the full implementation of Operation Rolling Thunder with massive bombings in both North and South Viet Nam.

In addition, on March 8, 1965, under President Johnson's orders, 3,500 U.S. troops of the Ninth Marines landed at Da Nang and stepped ashore on the beautiful palm-laden beaches aside the warm and breezy South China Sea. The marines, in full battle gear, fully expected defensive fire but instead were met by a friendly group of young Vietnamese girls dressed in their traditional soft white *au dai*, creating the impression that Viet Nam was a warm, friendly paradise and not the expected shrapnel-filled haze of a war-ravaged land. A young Marine named Phil Caputo was one of the first marines to land: "It was the astonishing heat, the incredible and exotic beauty of the country, and that it didn't look as I imagined a nation at war should look. . . . It was actually kind of pacific-looking when we landed there."[15] It was the first, but not the last, impression the American combat troops would find illusory.

General William Westmoreland was named commander in chief of all operations in Viet Nam. U.S. Ambassador Maxwell D. Taylor, alone in his dissent, warned that a big U.S. presence would make America look "like the old French . . . colonizer and conqueror."[16] Twenty thousand more U.S. troops were ordered to Viet Nam, and the air war in the North was expanded. In addition, LBJ implored other nations of the "free world" to assist the United States in stopping the spread of communism in Viet Nam. As a result, troops from seven other nations participated in the great troop buildup in 1965. Australia, South Korea, Thailand, New Zealand, the Philippines, Chinese troops from Formosa, and Spain added a total of 69,000 allied troops by 1969. On April 24, 1965, LBJ officially designated Viet Nam as a "combat zone."

The DRV and NLF responded with protest against the array of "foreign" invaders and stepped up their military effort. On May 11, 1965, PLA troops overran Song Be, the Phuoc Long provincial capital, and in the Central Highlands, the PLA destroyed two ARVN battalions. By the middle of June, the government once again was facing complete collapse.

The First Cavalry Division and thousands of troops from various other units arrived in August. By the end of 1965, nearly 180,000 U.S. troops, many of them now full combat units, were in Viet Nam, and thousands more became involved in the Pacific rim bases as planes and naval forces converged on Viet Nam. The last in a long series of political coups saw the establishment of President Thieu and Ky in Saigon as the Americans continued to flood the failing Southern government with financial support.

U.S. troops, tired of sitting on their "duffs" and waiting for the "Viet Cong," were spoiling for a fight. In August and November of 1965, they got their wish. General Westmoreland ordered the marine

garrisons at Da Nang to move out of their perimeter and seek out a
small force of sappers (special commandos trained in demolition) that
had snuck through the base, destroyed a few American planes, and
escaped with the loss of only one casualty. The marines, on August
18, 1965, launched Operation "Starlite," designed to trap PLA forces
against the sea. The PLA opened up first and, using a strategy they
developed against the French, ambushed reinforcements sent to rescue the initially besieged troops. In the tremendous tropical heat, the
marines engaged in a hard-fought battle for several days, which ended
on August 23 when PLA forces retreated in defeat.

Later that fall, Westmoreland ordered the newly arrived First Cavalry Division to intercept PAVN forces operating in the Ia Drang
Valley southwest of Pleiku. Two PAVN regiments had recently besieged Camp Plei Me, a U.S. Special Forces base, and Duc Co, a
remote village near the Cambodian border. The next day, Westmoreland ordered the First Brigade Seventh Cavalry into the area to
seek out and destroy the two PAVN regiments located near the Chu
Pong massif. On November 14, an entire battalion of U.S. troopers
were airlifted to the foot of the Chu Pong. The PAVN responded
with a sweep of the landing zones, and a platoon was soon surrounded, taking on heavy fire from the PAVN forces. Entire companies of U.S. troops were nearly overrun as PAVN troops ran
maneuvers around the raw U.S. troops. Vicious fighting flowed back
and forth across the jungle trails, representing one of the hardest-
fought battles of the war. The discipline and élan of the PAVN troops
surprised the U.S. commanders in the field. Captain Robert Edwards,
radioing for reinforcements, stated that "we are in heavy contact.
These guys are good!"[17] Counterattacking with intense U.S. artillery
and devastating air strikes, the PAVN attacks around the landing
zones were finally repulsed and the three PAVN regiments slipped
across the Cambodian border to lick their wounds. Both American
and Vietnamese commanders subsequently claimed victory.

The American Perspective

The U.S. high command felt that they had achieved a significant
victory as PAVN forces suffered three times the casualties as the
Americans. American firepower proved to be irresistible, and although
the PAVN forces put up a tough fight, the troops of the Seventh
Cavalry departed the fight confident that they could persevere over
the best PAVN forces. Using the tactic of airlifting the troopers by

helicopter, the mobility of the U.S. troops proved decisive. The Americans could take the fight to the most remote parts of Viet Nam and, establishing instant bases and landing zones, bring tremendous firepower to the enemy burdened by jungle trails and intense heat and usually operating without heavy weapons. Coordinating massive B-52 bomber strikes with fighter bombers with a variety of light and heavy artillery, the American forces could deliver, as demonstrated at Ia Drang and in Operation Starlite, a virtual wall of high explosives that no army on earth could stand against. Westmoreland had, by 1965, devised a military timetable for victory in Viet Nam, with a three-phase strategy foreseeing ultimate victory by 1967. Operation Starlite and the battle of Ia Drang were viewed by the American commanders as fitting nicely within that timetable. The American political view at the time was that the massive use of firepower both on the ground and in Operation Rolling Thunder would contribute to Westmoreland's timetable by convincing the Vietnamese leadership of the folly of standing against the United States.

Lieutenant Colonel Hal Moore, the Korean War veteran commander of the Seventh Cavalry at Ia Drang, related after the war that "morale was high, we knew we were facing a tough enemy. We had lost a lot of good men, but we had stopped them."[18] The battle at Ia Drang initiated the enduring belief that the United States never lost a major battle in Viet Nam. U.S. military and political leaders concluded that the Ia Drang battle was a decisive American victory.

The Vietnamese Perspective

An interviewer reminded General Vo Nguyen Giap, commander of all PAVN forces at the time of Ia Drang, that the Americans never lost a major fight with the Vietnamese. Giap responded with a smile by stating "that may be true, but it is also irrelevant."[19] When the bloodied survivors of the Sixty-sixth PAVN Regiment left the Ia Drang Valley and headed for their Cambodian sanctuary, they were, in fact, not a beaten army. Despite losing 50 percent of their numbers, the young Vietnamese men were full of fight and would return to combat again and again as their will to fight was never seriously threatened during the entire war. The peasant soldiers of the PAVN regiments stood their ground and performed well under an unimaginable maelstrom of American firepower. The events of the battle exemplified the war to come with the United States, and the PAVN commanders felt confident that their units were superior to the U.S.

infantry on the ground. The "L" ambush and wheeling movement performed against "A" Company of the Fifth Cavalry on the fourth day of the battle was a classic maneuver that gained the admiration of their American counterparts. Ho Chi Minh had predicted a thirty-year war against the Americans, and to win such a protracted war required a well-trained fighting force willing to stand and die in the face of superior firepower. In addition, the support of the peasants and PAVN commanders picking and choosing when and where battles would be fought, inflicting enough casualties on the Americans to erode political support at home as well as military morale at the front, were also essential. The battle at Ia Drang was thus considered a success by PAVN commanders. Although not victorious in the classic sense, Giap's troops survived to fight again, and in Viet Nam, as in most unconventional wars in history, merely surviving was the key to eventual victory.

Operation Starlite was also seen as a Vietnamese success. Although, as in the rugged mountain region of the Ia Drang, the PLA forces fighting in the tropical heat along the coast near Nho Na Bay suffered terrible casualties against the American war machine, the surviving PLA forces managed to slip away to regroup and fight another day. While the American commanders counted bodies and surveyed the battlefields where they stood victorious, the men and women fighters of the First PLA Regiment felt confident. Having stood and traded blows with the troops of a major superpower, inflicting casualties using creative ambush techniques, they were able to slip away undetected to fight another day.

There were also signs of the future: Antiwar protests, consisting of isolated incidents initially, questioned the legitimacy of fighting in Viet Nam. This movement gained strength on August 3, when men of the Ninth U.S. Marines were caught on film setting an elderly Vietnamese couple's house on fire by touching a Zippo lighter to their straw roof in the hamlet of Cam Ne. This image, along with those of stunned and crying Vietnamese villagers staring at the U.S. troops casually going about the destruction of their homes, were shown on national television in the United States, contrasting the image created by the Pentagon of going to Viet Nam to "save" the peasants from communism.

On October 15, 1965, nineteen-year-old David Millar became the first American to burn his draft card, and a young marine refused to go to Viet Nam in an act of protest. These incidents were the first of many representing the birth of an antiwar movement that would eventually erode the support and effectiveness of the U.S. military mission in Viet Nam.

THE AMERICAN WAR IN VIET NAM

After Ia Drang, Giap and his commanders gathered to discuss the new war against American troops, review lessons learned, and devise strategies to reduce the impact of the intense American firepower. The Americans responded to Ia Drang with growing confidence, and in December 1965, LBJ ordered a halt to the bombing of North Viet Nam in the belief that the damage inflicted was lesson enough to bring the DRV to the negotiating table. When the DRV leadership stood their ground, the bombings were renewed. In January 1966, the First Marine Division landed in Viet Nam and the massive buildup continued, total troop strength increasing to 389,000 by the end of the year.

PAVN and PLA troops avoided direct contact, and when they did fight, it was on their terms, resulting in increased U.S. casualties. Many were beginning to question the "body counts" that field commanders were reporting and also the strategy exemplified at Ia Drang in which shortly after the fight ended, U.S. troops left the area and returned to their base, leaving front-line troops, or "grunts," as they were called, frustrated. The political situation in Viet Nam also remained problematic. In February, LBJ met with Prime Minister Ky and solidified an agreement to end corruption and work together. Upon his return to Saigon, Ky, with American support, fired one of his rivals for power, General Nguyen Chanh Thi, a popular man within Viet Nam society. The firings provoked another Buddhist uprising in Da Nang, Saigon, and other cities and towns, resulting in a serious civil war within the South Vietnamese nation.

Although the American intervention after the Gulf of Tonkin had stopped the NLF short of its impending victory in 1965, consensus within the South Vietnamese government remained elusive, and the rebellions in 1966 were further testimony to the fragility of the political situation. As long as the South kept its ties to the United States and resisted land reform, the South government had little hope of winning over the peasants.

By the end of May 1966, the Buddhist uprisings appeared to be at an end after nearly a dozen Buddhist monks and nuns set themselves on fire in spectacular suicidal statements. But by the middle of 1966, it was becoming clear that there would not be a quick and easy victory over the revolutionary movement in Viet Nam. The U.S. Joint Chiefs of Staff now planned on an American troop strength of 500,000 men as draft callups doubled in 1966. Antiwar activism also increased. LBJ had always believed that by demonstrating the superiority of awesome American firepower, the leaders in the North would ultimately sue for peace—the failure of which both angered and frustrated him.

American troops settled into a war that was vastly different from the battles of World War II. There were no real "front," as PLA combat teams would sneak into Saigon or even within U.S. bases and create havoc with well-timed bombings helping to create an atmosphere of confusion and fear. Despite this, the growing American forces in Viet Nam continued to inflict greater casualties on their enemy than they themselves suffered and seldom failed to drive any PLA or PAVN force from the field.

The battle for Binh Dinh Province, a jungle-filled province along the coast, is an example of American futility. Using helicopter assault tactics developed at Ia Drang, the American troops waged a 111-day fight that thwarted PAVN and PLA goals and inflicted heavy casualties. With massive B-52 strikes along with naval support fire and flying over 1,000 fighter-bomber sorties, the First Cavalry troopers chased the enemy from one hamlet to another. At the end of February 1967, the "body count" for enemy soldiers was registered at nearly 4,000. Yet, despite these apparent victories, the PAVN and PLA forces still retained the initiative, and many after-action reports indicated an admiration of U.S. troops at their enemies' ability to continue operations almost at will.

Frustrated with the PAVN and PLA ability to drift in and out of the immense and deep jungles of Viet Nam, the Americans began operation "Ranch Hand." First initiated in 1960, it escalated as the United States began spraying huge tracts of land with various chemicals, crated in cans colored either white, green, blue, or orange. The most commonly used, and the herbicide that contained the deadliest chemical, dioxin, was crated in orange cans, thus the name "Agent Orange." At its peak, Operation Ranch Hand witnessed the destruction of 1.5 million acres of land in 1967 alone, of which nearly 40 percent was crop land, in Viet Nam, Laos, and Cambodia. Many Vietnamese became angered with foreigners destroying their beloved trees and crops. The devastation to the jungles also attracted international scrutiny to bear, which further intensified objections to the war at both home and abroad. The spraying quickly became a political liability, and by 1972, the U.S. military discontinued the program. The political stability of an already fragile South government was further damaged.

Westmoreland ordered another operation, "Attleboro," which began in Tay Ninh Province on September 14, 1966. Initial American attacks were ambushed, and isolated U.S. units were eventually saved by massive air and artillery support, eventually forcing battered PLA and PAVN units to retreat to jungle and tunnel sanctuaries in Cambodia and Cu Chi. Large body counts were cited, but American and ARVN troops were still unable to prevent their enemy from slipping to safety.

On January 8, 1967, Operation "Cedar Falls" began as a full-scale big-unit sweep against suspected PLA positions. The village of Cu Chi sits on the main road from Saigon to Tay Ninh in a district traditionally a major source of anticolonial resistance. The local population had spent years digging and maintaining an elaborate network of tunnels that spread to a total of over 150 miles in length by 1966. When the U.S. Twenty-Fifth Infantry Division moved into the area, the site chosen happened to lie directly above a section of tunnels, and the next weeks saw an amazed U.S. military being ambushed and shot at by PLA troops that seemed to appear and disappear like magic. While the Twenty-fifth Division spent the next weeks securing their own base, the local main force PLA units in the region stepped up attacks on Americans in and around Cu Chi and nearby Saigon.

A two-pronged attack was planned as a result. The military sweeps were to coincide with removal of the local villagers to "pacification" camps built closer to Saigon. The operation began with a helicopter assault on the village of Ben Suc located near a loop of the lazily flowing Saigon River in the morning on January 8, 1967, to the surprise of thousands of Vietnamese peasants. The villagers were rounded up, interrogated, and then transported to a newly built refugee center at Phu Loi. Those that tried to flee were shot dead by the troops surrounding the village, and when nightfall arrived, nearly 6,000 former residents in and around Ben Suc were now in government custody. Back at Ben Suc, huge Rome plows, or bulldozers, began the deliberate process of completely leveling the remnants of the village and surrounding jungle. Ben Suc ceased to exist. While Ben Suc was being destroyed, the American and ARVN troops swept the area known as the Iron Triangle and rubber plantations both north and south of the river without much enemy contact.

When Operation Cedar Falls ended, American commanders felt

confident that their efforts had been greatly successful. One noted that "it [was] a decisive turning point in the III Corps area; a tremendous boost to the morale of the Vietnamese government and army . . . a blow from which the VC [Viet Cong] in this area would never recover."[20] The entire Iron Triangle area was declared a "free fire zone," allowing for air and artillery fire into the area without prior authority from Military Assistance Command Vietnam (MACV) headquarters in Saigon.

The dropping of massive amounts of explosives in a contested area, along with chemical spraying, affected civilian morale and support for the Southern government. Rand Corporation studies revealed that nearly 80 percent of Vietnamese villagers surveyed blamed the United States for damage to their crops and homes, causing intense hatred of their enemy.[21] The implicit message in the U.S. and south government's inability to pacify certain regions in South Viet Nam was viewed as an ominous sign that the government was unable to guarantee the safety of its own people.

The tense situations that characterized U.S. operations placed individual soldiers at a great disadvantage. Not knowing the difference between Viet Cong and allied Vietnamese villagers, many GIs would often shoot first at any suspicious activity on the part of the villagers. Outside of Ben Suc, a U.S. unit guarding one of the access roads out of Ben Suc saw an elderly man on a bicycle who was shot off his bike. Major Charles Malloy, a commander at the Ben Suc operation, asked in frustration, "What are you going to do when you spot a man in black pajamas? Wait for him to get out his weapon and start shooting? . . . I'm not!"[22]

Cu Chi resident Huyen Van Chia, a PLA fighter for thirteen years of his life, reflected years later that the destruction of Ben Suc had galvanized the entire region against the Americans. "Even many of those who were previously neutral and tried to avoid taking sides in the struggle soon joined the NLF," said Chia.[23] James Henry, a soldier in the American Fourth Infantry Division, was quoted as saying that "a friend of mine in A Company told me that when A Company goes into a village, if it's not VC when they go into it, it's VC when they leave."[24] An American colonel summed up the operation by stating, "I don't think that we can afford any more Ben Sucs."[25]

THE AMERICAN HOME FRONT

The "turbulent" 1960s witnessed several, often violent, collisions between various cultures and three significant historical events: the post–World War II Cold War, the escalating war in Viet Nam, and the Civil Rights Movement in the United States. All three were symbiotically related and would combine to shake the cultural foundations of the American people.

On April 15, 1967, the largest antiwar demonstrations in American history took place as nearly 100,000 protesters gathered to voice their opposition to the war in Viet Nam. The growing antiwar movement was fueled by televised news that brought images of the war into American homes every night, contradicting images presented by the Pentagon and officials of the Johnson administration. Veterans returned home noticeably changed in the eyes of their friends and family and were found describing a war that was incongruent with historical images of America as the "good guys in white hats." In New York City, six Viet Nam veterans marched in a peace demonstration and afterward formed an organization called "Vietnam Veterans against the War" (VVAW). VVAW grew rapidly with the expressed purpose of "exposing the ugly truth abut U.S. involvement in Southeast Asia." Before the war's end, VVAW had over 30,000 dues-paying members, many of whom were still on active duty in Viet Nam.

On October 21, 1967, over 100,000 protesters marched at the Lincoln Memorial in Washington, D.C., and nearly 50,000 of them then marched to the Pentagon. The incident, immortalized by novelist Norman Mailer in his book *The Armies of the Night* (1968), portrayed a growing and increasingly militant antiwar movement that startled both Johnson administration officials and the great majority of Americans still supportive of the war in Viet Nam. Several organizations, however, promoted LBJ's war policies. The "Young Americans for Freedom," for example, had memberships on many colleges in direct conflict with antiwar protesters. Other incidents supporting the "war against communism" added to the social unrest that swept the nation in the mid and late 1960s. As 1967 came to a close, presidential candidates began calling for a return to "law and order," a message well received as Richard Nixon and George Wallace entered the national political scene.

1967: PRELUDE TO TET

By early March of 1967, the quick victory that American leaders initially envisioned had evaporated into numerous and, many times, futile "search-and-destroy" missions. On March 10, America bombed the Thai Nguyen industrial complex in the North, the first time that

U.S. planes were allowed to take the war to the heart of the Northern manufacturing center.

The impetus of the war turned toward the north along the demilitarized zone (DMZ) and to the Central Highlands to the west as several PAVN regiments began infiltrating the regions in anticipation of large-scale attacks across the often fog-shrouded and jungle-covered mountains toward the more heavily populated coastal regions to the east. These battles crested in the autumn of 1967 in fierce fighting between marine and army airborne troops and PAVN troops. These engagements represented General Giap's intention of enticing Westmoreland to send large combat forces out from their bases around highly populated areas for the planned January 1968 Tet Offensive. Westmoreland obliged, sending the First Air Cavalry Division north toward Hue and Quang Tri from months-long operations in coastal Binh Dinh. In the jungled mountains of the Central Highlands near the confluence of the Laotian, Cambodian, and Vietnamese borders, the "Sky Soldiers" of the 173rd Airborne Brigade had been attempting to prevent PAVN units from cutting across Viet Nam to the coast in anticipation of a large offensive since June of 1967. The 173rd found itself in a climactic battle in November in and around Hill 875 (875 meters high), with well-trained PAVN troops, expert in jungle ambush. For five days, the embattled American troops found themselves in a fight for their lives, and not until Thanksgiving Day 1967 did the reinforced American troops renew their assault on the hilltop, where they found that the PAVN troops had suddenly vanished into the jungle. In all, 27 percent of the 3,200 members of the 173rd Brigade deployed in and around Dak To during the week of fighting around Hill 875 had become casualties, a level reaching those incurred by U.S. combat units during the height of World War II.

The U.S. Marines had also been heavily committed to various operations and battles near Laotian and northern border regions near the DMZ. Following a series of battles near the remote village and nearby marine base at Khe Sanh, Khe Sanh was targeted as the western anchor of a series of strong points and bases along the DMZ frontier designed to stop PAVN infiltration of the Southern battle fronts. By August 1967, the American command ordered truck convoys stopped along Highway 9 to Khe Sanh as deadly ambushes made the journey too precarious. By January of 1968, a state of siege existed, with a total of 6,000 marine and ARVN forces cut off and needing to be supplied completely by air. Fears of another Dien Bien

Phu echoed throughout the Johnson administration and the media, although a closer look at the situation indicated that those fears were unfounded. The French in 1954 did not have access to the immense firepower offered by the U.S. Air Force, especially that of the devastating B-52s. LBJ had become obsessed with Khe Sanh, while others even wondered about the necessity of holding on to the remote outpost as its military significance was ambiguous at best. PAVN leadership was content with tying down large American forces that pulled Allied attention away from the real goals of their looming offensive.

While the battles for Hill 875 and Con Thien, near the DMZ raged, General Westmoreland had been called back to Washington to promote the war to the American public. The president had envisioned victory by the end of 1967, and two and one-half years later, the American effort appeared to be stalemated. The American high command countered this with statements to the media, one claiming that the Dak To battles were an "overwhelming success of U.S. arms."[26]

In just nine weeks, over 75,000 tons of explosives (the equivalent of four Hiroshima-sized atomic bombs) were dropped on enemy positions around Khe Sanh, the greatest amount of explosives used on any single target in military history. Yet PAVN and PLA forces continued to put up stiff resistance and, despite taking tremendous casualties, continued to hold the military initiative. Westmoreland, in November 1967, told an audience at the National Press Club in Washington, D.C., that the United States was winning the war and that "we have reached an important point when the end begins to come into view."[27] After Westmoreland returned to Viet Nam, he announced that the enemy had suffered so greatly and their morale was so low that they could not mount an assault anywhere in Viet Nam.

TET 1968: THE YEAR OF THE MONKEY

Tet Nguyen Dan, a large cultural festival celebrating the lunar new year, fell on the night of January 30, 1968, when nearly 100,000 PAVN and PLA troops launched a massive series of assaults on dozens of cities, military bases, towns, and almost all the provincial capitals throughout South Viet Nam. While most of the attacks were quickly beaten back, and the offensive can be considered a military defeat, the massive Tet Offensive significantly altered the course of the war. Televised for weeks on national news programs in the United

South Vietnamese National Police Chief Brigadier General Nguyen Ngoc
Loan executes a Viet Cong officer with a single pistol shot in the head, in
Saigon, Viet Nam, on February 1, 1968. AP Photo: Eddie Adams

States, Tet had a profound psychological effect on the American people that proved fatal to LBJ's efforts at nurturing popular support for
his war policies. Tet added to the confusion about the administration's claims for fighting the war in the first place. None of the images
of Tet watched across America in February 1968 had as dramatic an
impact as the stunning incident of a handcuffed man being publicly
executed on a Saigon street. The macabre event showed an ARVN
officer calmly walk up to a man called Bay Lop, raise his pistol, and
fire into the side of his head. The executioner was Nguyen Ngoc
Loan, chief of South Viet Nam's National Police, known as the "Terror of Saigon." Ultimately, the image tore at the core of a long-
nurtured image that America was fighting "evil" to save a defenseless
government from Communist terror. Many Americans, even long-
time supporters of the war, began openly to question why young
American men were dying 12,000 miles from home.

Fierce fighting raged throughout the beleaguered nation, especially
in and around the ancient imperial capital of Hue. At Hue, strong
PAVN forces took the entire city after having routed several ARVN

units, while fighting to retake the city lasted nearly a month. Massive artillery and air strikes helped destroy the mystical city with its ancient Cham and Nguyen Dynasty buildings as PAVN and PLA forces, dug in within the walls of the citadel, an ancient fortress, fought tenaciously for days. When U.S. Marines and members of the 101st Airborne retook the city, mass graves were discovered, holding nearly 4,000 Vietnamese bodies. Initially, Communist forces were blamed for the "massacres" as evidence of the brutality of the PAVN forces. Though later investigations found that the death tally included civilian casualties and ARVN executions victims in addition to those murdered by the PLA. President Nixon used these executions to justify his "blood bath" theory of what would occur in the event of a "Communist" victory.

The PLA, especially hard hit, saw its role diminished after Tet, resulting in subsequent increases in the number and influence of PAVN troops in the South. The hoped-for uprisings of the "people" never materialized at the level anticipated by PAVN leadership as most civilians simply attempted to flee from the fighting, hid, or were caught in the fire storm and died by the thousands.

By the summer of 1968, a majority of Americans had become convinced that the war was a mistake and the United States should pull out. LBJ had stunned the nation on March 31, 1968, by announcing that he would not seek reelection for another term and would dedicate his remaining months in office to finding a peaceful solution to the quagmire in Viet Nam. He announced that he would stop all bombing of Viet Nam north of the twentieth parallel, offered to halt all bombing in Viet Nam if the Northern leadership responded to offers to negotiate a peaceful settlement, and stated that he was ordering another 13,500 additional support troops to Viet Nam, and finally announced the beginning of a major effort to "Vietnamize" the war.

The 13,500-troop increase was far short of the 206,000 troops that Westmoreland had requested. Johnson had agreed to turn down this request after discussions within his cabinet and with officials at the Pentagon could not realize a concrete assessment of how long it would take to win the war. Robert McNamara officially resigned as the secretary of defense on February 29, 1968. McNamara had opposed Westmoreland's request for more troops on "economic, political, and moral grounds"; he told LBJ that American objectives in Viet Nam could not be obtained "through any reasonable military means"[28] and advised him to seek a political settlement. His successor, Clark Clifford, arrived at the new position of secretary of defense with a similar perspective on Viet Nam. Clifford had formed a task force, initially to assess Westmoreland's troop request, that soon addressed the entire issue of America's involvement in Viet Nam.

Without clarification from the Pentagon or the White House about what their role was or when the war would end, the patience of the American people had dissolved after eighteen years. Military analysis, revealed during discussions between Clifford and General Earle Wheeler, the chairman of the Joint Chiefs of Staff, shocked Clifford and cast doubt on the entire status of the war. The report revealed that after three years of intensive bombing, more men and supplies were coming down the Ho Chi Minh Trail than ever, that the spirit and determination of the enemy remained, and that the fighting capability of ARVN troops, while improved, was still deficient, especially if U.S. air power was absent. In effect, the U.S. military was stalemated against a peasant army without air support and outnumbered nearly five to one. Fearing involvement by China or the Soviet Union if the United States escalated the war, the military and political leaders in the United States could not, at that time, figure out how to resolve the conflict without abandoning their allies in the South.

The year of 1968 witnessed other dramatic events that rocked the American people. On April 4, in Memphis, Tennessee, Martin Luther King, Jr., the spiritual leader, a strong advocate of nonviolence seeking equality and civil rights, was murdered. As word of King's murder spread, violent riots erupted across the United States. National Guard troops numbering 75,000 assisted local and state police forces in quelling the angry response to King's murder in over 130 cities.

On June 5, after a victory in the California Democratic presidential primary, Robert F. Kennedy, the idealistic brother of the late President John F. Kennedy, was also murdered in full view of hundreds at a victory celebration in Los Angeles. Bobby Kennedy had become the inspiration of both the civil rights as well as the antiwar movements, and his death left the nation uncertain about who could end the war and unify the nation. By August of 1968, with news of Russian troops brutalizing Prague, Czechoslovakia, hundreds of students were shot in the streets of Mexico City. Even the usually apolitical Olympic Games saw controversy when American black athletes raised their clenched fists in solidarity after winning track and field events. In Chicago, where the democratic convention ironically attempted to play out a theme of "The Politics of Joy," Chicago police attacked thousands of antiwar protesters in full view of rolling cameras in a police riot. As the police charged into groups of protesters and un-involved bystanders, the eerily lit night echoed with chants of "The whole world is watching." The spectacle left millions of Americans wondering if the nation was not headed for civil war. Chaos seemed to rule everywhere.

While the nation agonized over events in 1968, Richard M. Nixon, the former vice president to Eisenhower, declared his intention to run for the presidency. With LBJ pulling out of the race and the death of Bobby Kennedy, a political vacuum had been created. Hubert H. Humphrey, Johnson's vice president, took the Democratic nomina-tion, while George Wallace, the Alabama governor made famous for his antidesegregation tactics during the 1960s, ran on an independent platform that appealed to many working class Democrats fed up with the war and protests. Nixon, a controversial politician not unfamiliar with political scandal and overzealous campaign tactics, promised to unify the American people. He began attacking the antiwar move-ment and promised to end the Viet Nam War with "honor." Nixon's campaign appealed to enough voters to give him one of the narrowest margins of victory in American history.

NIXON'S WAR

On January 20, 1969, Richard M. Nixon, the fifth president to preside over the conflict in Viet Nam, was inaugurated and inherited stalled peace talks, increasing U.S. involvement, and growing casu-alties with no clear sense about the war's mission. Nixon had prom-ised a "secret" plan to end the war, a phrase more political than substantive, but it involved turning more of the fighting over to the South Vietnamese government, expanding the war with secret bomb-ings and undercover special forces operations, and initiating talks with North Viet Nam's leadership. Nixon had developed his strategy so as to "not," as he stated, "be the first president to lose a war."[29]

Nixon would eventually be driven from office in 1974, and the first steps to national disgrace were taken within hours of his inauguration. He assembled a foreign policy team led by Henry Kissinger, who was named as secretary of state, and planned his war strategy. Within days, Nixon gave permission to the military to widen the war into Laos and Cambodia and sent Ho Chi Minh a letter indicating a willingness to negotiate within American conditions. He warned Ho that he would use massive force from the air force if Ho did not concede to his plans and, to add credibility, ordered a massive B-52 bomb raid of neighboring Cambodia. Nixon had given the Joint Chiefs of Staff what they had sought since the war's beginning: authority to bomb PAVN and PLA forces wherever they were found and elimination of the long-held border sanctuaries used by fleeing PAVN forces. The "secret" bombings, called Operation "Menu," initiated on March 18, 1969, violated Cambodian neutrality and caused PAVN forces to move deeper into the Cambodian and Laotian jungles to avoid the awesome devastation of the B-52s. Not surprisingly, the attempts to keep such an immense policy quiet were doomed from the start. On May 9, 1969, the *New York Times* broke the story. The next day, Nixon ordered Federal Bureau of Investigation (FBI) wiretapping of members of the national security council as well as suspected informants from the news media.

Over the next several months Nixon's frustration led him to order more wiretaps and other activities designed to stop "leaks" to the press and to undermine his political "enemies." In the meantime, the Soviet Union rejected Nixon's plea to force the North into a negotiated settlement, and Thieu's regime rejected any settlement in which PAVN forces would be allowed to remain in the South. Frustrated, Nixon met with Thieu on Midway Island in the Pacific Ocean and, on June 8, 1969, announced the first U.S. troop withdrawal from Viet Nam, with units of the Ninth Marine Division being sent home on July 7, 1969. A few months prior to that announcement, U.S. forces, along with ARVN troops, had fought a bitter battle for the control of a hill (Dong Ap Bia) near the Laotian border. It took ten days of savage fighting to wrest the hill from determined PAVN troops that vanished into the jungles, leaving the exhausted victors once again in control of a hill that the U.S. high command soon abandoned. The battle for what was called "Hamburger Hill" again focused antiwar sentiment at home on the futility of the fighting. Nixon's policy of troop withdrawal also deepened morale problems by giving troops in the field the impression that America was leaving Viet Nam, victory or not, with few soldiers willing to be the "last man" to die in a lost war. In August, Kissinger began the tedious process of "secret" negotiations with Xuan Thuy, which began in addition to, and outside of, the ongoing but stalled Paris Peace Talks.

Truong Nhu Tang, who had risen to the position of minister of justice for the NLF at the Central Office South Vietnam (COSVN), the Southern headquarters for the revolution, believed that the early spring of 1969 was a crossroad for the revolution. Nixon's new policies had created a paradoxical situation. With the expanded air war in Cambodia and Laos against PAVN bases, the fight for reunification became a deadly serious adventure with massive B-52 bombings capable of instant and total destruction. COSVN was now a hunted target, and escaping into the jungles of Cambodia was no longer a guaranteed sanctuary. The COSVN camp, designated "base area 353" by the American military, was hit several times, but the NLF leadership, always forewarned of impending air strikes, escaped death and capture throughout the war.[30]

Nixon's moves were seen as a willingness to compromise and gave the revolutionaries the knowledge that antiwar sentiment in the United States in both Congress and a majority of the American people was now directing American policy in Viet Nam. Although Nixon's adopted policy of Vietnamization was not new to the Vietnamese (the French called it *jaunissement*, or yellowing), NLF and PAVN leaders were now confronted with massive political and military pressures that the French had been incapable of creating in their defeat in the 1950s. To add credibility abroad, the NLF organized a new coalition government, called the Provisional Revolutionary Government (PRG), which could vie for legitimacy as the government in power in South Viet Nam. On August 15, 1969, Ho Chi Minh formally replied to Nixon's settlement offers by refusing any negotiation until U.S. troops had departed Viet Nam. Hanoi radio then wished the American peace movement an enduring success. Nixon and Kissinger had now joined the ranks of previous American administrations in underestimating Hanoi's resolve to win. On September 2, 1969, that resolve was tested even further as Ho Chi Minh, the spiritual and political leader of the anticolonial revolution in Viet Nam, died. His death stunned Vietnamese in both southern and northern parts of Viet Nam, but his passing had no effect on the fighting or final outcome of the war.

The war raged on, and the autumn saw millions of Americans and individuals from dozens of countries abroad assemble for massive antiwar demonstrations on October 15, called "Moratorium Day." The day also saw thousands of U.S. soldiers in Viet Nam wear black arm bands in solidarity with the peace movement. Now soldiers in uniform as well as labor unions, politicians, and other professionals joined students in demanding that the war end.

President Nixon then pulled off a major political victory with a nationwide television address to the American people on November 3, 1969, when he called upon the great "silent majority" of Americans to pull with him in finding peace with honor in Viet Nam. Nixon used the killings in Hue during Tet 1968 to illustrate what he called an impending "blood bath" if the Communists were to win in Viet Nam and urged Americans to back his Vietnamization policy. A solid majority of Americans approved of Nixon's plea.

Troop morale, however, sank with each passing month. A sharp lack of willingness to die for a dubious cause spread among the troops, as incidents of desertion, protest, drug usage, and even refusals to fight in the field became widespread. The 1960s' youth counterculture was now mirrored in Viet Nam as, for the first time in the war, draftees outnumbered volunteers there. Evidence of discrimination compounded the many racial issues that mirrored those back in the states, especially after 1968 with the death of Martin Luther King. In addition, assaults upon officers by their own men, known as "fragging," from fragmentation grenades, a commonly used weapon in incidents against officers, increased dramatically after 1968. These assaults were directly related to the perception that officers were either incompetent or out of touch with the reality of a war that was no longer perceived as winnable by most troops in the field.

Several incidents in which field troops even disobeyed direct orders occurred, with many of the refusals being race related. In 1970 members of the Americal Division refused another order to renew an attack up a hill. Infantryman Charles Trujillo, a Chicano, stated that "the black soldiers were saying that the war was at home. . . . This made me think. . . .I was very angry at the officers. . . . We argued through the night, the majority being against going in."[31] Racial incidents occurred on the U.S.S. *Kitty Hawk* in 1972 as the *Kitty Hawk* was ordered back to Viet Nam after its replacement ship was delayed because of sabotage. Not wanting to return to Viet Nam duty, sailors demonstrated on board and were attacked by a marine detachment, resulting in fighting between black and white sailors and marines.

By the spring of 1970, opposition to the war at home, in Congress, and in Viet Nam grew while Vietnamization proceeded very slowly. In Cambodia, the neutralist Prince Sihanouk was overthrown by a pro-Western coup, which put Lon Nol in charge. Although Sihanouk had reluctantly agreed to allow Nixon's air war in Cambodia, an agreement that Sihanouk allowed only with a promise to bomb uninhabited areas of Cambodia, Nol agreed to let Nixon invade the PAVN sanctuaries along the border in Cambodia in an attempt to end the revolution's command structure. The massive air campaign did not alter the war effort or the PAVN and NLF determination to continue the war against the Southern government and their American allies. As a result, Nixon ordered a massive U.S. and ARVN operation into Cambodia on April 29, 1970. Hanoi's determination to wage war was undeterred, Lon Nol failed in gaining popular support and pacifying Cambodia, the PAVN and NLF leadership simply melted into the endless jungles away from the American troops, and their troops avoided contact whenever possible. Large amounts of weapons and food storage were captured, but it had no long-term effect on the outcome of the war. In addition, the international community as well as the antiwar movement in the United States exploded against what was now seen as Nixon's war, which he expanded into Laos and Cambodia. Nixon had ordered American troops to advance no more than nineteen miles into Cambodia, and as a result of the significant protests to his invasion, even those troops were back in Viet Nam by the end of May.

The violent reaction to the invasion of Cambodia surprised President Nixon in its ferocity and its consequence. On the evening of April 30, 1970, Nixon tried to explain his reasons for invading the small Buddhist nation on Southern Viet Nam's western border. Nixon opened his speech to the nation by falsely proclaiming that America had, until then, honored Cambodian neutrality. He indicated that it was not to be seen as an expansion of the war but rather a military necessity to prevent Communist success in Indochina and to protect U.S. troops that were being withdrawn in increasing numbers. Nixon was in no mood to be apologetic for his actions. His attitude toward potential critics was antagonistic, referring to student protesters as "those bums, you know, blowing up the campuses."[32] Student protest over the invasion rose to the highest in American history. One was at the usually sleepy college town of Kent, Ohio, which harbored Kent State University. On Monday, May 4, a peaceful calm had returned to the campus after several nights of violence in which the Reserve Officers' Training Center (ROTC) building had been burned. National Guardsmen then declared that a peaceful protest violated a ban on rallies and swept students from a campus green, using bayonets, tear gas, and swinging batons. In the ensuing melee, the guardsmen opened fire into the student crowd, killing four and wounding nine. The killing of students ignited other volatile college campuses, with over 1 million students walking out of classes and joining the spreading rebellion. Over 50 percent of colleges in the nation recorded some form of protest, and strikes were called at another 25 percent. Over 75 colleges were shut down for the remainder of their spring semester.[33] Thousands of students were arrested and hundreds were injured, creating an atmosphere bordering on civil war. Over 100,000 people descended on Washington, D.C., on May 9, and on May 14, two black students were shot to death by police at Jackson State College in Mississippi. In all, National Guard troops were in action on twenty-one campuses in sixteen different states. Bombings began to occur, and a total of 34 ROTC buildings were burned to the ground. Protests also erupted in government agencies where, for example, 250 state department employees signed a statement condemning Nixon's policies. In the U.S. Senate, the Cooper–Church Amendment was passed, cutting off funding for the Cambodian invasion, and the Gulf of Tonkin Resolution was repealed. Henry Kissinger reflected later that "the very fabric of government was falling apart."[34] Protests were also held in many cities in other nations as well, and it soon appeared to Nixon that he had badly judged the political mood at home as well as abroad. Though the great majority of protests were against Nixon's policies, there were also demonstrations in support of Nixon. On May 9, hundreds of demonstrators in downtown New York City, many of whom were wearing construction hard hats, rallied in support of the president and then, after hearing of an antiwar protest nearby, ran toward the protesters, shouting and severely beating many in front of nonintervening police. Disillusionment with the president increased because Nixon was, after all, elected on his promise to end the war. Vietnamization was failing, protests, though diminished over the summer, continued both at home and in Viet Nam itself, and the peace talks in Paris were stalled.

By early 1971, Vietnamization had progressed to a point where Allied military leaders prepared to launch a massive operation primarily with ARVN forces. Coinciding with renewed announcements of U.S. troop withdrawals, the operation, code named Lam Son 719, was designed to destroy PAVN bases near the Laotian and Vietnamese borders west of Khe Sanh. Despite massive air campaigns, PAVN supplies along the now-expanded Ho Chi Minh Trail increased every month of the war, and by the spring of 1971, large and well equipped PAVN troop concentrations occupied the border regions. The operation was launched on February 8, 1971, as men of the ARVN First Infantry and Airborne Divisions, reported to be some of the best-trained and finest troops in South Viet Nam's military, advanced into Laos along Route 9 west of Khe Sanh. PAVN forces counterattacked viciously, sending the invasion force heading back to Viet Nam in a month-long fighting retreat. By the first week in April, the operation had ended in complete defeat for the ARVN. American troops that had entered the border region in Operation "Dewey Canyon II" to secure the launching areas for Lam Son 719 were forced to abandon several supporting firebases as they, too, fell back toward Khe Sanh. In all, 7,000 ARVN troops were killed and wounded, with nearly 1,400 U.S. casualties and 107 American helicopters, flown in support of the operation, being downed. The loss was a defeat for Vietnamization, although many of the ARVN troops fought rather well.

Other events in the spring of 1971 proved equally embarrassing to America and to Nixon's war policies. On March 16, 1968, units from the Americal Infantry Division had launched an attack against the villages of Song My near the coast in Quang Ngai Province and massacred 504 residents at the hamlet of My Lai; almost all were women, children, and the elderly. The slaughter had raged for several hours, and at no time did U.S. troops receive any incoming fire from PLA forces. The massacre was initially covered up, but word eventually reached the news media a year later, accompanied with graphic photos of dead Vietnamese lying in ditches. At the time it occurred, the event was reported by the U.S. news media as a "major U.S. victory over the Viet Cong"; when the story broke in 1969, with reports of rape and mutilation in addition to the killings, it shocked the war-weary American nation. Several GIs were tried, although only one, Lieutenant William Calley, was convicted. Nixon would eventually pardon Calley, but the trial, during January and February 1971, added to the deepening cynicism of the American public. In addition, when some "hawk" politicians began to make public statements that My Lai was an aberration and not representative of usual U.S. treatment of Vietnamese civilians, many American veterans of the war demanded, and got, a hearing in which hundreds of GIs testified of other atrocities and massacres that they had witnessed or committed themselves. The hearings, known as the Winter Soldier Hearings, contributed to a deepened cynicism about the war. Although student protests had declined somewhat by the spring of 1971, protests by American servicemen were increasing to a near-crisis level. Fraggings and combat refusals, as well as "search-and-evade" tactics, increased dramatically. Thousands of GIs were deserting, and thousands more young men were openly resisting the draft, either by refusing induction or fleeing to Canada and other safe countries. For five days in April, thousands of Viet Nam veterans descended on Washington, D.C., to protest the continuation of the war and to demand jobs and better treatment by their own government. In an emotional display, hundreds of veterans hurled their medals and ribbons from their service in Viet Nam onto the nation's Capitol building steps. A few days later, the largest demonstration in American history was held in Washington, D.C., as a crowd estimated by park police to number at nearly 750,000 demanded an immediate end to the war. Nixon's reaction was defensive and antagonistic, and Vice President Spiro T. Agnew referred to the protesters as "an effete corps of impudent snobs."[35] A sizable percentage of the protesters were now union members, professionals, church officials and ministers, and homemakers in addition to the antiwar veterans and student protesters. A middle-aged mother and her two daughters carried a banner that read: "The majority is not silent, the government is deaf!"[36] Polls gave credibility to their banner as 69 percent of Americans felt, by then, that the United States should pull out of Viet Nam within one year.[37]

Further national agony was endured on June 13, 1971, when the *New York Times* published a series of documents called the "Pentagon Papers," a collection of official government documents on the war from 1946 through 1967. These documents portrayed a reality of the war that differed greatly from what every administration had portrayed to the American public. The documents served notice to the American people that they had been lied to repeatedly from the beginning, giving credibility to those who had portrayed U.S. policies as primarily responsible for the war and for spurning peace initiatives from the beginning.

Nixon's reaction toward dissent of his policies was two pronged: In public, Nixon and others in his administration attempted to divide the public between "patriotic" Americans and those in the antiwar movement who were considered traitors by many Americans at the time. In private, Nixon worked with FBI Director J. Edgar Hoover in developing a Counter Intelligence Program (COINTELPRO) designed to employ a wide range of activities against what they believed were "subversives." Antiwar groups were infiltrated with agents and informers and subject to numerous dirty tricks and illegal wiretaps. VVAW was especially targeted as decorated Viet Nam veterans were viewed as potentially harmful to Nixon's war policies. An organization called "Plumbers" was formed, designed to illegally retrieve damaging war-related documents and to plug "leaks" to the media from insiders such as Daniel Ellsberg, who had leaked the Pentagon Papers to the press.

By early 1972, with American troop levels under 100,000, the presidential campaign began. Initial polls showed Nixon behind Senator

Edmund Muskie of Maine. To counter the appeal of Muskie and McGovern, both of whom were peace candidates promising to end the war, Nixon, on January 25, 1972, told the American public of the ongoing secret talks between Kissinger and the North Vietnamese and reported that it was the North that had stalled a peace initiative. The DRV responded to Nixon's announcement by condemning Nixon for exposing the secret talks, and the talks soon collapsed. Nixon was at a political crossroad and came up with a brilliant strategy that he hoped would dramatically change America's antiwar and anti-Nixon sentiment: He told the public that he was headed for China to meet with Chairman Mao. As a life-time Republican who had made his political career on anti-Communist rhetoric, Nixon's bold move to capture the initiative was a striking success. He then flew to Moscow to meet with Soviet leader Leonid Brezhnev in late April. His overall strategy was to widen an existing wedge between Moscow and Beijing and to push the two superpowers into pressuring Hanoi into accepting his settlement in exchange for improved relations and trade with the United States. Although the visits gained him great popularity at home, Nixon's efforts to scare Hanoi to the table failed. China's support for Hanoi actually increased, and Hanoi was little affected by Nixon's ploy. In fact, a massive offensive was launched on March 30, 1972, in which thousands of well-trained and quipped PAVN and PLA forces sent ARVN forces reeling at a time when U.S. troop strength was greatly diminished. Known as the "Easter Offensive," this move began with large unit movements across the DMZ with tanks, artillery, and other components that characterized conventional warfare. Other attacks raged in the Central Highlands and along Highway 13 northwest of Saigon. Many ARVN units in place to stem this flood of PAVN military might collapsed or simply ran away, and one entire regiment defected to the PAVN side. On May 8, Nixon ordered the mining of Haiphong Harbor, long used by Russian ships to deliver supplies to the DRV. Antiwar protests once again broke out all over the United States in numbers almost as high as in 1970. In August, while Nixon was being nominated by his party to run against McGovern, thousands of protesters descended upon Miami Beach, Florida, and ran through tear gas–filled streets, fleeing police sweeps that led to a total of 885 arrests. The protesters, who camped out in Flamingo Park with Viet Nam veterans, were outraged that while Nixon accepted his party's nomination, B-52s were still bombing Viet Nam in what was being labeled "the endless war."

Russia and China, seeking détente, did not react militarily. They did, however, increase military supplies across the Chinese border in the greatest number of the entire war. The air assault carpeted Viet Nam with enormous amounts of explosives, bringing the PAVN offensive to a halt. By September 1972, ARVN forces retook the city of Quang Tri. "Vietnamization" was again questioned as without U.S. air, artillery, and naval support, the South's forces could not compete with their highly motivated counterparts.

Nixon was then motivated to negotiate with the North. What had been holding up negotiations was Thieu's reluctance to sit with the NLF and Hanoi's reluctance to grant security to a Thieu regime. They had, instead, hoped for a coalition government in the South, which Kissinger had refused to consider. The war-weary leaders in Hanoi and in the PRG also began to reconsider their positions at the negotiating table. On October 8, 1972, Le Duc Tho presented Kissinger with a proposal that basically was a reinvention of the 1954 Geneva Accords. This proposal called for free elections in six months and a promise by the United States to "respect the independence, sovereignty, and territorial integrity of Viet Nam as recognized by the 1954 Accords," although it did include the concession that would allow Thieu to remain in power. Kissinger began a series of meetings between Washington, Paris, and Saigon, attempting to negotiate this latest offer and to bring Thieu into the fold. On October 26, 1972, Kissinger proclaimed to the American people that "peace is at hand."[38] Coming a few days before the elections, Kissinger's claim had dramatic success with the American people, helping Nixon to defeat McGovern by one of the largest margins in American history. Nixon's appeal to the "silent majority" proved successful as the American public leaned more to Nixon's conservativism.

Unfortunately, peace was not at hand. Thieu had misgivings about the proposal, and it was Nixon, who agreed in part with Thieu, who delayed the signing until after the election. With his landslide election behind him, Nixon felt more confident to rewrite the terms that he had previously agreed upon and sent a reluctant Kissinger back to Paris with the new demands. Le Duc Tho was outraged, and Hanoi felt deceived by this latest change of events and promptly refused to reconsider their already compromised agreement. Kissinger and Le Duc Tho talked for weeks until Nixon directed that the talks cease on December 13.

Concerned that the next Congress, to be convened in January, would finally cut off all funding for the war, Nixon attempted to force Hanoi into the new agreement by unleashing the full might of Amer-

Battle gear and clothing discarded near Hoc Mon, Viet Nam, by Army of the Republic of Viet Nam troops in retreat, April 29, 1975. Courtesy of Duong Thanh Phong.

ican air power against Hanoi and Haiphong. To the chairman of the Joint Chiefs, Admiral Tom Moorer, he said emphatically: "I do not want anymore of this crap about the fact that we couldn't hit this target or that one. This is your chance to use military power to win this war, and if you don't, I'll consider it your responsibility."[39]

On December 16, 1972, a massive air campaign was launched against the two Vietnamese cities with huge B-52s in Operation "Linebacker II." For the next eleven days and nights, over 15,000 tons of high explosives were dropped on a wide array of targets including oil depots, rail yards, power plants, and SAM-2 (surface to air missiles) sites. Generally, the bombers were highly accurate; civilian casualties, however, were inevitable. Estimates of as high as 7,000 civilian deaths prompted another wave of domestic and international protest, and Nixon was accused of waging a war of terror against civilians. The Swedish prime minister correlated the bombings to Nazi atrocities as Nixon's approval ratings dropped.

American losses were high as well. The Pentagon admitted to fif-

Lieutenant Colonel Robert L. Stirm is greeted by his family at Travis Air Force Base in California after his release in March 1973. Photo: AP/Wide World Photos

teen B-52s shot down and twenty-five more damaged and another twenty-three fighters and fighter-bombers lost. Within the American military, debate raged about continuing with such high losses with one Air Force historian claiming that at Strategic Air Command Headquarters in Omaha, Nebraska, officers were imploring Nixon to "stop the carnage."[40] Hanoi signaled Nixon that they would once again talk in Paris. Thieu, feeling confident that Nixon would keep his written promise to intervene militarily if Hanoi violated the peace agreement, agreed. The parties consented to a settlement that differed very little from what was originally decided back in October. One of Kissinger's aides remarked sardonically that "we bombed the North Vietnamese into accepting our own concessions."[41] The Paris Accords were signed on January 27, 1973, exactly one week after Nixon was inaugurated for his second term as president. His inauguration was accompanied by over 350,000 demonstrators, the last large antiwar protest of the Viet Nam era.

Without much fanfare and little joyous celebration, a temporary calm descended upon the devastated tropical country. Shortly after

People's Army of Viet Nam tanks storm the presidential palace on April 30, 1975, to end the war in Viet Nam. Courtesy of Duong Thanh Phong.

the accords were signed, the United States got their POWs from Hanoi and, with the exception of special units, the remaining U.S. troops in Viet Nam were sent home. In October of 1973, Kissinger and Le Duc Tho were awarded the Nobel Peace Prize by the Norwegian committee.

While both Hanoi and Thieu consistently violated the Paris Accords, there were no major battles until late in 1974 when, in December, two divisions of PAVN and PLA troops moved against ARVN positions northwest of Saigon near Cambodia. The ARVN forces collapsed after heavy casualties without U.S. support. The PAVN and PLA forces captured the entire Phuoc Long Province. It was a test of Nixon's promise, although by then, Nixon had resigned in disgrace for his many illegal and unethical transgressions, which came to light with the extensive "Watergate" hearings. Thieu panicked and ordered his forces in the Central Highlands to abandon the entire northern region. This set off a disastrous retreat by his ill-prepared forces who tossed their gear onto the highway and fled, with thousands of refugees clogging the few roads to the South. Kontum

A young man's joyful reunion with his mother is caught on film. The man was at the famous Con Doa Island Prison when he was released by victorious People's Army of Viet Nam troops in 1975. Courtesy of Southern Women's Museum.

and Pleiku fell, and by March 26, Hue had been taken by PAVN forces on the coast. More panicked retreats followed as the ARVN rapidly collapsed throughout Southern Viet Nam. On March 29, 1975, Da Nang fell, while escaping ARVN troops were flown out on an overcrowded and damaged TWA 727. The collapse of Thieu's army surprised the PRG and DRV leadership, which had anticipated a two-year fight for reunification. They proceeded cautiously down crowded Highway 1 and by mid-April were outside Xuan Loc, only thirty-five miles from Saigon. There, ARVN units put up their best fight of the entire war. Outnumbered, they held off the PAVN onslaught for one full week, inflicting, and suffering, ghastly casualties before collapsing and retreating toward the capital. Khmer forces in Cambodia were also on the move, and on April 17, 1975, the American-supported government there fell.

Last-ditch efforts by Henry Kissinger and President Gerald Ford to save the dying republic failed when the U.S. Congress voted down a bill calling for $722 million in military aid. PLA and PAVN forces launched from Cu Chi District more assaults, and within days the capital of Saigon was surrounded. A massive attempt to destroy secret documents and evacuate civilians and military personnel got underway as PAVN and PLA troops swarmed into Saigon. Thieu abandoned his country on April 21 and, after looting much of the gold reserve, flew to Taiwan. On April 29, 1975, two U.S. marines became the final casualties in the Viet Nam War when they died in a rocket barrage at Saigon's airport. The next day, PAVN tanks broke down the iron gates of the presidential palace in Saigon and stormed into the grounds. As the last helicopter flights flew from the tops of buildings, including the U.S. Embassy and the CIA house in Saigon, to whisk away CIA workers, embassy guards, and some Vietnamese, thousands of Vietnamese civilians poured into the streets. Carrying NLF and DRV flags and marching alongside PAVN armored columns, they celebrated while surviving ARVN forces and their supporters cast aside their uniforms and papers and melted into the frenzied throngs of civilians. The war in Viet Nam was over.

NOTES

1. Edward Doyle and Samuel Lipsmann, eds., *The Vietnam Experience: Setting the Stage* (Boston: Boston Publishing, 1981), 179.

2. Edward Doyle, Samuel Lipsmann, and Stephen Weiss, eds., *The Vietnam Experience: Passing the Torch* (Boston: Boston Publishing, 1981), 17.

3. James William Gibson, *The Perfect War* (New York: Atlantic Monthly Press, 1986), 55.

4. Doyle, Lipsmann, and Weiss, *Vietnam Experience*, 25.

5. Ibid., 84.

6. John Prados, *The Hidden Story of the Vietnam War* (Chicago: Elephant Paperback 1995), 11.

7. Nguyen Vien Khac, *Viet Nam: A Long History* (Hanoi: Gioi Publishers, 1993), 345.

8. Neil Sheehan, *After the War Was Over* (New York: Random House, 1991), 77.

9. Doyle, Lipsmann, and Weiss, *Vietnam Experience*, 114.

10. Ibid.

11. Ibid.

12. George Donelson Moss, *Vietnam: An American Ordeal* (Upper Saddle River, NJ: Prentice Hall, 1998), 145.

13. Ibid., 180.

14. Ibid., 173.

15. CNN, "The Cold War," CNN television series (June 1996).

16. Stanley Karnow, *Vietnam: A History* (New York: Viking Press, 1983), 417.

17. John Plimlott, *Vietnam: Decisive Battles* (New York: Barnes & Noble, 1990), 48.

18. "Untold Story of the Road to War in Vietnam," *US News & World Report*, October 1983, vn 1–vn 24.

19. Ibid.

20. Edward Doyle and Samuel Lipsmann, eds., *The Vietnam Experience: America Takes Over* (Boston: Boston Publishing, 1982), 108.

21. L. Goure, A.J. Russo, and D. Scott, "Some Findings of the Viet Cong Motivation and Morale Study." *Memorandum* (Santa Monica: Rand Corp., 1966), 7.

22. Doyle and Lipsmann, *Vietnam Experience: America Takes Over*, 105.

23. Huyen Van Chian, taped personal communication, translated by Hanh Thi Ngoc Trinh-Vadas (January 2001).

24. Gibson, *Perfect War*, 145.

25. Doyle and Lipsmann, *Vietnam Experience: America Takes Over*, 108.

26. Arnold R. Issacs, Gordon Hardy, and MacAlister Brown, eds., *The Vietnam Experience: Pawns of War* (Boston: Boston Publishing, 1987), 183.

27. Moss, *Vietnam*, 262.

28. Robert S. McNamara, *In Retrospect* (New York: Random House, 1995), 313.

29. Karnow, *Vietnam*, 582.

30. Truong, Nhu Tang *A Viet Cong Memoir: An Inside Account of the War and Its Aftermath* (New York: Vintage, 1985), 289.

31. Richard Moser, *The New Winter Soldiers: GI and Veteran Dissent during the Vietnam Era* (New Brunswick: Rutgers University Press, 1996), 47.

32. Maurice Isserman, *Witness to War: Personal Narratives from the Conflict in Vietnam* (New York: Perigee, 1995), 167.

33. Todd Gitlin, *The Sixties: Years of Hope, Days of Rage* (New York: Bantam Press, 1987), 409.

34. Ibid., 410.

35. Ibid., 414.

36. Clark Dougan, and Samuel Lipsmann, eds., *The Vietnam Experience: A Nation Divided* (Boston: Boston Publishing, 1984), 177.

37. Ibid., 183.

38. Gibson, *Perfect War*, 413.

39. Moss, *Vietnam*, 391.

40. Gibson, *Perfect War*, 416.

41. Moss, *Vietnam*, 394.

Chapter 2

Understanding the Cultural Conflicts between the United States and Viet Nam

THE UNITED STATES AFTER WORLD WAR II

"I saw things that you cannot ever imagine," wrote Martin Bolha, a World War II combat veteran in Europe. "When the war ended in Europe I was sent home, and when I landed in New York, in my exhilaration, I felt that for the very first time in my life I truly understood how great America was."[1]

Martin Bolha, whose carpenter father had immigrated to the United States from Slovenia in 1909, grew up in northern Ohio and starred as an athlete in high school. Coming from a peasant farm in Slovenia, Martin's father had left his home in 1909 to escape the conflicts and coming World War I in what was to be called Yugoslavia. Fleeing one of the many "Balkan Crises," he left Franz Josef's army and headed for the security of the United States.

Martin had a job making thirty-five cents an hour and was playing football for Akron University when he got his draft notice in 1942. Martin had grown up in near poverty in Mogadore, Ohio, a small working class community southeast of Akron. His older brother died during the great influenza epidemic at the age of only eighteen months, and he, and his three surviving older sisters, learned about hard work and strict discipline. Politics did not interest him, but when he got his draft notice, he was ready to serve. "You have to serve your country," he wrote. "We all talked about the war, we hated Hitler. . . . All the guys were ready to go."[2]

After getting his airborne rating in Georgia, Martin Bolha was sent to the European theater in 1944. Coming ashore in France at Utah Beach weeks after the Normandy Invasion, Martin fought his way toward Germany with the 104th Infantry Division (the "Timberwolves"). After being wounded by shrapnel near Aachen, just prior to the Battle of the Bulge, Martin engaged in a firefight in which he was ultimately awarded the Bronze Star for valor and meritorious conduct as well as the Purple Heart.

Two incidents deeply moved Martin during the war, the first near a German concentration camp outside Nordhausen, Germany. He remembers standing in a slight drizzle while watching a long procession of recently liberated inmates, emaciated, looking hollow and desperate, slowly walk by. At one point, a young woman in line passed by and shouted a grateful greeting to him in Slovene, his own native language. She was in tears and exuberant meeting someone who could speak her native tongue. She told him she had been taken from her home three years earlier and was used by two German officers at the camp as a servant. Suddenly, those same two officers appeared in another line of prisoners of war being marched from the camp, and the woman, to Martin's surprise, took his pistol, ran up to these two men, and shot them both in the head. "I was shocked and stunned and could only then begin to understand the horror that she had lived through," wrote Bolha. She returned his pistol while hugging him in tears and thanking him over and over again. At that moment, the significance of fighting Hitler hit home.

Martin had also met the Russian troops on the Elbe River in April of 1945. He was there as an interpreter as Slovenian is similar to the Russian language. He was appalled at the vengeance and ruthlessness he saw in the manner and talk of the Russian soldiers, two of whom were women soldiers who had sprayed a German refugee column on a bridge with gunfire. This ruthless execution of civilians made him leery of the Russians, a wariness that stayed with him for years.

Martin steamed into New York Harbor on the way home from the war and passed the Statue of Liberty. "I became almost overwhelmed with emotion. I had come from a terrible place," he wrote years later, "a place where the world seemed to be upside down, a place of great pain and sadness. I was very happy to be an American." At that moment, he and one of his buddies walked to the rail and saluted the majestic statue.

The night he finally returned to his home in Mogadore, he celebrated and "danced the polka" with his family to whom he had writ-

Martin Bolha (top left), leaves Germany in July 1945. Although not greeted by a victory parade, Bolha, unlike many Viet Nam veterans, returned home with a strong sense of accomplishment. Courtesy of Martin Bolha.

ten prodigiously throughout the war. His respite at home was brief, however, and soon he was back in service near San Luis Obisbo, California. There, while training for duty in the Pacific theater, he became ecstatic upon hearing of the dropping of atomic bombs on Hiroshima and Nagasaki. "It ended the war for all of us who were very exhausted and worried about being sent back over."

His thoughts reflect those of an overwhelming majority of Americans at the end of World War II. His patriotic emotions exemplified those of an entire generation of GIs who returned from the war with bitter feelings about totalitarian regimes, a generation of Americans whose suffering during the war and the Great Depression welded a powerful sense of patriotism and respect for the "American way." This patriotism stemmed from a sense that capitalism and American democracy were the hope for the rest of the world in a chaotic and violent time. Martin Bolha, like most of his fellow countrypeople, was psychologically ready to wage a "Cold War" to keep the "American way" strong against communism.

In 1947 Martin migrated west where he married, raised four children, and found the "American dream" his father had long sought among the mystical Joshua trees in the high desert community of Yucca Valley, California.

Martin lived through the Korean War years, concerned about the rise of communism, a philosophy that he "never cared for," and when the McCarthy hearings made the news in the early 1950s, Martin paid little attention. He figured that Senator Joseph McCarthy was a bit extreme, but he trusted President Dwight D. Eisenhower, having fought under his command in Europe. He had total trust in the government to keep the peace and to keep "Russia, and China, or any government that threatened people's freedom" in line. Martin was convinced that great sacrifice was warranted to prevent the world from allowing another Hitler to rampage as he had done in the 1940s. So when President Eisenhower talked about "falling dominoes" in Indochina in 1956, he went about his business, having "complete faith in Ike."

The postwar United States witnessed an unprecedented prosperity throughout most of the country as the nation turned to a seductive peacetime consumer society. The advent of television reduced isolation and strengthened America's cultural identity. The culture of the 1950s saw women return from their wartime jobs to raise children in sprawling new suburban communities. The new prosperity reduced, to a degree, the prewar tensions that had existed between business and labor, as the resulting increase in the overall standard of living created a stable confidence in capitalism and the American system. Events in Europe and Asia, coinciding with the Soviet Union's development of the atomic bomb in 1949, had great impact on Americans in the 1950s as the fear of communism and the darker side of human nature in a nuclear age resulted in a wide variety of allegories against the spread of "Communist evil." William Golding's 1954 novel, *The Lord of the Flies*, warned us of what lay ahead if we were left to "recreate" society and George Orwell's *Animal Farm* (1945) satirized the Communist concept of equality.

While American politics was uniformly anti-Communist, the growing pop culture of the 1950s expounded a growing individuality. Walt Disney created a huge fantasyland out of a California orange grove called "Disneyland" in 1957, Elvis Presley rocked into the national scene in 1954 with his first recording called "That's All Right Mama," and Dr. Suess tweaked the imagination of both young and old with his *How the Grinch Stole Christmas* and *The Cat in the Hat* (1957). American culture in the 1950s was transforming itself almost exponentially as the new prosperity fed a nation hungry for entertainment.

The peaceful solace that Martin Bolha had perceived in the 1950s came to an abrupt end one November day in 1963 when President John F. Kennedy (JFK), a man Martin "liked a hell of a lot," was murdered in Dallas, Texas. The ensuing events of the 1960s confused and angered Martin as he could not comprehend his nation in such turmoil, nor could he understand what young people across America were all about during the waves of protest, drug use, and rock music that typified the 1960s and seemed alien to him.

The death of President Kennedy proved traumatic for the entire nation as the American people entered an era where cynicism and mistrust replaced the nearly universal and historical faith that Americans had in their government. Lyndon B. Johnson became frustrated by Viet Nam as it took the limelight and funding away from his "Great Society." He envisioned the new prosperity to deliver the United States into an egalitarian industrial giant that would be the envy of the world. The Civil Rights Movement, galvanized by court decisions that outlawed racial segregation, had snowballed with such a momentum that it would no longer take a back seat in American politics. Charismatic and spiritual leaders such as Martin Luther King, Jr., catapulted the pain and poverty of Black America onto the national conscience. Isolated moments of courage and dignity such as Rosa Parks's refusal to give up her "white" seat on a Montgomery, Alabama, city bus in December 1955 grew into a national movement of Americans of all races demanding equal justice and an end to discrimination. The agonizingly slow progress that the movement made tested the patience of many blacks and other minorities as groups such as the Black Panthers, representing radical alternatives to the nonviolent civil disobedience advocated by Martin Luther King, began to come into violent conflict with local and national police agencies. By 1965, cities across America had erupted into violent confrontation, with death and destruction increasingly common. Riots in the urban centers of Los Angeles, Newark, Detroit (where open battles between troops and blacks resulted in forty-three deaths), Cleveland, and other American cities broke out as Americans witnessed the apparent tranquil prosperity of the 1950s rapidly fading from national memory.

The exquisite image of white "suburbia" was questioned by a new generation of youths who, identifying with the romantic notions of artists and celebrities such as Jack Kerouac (beat poet), Timothy Leary (LSD proponent), the Beatles (rock-and-roll musicians), and Ken Kesey (author of *One Flew over the Cuckoo's Nest*) turned in increasing numbers to a growing counterculture where drug use, sexual freedom, and music became the vehicles of individualistic expression. The rise of the counterculture represented an unusual collision of several variables including rapid development in technology, the Great Depression and World War II generation, exemplified by Martin Bolha; and the expansion of worldwide access to media and cultural traditions never before seen—all of this under the compelling threat of nuclear war. Through it all, the Viet Nam War became transfixed onto the national and global scene, becoming the focal point with which two diametrically opposite cultural generations clashed. Viet Nam became, by twist of fate, the very definition of what separated the depression era babies, such as Martin Bolha, from the Cold War–era babies, which included Martin's four children: A war to protect the American way of life or an outdated colonial reaction to inevitable movement toward independence, Viet Nam had become *the* event of a new generation of Americans.

A close look at the Civil Rights Movement of the 1950s and 1960s reveals an American culture not as docile as generally thought but rather a culture with serious problems that were ready to explode by the time the war in Viet Nam had mesmerized national attention. In 1963, for example, some 930 civil rights demonstrations had occurred, resulting in over 20,000 arrests and culminating in the massive march on Washington, D.C., in which Martin Luther King, Jr., was immortalized with his "I Have a Dream" speech.[3] Antiwar sentiment has long been part of American politics, with massive and violent antidraft demonstrations occurring in New York City during the Civil War. American literature and music that advocated antiwar perspectives, revolution, union organizing, or other acts of civil disobedience had long become an integral part of American culture. This includes the works of writers such as Jack London, Henry David Thoreau, and John Reed, of the socialist politician Norman Thompson, and the folksy union supporter Woody Guthrie—author of the tune, "This Land Is Our Land," a song written to declare ownership of America by all its citizens, not just the wealthy and powerful. People whom Martin Bolha's father had grown to admire. This had evolved from the rather strong elements of the socialist, unionist, and Communist movements of the early decades of the 1900s but had been relatively shattered by the turn of events of the 1950s, more specifically, the McCarthy hearings, the postwar growing prosperity of the middle and working class in America, and the moral repulsion toward the Soviet Union's debacles such as in Hungary in 1956 and the Cuban missile crisis of 1962.

The 1960s counterculture had its immediate origins in the beat and jazz movements of the 1950s as characterized by artists like poet Jack Kerouac, comedian Lenny Bruce, jazz musician Charlie Parker, and even actors Marlon Brando and James Dean. The common denominator appears to be the lost or restless soul, outcast, antihero, or pained artist who sought spiritual solace lacking in the material expansion that represented suburban growth coinciding with inner city decay in the late 1950s. A large part of an entire postwar American generation, reared with the fantasy worlds of Walt Disney, *MAD* magazine, and the television show "Howdy Doody," were very ready to be seduced by the listless spirits that resided on the cultural fringe of post–World War II America.

As Viet Nam arrived, a new generation of American youths were ready to take on and challenge longstanding American traditions. This "revolution" became politicized by the draft and the war at a time when the nation was reeling from the murder of JFK and the urban riots in mid-1960s. On July 21, 1965, a relatively unknown folk singer from Minnesota who called himself "Bob Dylan" seized the moment at the usually apolitical Newport Jazz and Folk Festival with prophetic words about changing times that Martin Bolha could sense but not understand.

VIET NAM: ITS PEOPLE, ITS LAND

"Oh East is East, and West is West,
And never the twain shall meet."

Rudyard Kipling, "White Man's Burden"

When Martin Bolha, like virtually all the nearly 180 million Americans in the early 1960s, first heard about Viet Nam, he initially "had no idea where in the world it even was." He knew even less about Viet Nam's history and nothing of its land, culture, or traditions— "It didn't really matter to me one way or another." Americans who fought in Viet Nam lacked the time and opportunity to see and understand Viet Nam as anything other than a hot, humid, dangerous, and often hostile place. John Lancaster, a U.S. marine who fought near Hue in 1968, related: "I never had the time to really interact with the Vietnamese; I was always on the move, or, when not, I was too tired to really see what was before me."[4]

The "East" or "Orient" has always intrigued Westerners as Kipling's poem symbolizes an imaginary wall separating Asians and Americans who are seldom able to fully comprehend or tolerate the other. A 1971 poll taken of supposedly Allied Vietnamese civilians by U.S. officials found opinions of Americans as "drunkards, haughty, licentious men who . . . seemed indifferent."[5] An American officer summarized the lack of cultural understanding when he reported that "the GI isn't tolerant. Never has been. . . . Our boys are full of fighting spirit, whiskey, women. . . . They disrupt civilian communities here . . . wherever they are assigned overseas."[6]

Viet Nam is a nation with ancient histories and traditions that have had significant impact on the Vietnamese resolve to fight foreigners. It is located in an area of Southeast Asia bordered by Laos and Kampuchea to the west, China in the north, and the South China Sea to the east and south. It is roughly 1,200 miles from north to south and ranges in width from 300 to just 50 miles near the seventeenth parallel. Viet Nam is a tropical nation with beautiful mountains and cave-filled bays along the coastal regions that have, for countless generations, inspired traditional myth and folklore.

Viet Nam has five distinct geographic regions: the coastal plains, the Red River Valley, and delta region in the north; the rugged mountain regions of the north bordering China; the Central Highlands, which range primarily in the west central areas near the border region between Laos, Viet Nam, and Kampuchea; and the Mekong River and delta regions in the far south, with little elevation and mostly flat lands interspersed with numerous canals and rivers that are affected by seasonal floods and ocean tides.

Viet Nam has two seasons: the rainy season, usually from mid-June through November for the southern parts, and the dry season, which is usually in effect from January through April. The highlands can see rain on any given day even in the dry season, with relatively cool weather, especially at night. The temperature along the coasts can be extremely hot with high humidity, sometimes reaching 110 degrees Fahrenheit.

Primordial Viet Nam was covered mostly with dense jungle growth, sometimes with triple canopy, along with mangrove swamps, fertile plains, and long sandy white beaches bordered for miles with palms. Marine, plant, and animal life is extremely varied and includes five major fruits that thrive yearlong: banana, guava, papaya, coconut, and pineapple. Mango, melons, oranges, pomelo, jufube, longan, litchi, grapes, and tangerines are some of the seasonal fruits. Crocodiles, gibbons, tigers, elephants, wild boars, deer, rhinoceros, bears, cobra snakes, and wild ox are examples of its varied wildlife.

The jungle- and fog-shrouded Central Highlands have long been a barrier between the north and south, allowing for distinct cultures to develop: northern, southern, and various ethnic populations in the highlands the French referred to as Montagnards.

The earliest sites of human habitation are found along the Ma River southwest of Hanoi and have been dated to approximately 450,000 years ago. By the end of the neolithic era, about 5,500 years ago, rice-cultivating cultures had spread throughout Viet Nam, especially along the coasts and major river delta regions. From ancient Chinese historical annals, there is a fairly concise account of the spread of what the Chinese called the Lac Viets, a people who inhabited southern China and what is now northern Viet Nam, who continued to migrate further south. The Lac Viet comprised fifteen major tribes who developed an existence that depended upon rice and certain traditions, some of which, like the chewing of betel nuts and the darkening of teeth by women, are still found today. Legend puts the first major Viet dynasty, the Hung, at around 3,000 B.C.E, ruling in a kingdom called the Van Lang. Another federation of tribes, the Tay Au, developed their culture primarily in the mountainous regions in the north, and eventually they defeated the last Hung king and merged the cultures into the kingdom of Au Lac in 258 B.C.E. Fifty years later, Trieu Da unified the northern parts of Viet Nam and southern China into the kingdom of Nam Viets (literally, Southern Viets). The spread of Chinese influence upon the Viets established a pattern of subjugation, revolt, independence, and renewed subjugation that would mold Vietnamese history and national identity in a series of wars for independence over a 2,000-year period.

The Han, in 111 B.C.E., conquered the kingdom of Nam Viet,

initiating two parallel developments in which Chinese literature, Mandarin government organization, trade, and military control spread throughout northern Viet Nam, while the Viet population developed a strong sense of national identity built of resistance and armed insurrection.

Local Viet nobles collaborated with the Chinese for land and power but were able to help the Viets retain a strong national identity. The Viets benefited from Chinese irrigation and dike-building technology, enabling them to harness the powerful Red River. In addition, the teachings about life and government rule of Confucius helped Viet scholars organize local and regional political structures to facilitate trade and education.

Despite many benefits of Chinese influence, a burning passion for independence thrived, leading to a series of revolts. In 39 C.E. two sisters, Trung Trac and Trung Nhi, collectively known as Hai Ba Trung, led a peasant army that defeated the Chinese. A Chinese army later defeated the Trung alliance near the present Hanoi, and the sisters committed suicide in the Song Hong (Red River) rather than allow themselves to be captured. The Trung sisters, exemplifying the great respect Vietnamese women are accorded in both literary and political realms, became national heroines in Vietnamese lore. Almost constant warfare between the Chinese and Vietnamese followed until relative peace descended under Chinese rule again in 603 in what the Chinese called An Nam.

The first Vietnamese dynasty in 939 eventually saw the establishment of Buddhism by Khuong Viet. Vietnamese peasants were attracted to the Buddhist promise of a painless afterlife in lieu of the teachings of Confucius. The strict lessons of Confucius were, however, retained in the administration of governments and education. Buddhism was first introduced to Viet Nam from Indian and Chinese monks in second century C.E. and helped the Vietnamese develop a spirituality integrated into their daily lives that stressed unity, conformity, and forgiveness and emphasized the future and present over the past, qualities that would serve the Vietnamese well in their endless series of struggles against foreigners.

In 1284, the Mongols sent an army of 500,000 warriors southward to conquer Viet Nam. The Vietnamese general Tran Hung Dao met the invasion by engaging in a fighting retreat from the north border region with his outnumbered army of 200,000. Inspired by Tran Hung Dao's resistance, many Vietnamese peasants tattooed nationalist slogans on their arms in defiance of the invading horde. This practice endured until the 1970s when Northerners tattooed the words "Born in the North to die in the South" on their arms before traveling south along the Ho Chi Minh Trail.

Tran Hung Dao mercilessly harried the invading troops. He finally lured them to defeat at the battle of the Bach Dang River and sent them reeling back to China. The survivors, captured in battle, were shown mercy: They were told to leave but were always welcome to return as guests.

The next nine centuries witnessed a strengthening of Vietnamese nationalism amidst warfare, revolt, migration southward to the Mekong River areas, and civil war. Throughout this period, Chinese influenced Vietnamese culture with feudal rulers endowed with Confucian philosophy. This philosophy integrated the concepts of authority (usually at the village level), conservatism, dogmatism, and scholastic education. All the while, the educated Vietnamese class integrated an emphasis on Confucianism's rational and positive elements. One of the traditional Confucian principles, the concept of *chun* (loyalty), referred to unquestioning obedience to the emperor. The Vietnamese feudal lords adapted this concept into their own version, *trung*, which added a significant reservation to *chun*, that being that loyalty to the emperor was merited only if the emperor was a Vietnamese patriot first. If the emperor bowed to "foreigners," then loyalty was not obligatory. Obligation was seen, as a result, as being owed mainly to Vietnamese independence. This deviation from traditional Confucian thought was significant, especially to the continuing rise of Vietnamese nationalism. As a result, most resistance movements over the centuries were led by Confucian scholars tied to the masses of Vietnamese peasants. Confucianism grew to be seen as symbolic of everything Vietnamese. This was true even as Buddhism spread throughout Viet Nam as a spiritual replacement to Confucian philosophy. The educated Mandarin scholars, ruling with Confucian rationality, articulated the vision of independence and freedom generation after generation until the French arrived in the 1800s. The concept of *trung* was to become a significant and fundamental obstacle to the American effort in the twentieth century at nation building with its support of Diem and later Thieu. The strong traditional sense of loyalty to those in power vanished as neither Diem nor Thieu could illicit strong support from the majority of Vietnamese during the 1960s and 1970s, being tied to corruption and affiliation with a "foreign" power: the United States.

The Nguyen Dynasty, Viet Nam's final monarchy, began in 1802

Traditional musicians perform at a hotel in Viet Nam. Courtesy of Molly Cook.

with the rule of Nguyen Anh who resuscitated Confucian principles into the ruling of Viet Nam, which also witnessed a rise in anti-Catholic sentiment. The French who moved to Viet Nam ruled harshly while setting up a government and society that favored Catholics and those Vietnamese willing to study European ways of trade, law, and commerce. French landowners were able to live a life of luxury, more so than in France itself, as they profited greatly from Viet Nam's new economy and cheap labor. The French introduced architecture in the building of schools, government buildings, and homes for the ruling class, many of which stand to this day. In addition, French colonialists also brought clothing, music, literature, language, tourism, legal systems, opera, food, and more missionaries to Indochina. While many Vietnamese were able to thrive alongside the French colonialists, usually by converting to Christianity, most Vietnamese suffered greatly under a French rule whose cruelty continuously spawned endless revolts. Those willing to work for the French were soon to be educated, often in Paris, and developed the basis for a pro-Western middle and upper class within Vietnamese society that would later be the foundation of support for the Americans as well. Although their numbers never represented much of Viet Nam's populace, they were given substantial holdings of land and business and government positions. With the defeat at Dien Bien Phu

An elder waits for his noontime prayer at the Cao
Dai Temple near Tay Ninh City, Viet Nam.
Courtesy of Robert E. Vadas.

in 1954, this class of educated Vietnamese, straying from the traditional Confucian identity of Vietnamese nationalism, became the
foundation for the new nation being built with the support of the
United States in America's fight against communism. French influence came to an abrupt end in the mid-1950s, while American involvement intensified. These first Americans found themselves among
a Vietnamese people rich in history with a 2,000-year tradition of
resisting foreign interference. The first American soldiers and poli-
cymakers of the Viet Nam involvement generally ignored this tradi-

tion, seeing the Vietnamese as mere pawns in a global "Cold War." Americans generally felt that the revolution was inspired by "Communist" pawns of China and Russia and would be quickly overwhelmed by American firepower and economic influence. French President Charles DeGaulle warned John F. Kennedy about underestimating the Vietnamese ability to persist; Kennedy, like most Americans, ignored him.

THE AMERICANS IN VIET NAM

Roughly 2.7 million Americans served in or near Viet Nam. Most of the first troops sent between the years 1950 and 1964 were older professional soldiers, many of whom fought in World War II and/or the Korean conflict.

By 1966, the number of those serving in Viet Nam who were drafted rose dramatically, although the troops were still, for the most part, volunteers, well trained, with high morale. After 1969, the make-up of the troops more closely resembled the 1960s generation, with high percentages of draftees who were less than enthusiastic about the war, many of whom brought to Viet Nam behaviors that were common in the states: drug use, long hair, and a protest spirit representing the rock-and-roll culture sweeping the nation.

The men who fought in Viet Nam, to some degree, represented the cultural diversity of the nation (see Appendix C). Despite variations in age, race, gender, and overall "culture" of the troops in Viet Nam, there were significant patterns of behaviors and "cultural" identities that can be used to describe the "average" American GI. Soldiers serving during the time period from 1964 to 1972 represented, for the most part, those coming of age in the 1950s—"baby boomers," born after World War II, when millions of GIs, like Martin Bolha, returned home from the war to raise families, deeply inspired by visions of realizing the American dream.

The first generation to grow up entirely with television, they were introduced to a massive bombardment of commercial products and grew up with a highly developed sense of consumerism. The nation engaged in great changes in the 1950s as blacks and poor whites migrated from the South to jobs in Northern cities, resulting in "white flight" to housing tracts in new communities referred to as "suburbia." By 1959, 25 percent of all Americans lived in suburbia in what could be described as "cookie cutter" houses that were built with limited variations and color. Eleven of 13 million homes built in the United States between 1945 and 1955 were built in the suburbs. This cookie-cutter image represented the corporate ideal or "team," in which conformity with the goal of achieving social stability coincided with a massive growth of the American middle class. Exemplifying this corporate hegemony is the statement that businessman Ray Kroc put out to his staff in the early years of his newly purchased McDonald's hamburger chain in 1955: "We cannot trust people to be nonconformist. . . . The organization cannot trust the individual."[7]

Television shows like *Leave It to Beaver* reflected the new suburban values, and even shows that catered to urban residents, such as the comedy starring Jackie Gleason and Art Carney, *The Honeymooners*, had as a theme Ralph's and Norton's endless hilarious schemes to escape the working class to find the American dream.

World War II and the depression had greatly impacted American life, with hundreds of thousands of children left fatherless and widowed women moving into the work force in great numbers for the first time. The almost surreal fantasy world that 1950s America witnessed was perhaps a way to tranquilize the trauma experienced during those frightful times. Nothing exemplifies that fantasy world better than the imaginary world found in the beginner reading books that told the story of "Dick and Jane." The always sunny, always happy and fun-filled world of Dick and Jane urged first-time readers to "look" and to "run," to wonder and to behave. They lived in a world with white picket fences, a forever-green lawn, a dog named Spot, and a father who was eternally patient and understanding and a mother loyal and nurturing, model parents in a model world where there was no anger or frustration. Millions of baby boomers, first learning to talk or read, awoke to this fantasy world also on television. The *Captain Kangaroo* TV show, created by Bob Keeshan, aired in 1955, seduced millions of growing baby boomers into reading and exploring a painless life inside the parameters of the TV. Bob Keeshan wrote: "It was for me the world of Dick and Jane, the world that every child should inhabit, a world with yellow brick roads, the security of parental love, full stomachs and overflowing hearts filled with warm feelings. . . . Dick and Jane could only be a wonderful dream, a dream of what might be."[8]

This utopian sense of love and childhood fantasy was promoted and sheltered in schools that tried to avoid controversy and neglected to discuss serious global issues. The men who fought and died in 1968 in Viet Nam were five or six years old when *Captain Kangaroo*,

Disneyland, McDonald's hamburgers, and the *Howdy Doody Show* first came on the national scene. They went to elementary and secondary schools that taught them nothing about politics and revolution, about faraway lands and cultures like Viet Nam. Their parents, for the most part, stayed married and had great faith in their politicians.

The most impactive cultural change of the 1950s and early 1960s was, by far, the dramatic transformation of American life caused by the rise of the institution of the automobile, a natural consequence of migration to the sprawling suburbs. Large and powerful cars made their way into millions of driveways across America as the nation responded to TV ads such as Chevrolet's "See the USA in a Chevrolet." The national interstate and highway system was begun in 1956, creating an instant love affair as Americans fused their ideals of individual freedom with owning a car. By 1960, one in seven jobs in the United States revolved around the auto industry, coinciding with development of "fast" food restaurants such as McDonald's and Burger King, which catered to America's new sense of identity in the "fast lane."

Although these baby boomers had not experienced World War II or the Great Depression, they were heavily influenced by these dramatic events. Their parents devoted significant amounts of time to instilling in the new generation a strong sense of national pride and work ethic. For the first time ever, an entire generation came of age with the real threat of nuclear annihilation hovering like some foreboding cloud—behind which was a sinister and "evil" empire intent on destroying everything sacred to all Americans: religion, capitalism, and freedom. In large and small schools throughout the United States, in cities, in towns, and in rural areas, teachers and guest speakers showed films and handed out posters depicting the evils of communism behind what was ominously called the "Iron Curtain."

Many students engaged in "duck-and-cover" air raid drills while eerily screeching air raid sirens wailed outside. Parents talked quietly at home about "fallout" shelters and what to do if "it" started, referring to the "third and final world war." Such talk filled dinner table discussions during the now-infamous Cuban missile crisis in 1962.

The incessant anti-Communist onslaught that pervaded the 1950s helped create a patriotic zeal that inspired many American youths to enlist to fight communism and to fight it where their government was telling them to fight: in a small corner of the earth called Viet Nam. Representing a culture steeped in a tradition of free enterprise, a perception of individualistic freedom, and a Judeo-Christian ethic, the American soldiers who went to Viet Nam were told that the "enemy" in Viet Nam was communism that threatened their own "way of life." It was an attitude that, at times, resulted in excessive and extreme behaviors such as the McCarthy hearings in the early 1950s, the exposure of soldiers to atomic bomb tests in the Nevada and Arizona deserts, and Central Intelligence Agency interference in foreign affairs. This attitude, mixed with general ignorance of Vietnamese culture, often led to a serious conflict of cultures between Viet Nam and the United States. During his trial for the massacre of innocent Vietnamese civilians, at the village of Song My in 1968, U.S. Army Lieutenant William Calley spoke of this when he stated:

When my troops were getting massacred by an enemy I couldn't feel, I couldn't see, I couldn't touch, that nobody . . . ever described as anything other than communism, they didn't give it a race, a sex, or even an age; they never let me believe that it was a philosophy in a man's mind. . . . That was my enemy out there.[9]

The thousands of young American baby boomers who went to fight in Viet Nam had a new sense of cultural and national identity. Mixed with a general ignorance of Vietnamese traditions, this was the foundation for the national crisis that Viet Nam became in the 1960s.

THE PEOPLE'S LIBERATION ARMY

Most Americans refer to members of the National Liberation Front (NLF) and its military wing, the People's Liberation Army (PLA), as "Viet Cong." The term elicits images of black-pajamaed men sneaking around at night, killing and fighting in almost mythical dimensions. In songs and poems, books and school papers, the Viet Cong have been ingrained in the American psyche as the "enemy" and portrayed in movies as nameless and evil harbingers of the sinister "Communists." Those who fought in the PLA were, in truth, much more complex and diverse than how they have been presented. Although most of the leadership were Communist party members, the majority of PLA and People's Army of Viet Nam (PAVN) fighters were Buddhist or traditionalist Vietnamese, some were Catholic, with a sizable majority coming from small farming and fishing villages. Most had little formal education and had spent most of their lives working in the hot sun or unending monsoon rains in traditional seasonal cycles of rice farming. Most were poor, but not all. High-ranking officials could get their children into good schools, even in Russia or China, but many of their sons and daughters also volunteered to fight. Minh Tien Viet, whose father was the Vietnamese ambassador to Cambodia, reenlisted in 1965 with the Twenty-Fifth PAVN Regiment and was killed during the U.S. invasion of Cambodia in May 1970.[10]

Used to hard, cooperative work with their clan or village members, the typical PLA fighter was about twenty-three years old with six years of combat experience. Their training ranged from minimal in the local militias to highly trained commandos with several months spent in specialty training camps in the North. Although the Viet Cong's legend as "jungle" fighters grew as the war progressed, most Vietnamese, in fact, avoid the dangerous jungles, and few had real experience living off the land. These were skills that were developed out of necessity as the war progressed.

PLA fighters ate mostly rice, fish, tarot root with cups of tea, vegetables and fruits, sometimes washed down with traditional herbal "snake" wine or rice wine. They played cards often and sang and listened to the traditional music sometimes offered by traveling music troupes. They wrote letters or kept journals, many of them written as poems to family or lovers. Whenever they wrote, they had to be wary of army censors.

In battle, they usually fought with extreme courage and tenacity, enduring casualties that would break most armies in the field. A major concern was for their bodies to be retrieved for proper burial to permit their soul to leave their feet and ride with the large stork to heaven. They feared being left on a battlefield and went to supreme effort to carry away their dead and wounded, a behavior that impressed Americans in the field and stymied U.S. officials obsessed with "body counts."

Occasionally they would get "Dear John" letters from a lost love, but usually Vietnamese were very faithful to their parted lovers, and stories of returning veterans being reunited after ten or even fifteen years were not uncommon. They carried photographs of their families and children and fell to homesickness and loneliness as well as diseases that thinned their ranks nearly as much as American weapons. They seldom got paid; most, especially in the early years, were volunteers and often fought alongside friends or relatives, even sons and daughters. After battles, they would have to face their cadres in atonement sessions in which their behavior was critiqued.

Although American troops could look forward to leaving Viet Nam after a year, the PLA and PAVN fighters fought until dead, wounded, or victorious. They had about nineteen ounces of supplies per day available to them compared with nearly fifty pounds of supplies per American soldier per day. Their intelligence was excellent for the most part, as even high-ranking Army of the Republic of Viet Nam (ARVN) generals were often PLA agents. They knew of most B-52 raids, most operations and sweeps, and were usually able to leave an area quickly, before an assault began. They went to great lengths to prepare for an assault and usually engaged only when they had the element of surprise. Their basic goal was simply to survive and to wait out the U.S. resolve to carry out a war without popular support at home. Their primary military strategy was to inflict casualties on the Americans, destroy installations, and deny a sense of security to the Government of Viet Nam and their American allies.

As the war progressed and Russian and Chinese supplies got to the Southern fronts, their technological support improved greatly. By the end of the conflict, most were armed with the modern AK-47 assault rifle. They had a wide array of homemade bombs and mines and were able to utilize booby traps in ingenious manners. They often would obtain most of their explosives from the dud American shells lying around almost everywhere, they would turn them into weapons to use against their former owners.

Rand Corporation studies of motivations and morale indicated that the majority of PLA members joined because of mistreatment of the villagers by the South government troops and police. Overall, the Vietnamese who turned to the revolution and sided with the PLA did so for a variety of reasons, and ideological communism was the motivation of a rather small percentage. Anger at the bombing, shelling, and spraying of defoliants was a significant reason for joining, especially if the villagers felt that those actions were done without the justification of responding to PLA attacks.

Life in the PLA was difficult and, as the war progressed, became nearly intolerable as massive American firepower and sweeps of NLF-controlled territory made life in the underground resistance extremely perilous. Despite having to face the awesome firepower and technology of the United States, the PLA continued their fight until April 30, 1975, when PAVN and PLA forces captured Saigon from ARVN troops. General Maxwell Taylor told American officials in a briefing that

the ability of the Viet Cong continuously to rebuild their units and to make good their losses is one of the mysteries of this guerrilla war. . . . Not only do the Viet Cong units have the recuperative powers of the Phoenix, but they have an amazing ability to maintain morale. Only in rare cases have we found evidence of bad morale among Viet Cong prisoners or recorded in captured documents.[11]

However, the Rand studies indicated an increasing willingness to defect from the PLA as the war grew in intensity. According to U.S. statistics, nearly 70,000 Vietnamese rallied to the South side during the war, although many of those were, in fact, simply taking a break to get food and supplies and then returned to their comrades. The major reasons for these defections were, as stated in the Rand study, either a lack of belief in their ability to win, anger at the PLA for its terror tactics and lack of promised support for families, and the inability to stand up to the draconian conditions that the front fighters had to endure. Their PAVN brethren, coming from the North, rarely suffered from these issues and exhibited extreme discipline throughout the conflict. Fewer than 1,700 PAVN regulars defected during the war, most of whom identified escape from punishment for infractions as their primary motivation.

Growing up in a culture immersed in centuries-old struggles against foreign rule made recruitment that much easier for the NLF leadership. The war against the Americans was more a war of independence and nationalism than it was of promoting Communist theory. When the PLA cadres traveled through the countryside, usually at night, to talk to the villagers, they invoked traditional loyalty to the motherland with stories of Hai Ba Trung, Le Loi, and Tran Hung Dao, all Vietnamese heroes that overcame great odds to defeat foreign enemies. In addition, the Vietnamese tradition of *trung*, which qualified loyalty to the emperor or any reigning government as being merited only if the authority was a Vietnamese patriot, was ever present. If the rulers bowed to "foreigners," then loyalty was not obligatory. Thus, Diem's, and later Thieu's, policies of oppressing the villages in the countryside while catering to the mostly Catholic urban governmental officials elicited a strong and negative response by most rural Vietnamese who felt that the traditional authority of the village had been compromised by the South government. One Vietnamese villager stated that he

hated the soldiers of the Ngo Dinh Diem regime. . . . The villagers were already very poor, and yet, the soldiers commanded them to build roads and bridges. . . . Under . . . Diem's regime, people had to pay all kinds of taxes. . . . A person even had to pay a tax . . . if he wanted to sell a buffalo. And yet, the soldiers carried weapons to protect him and his regime. Therefore, [he] hated the soldiers.[12]

Thus, regardless of the intent or even behavior of the Americans, the villagers viewed them as controlling Diem and most simply wanted them to leave. To the Vietnamese villagers and the PLA fighters, ancient and powerful traditional attachment to their lands was the foundation of their culture. It is believed by villagers that the souls of their ancestors roam about their sacred soil near the village. To leave means to abandon their soul, to lose their status. Thus, when Vietnamese were brought to newly built towns after their removal from ancient grounds, they, especially the elders, fermented anger and hatred, this despite the new schools, homes, and sanitary facilities usually missing in their own villages. The resultant attitude was seen as arrogance by many U.S. troops, which often came to feel that "they do not appreciate what we're doing for them."

Though many Americans made efforts to treat the Vietnamese with respect, many did not. This was true even when intentions were benign. With the arrival of over 600,000 foreign troops from several nations, conflicts in culture were inevitable.

When the Americans first arrived, many Vietnamese remarked that the only difference between them and the French was their language. This did not bode well for the Americans as deep-rooted hatred of the French played over to the U.S. troops as well. Trinh Dai, an ARVN soldier for eight years, has since said that "to us, they were the same, only they had more money, and there were more. . . . We took their money, of course; we accepted their presence—we had no choice. Why are they here? It was a question we couldn't answer."[13]

The Americans tended to refer to the Vietnamese as gooks or slopes, but the Vietnamese also had racial or derogatory terms for the Americans: Monkeys and crooked noses were two of the common terms, both insults in Vietnamese.

Steve Hassna, an American veteran of the 101st Airborne, wrote that "we certainly caused many Viets to go over to the VC [Viet Cong] with our treatment of them and their land."[14] Few issues conflicted more with traditional Vietnamese society than the issue of sex. The war brought half a million or more foreign men to a country traditionally bounded by prudent Buddhist morals regarding dating, marriage, and sex. The war changed all of that, and the sight of Americans spending time with Vietnamese women, in brothels or in amorous relationships, caused great anger among the men of Viet Nam, and more than a few used vengeance against American males as a reason to join the PLA. As traditional values broke down under the strain of war, more and more Vietnamese women became pregnant by American men. The resultant children, called "*my lai*" (mixed blood), were many times tormented by the villagers. The mothers were scorned for "sleeping with the enemy." Many women were forced from their villages or, having been abandoned by their American lovers, opted for prostitution as a means of supporting their child. The men did not have that option and took to ambushing lone GIs walking streets or to joining the PLA and getting their revenge in combat. Estimates run as high as 40,000 to 60,000 *My Lai* children were fathered by American men. Rape was also not uncommon, especially after battles when emotions were high. The *My Lai* massacre in 1968 involved numerous rapes of girls and women before their execution. In 1967, four Vietnamese students approached their teacher to say good bye, that they were joining the PLA: "We must fight for our country. . . . We must fight the Americans . . . because their presence is destroying our native land . . . culturally and morally."[15]

The NLF infrastructure permeated all aspects of village life, even within villages in so-called "pacified" zones. The PLA, manipulating general positive support for Ho Chi Minh, spent long hours, even weeks, talking and discussing politics with cadre members or potential recruits to explain their cause. Whenever possible, they would utilize propaganda techniques to manipulate the population to view American and government bungling or atrocities quite effectively. Ho Chi Minh's popularity was real and ever present. The simple Buddhist villagers took to Ho because of his patriotic appeals and his simple monk-like lifestyle. Ho had spent many months in prison and had become quite a poet. Poetry is a national pastime in Viet Nam, and Ho's poems endeared him to the people. While in prison in China, he wrote,

On the Road

Although they have tightly bound my arms and legs,
All over the mountain I hear the songs of birds,
And the forest is filled with the perfume of springflowers
Who can prevent me from freely enjoying these,
Which take from the long journey a little of its loneliness?

Ho Chi Minh[16]

His words of enduring pain colored with rays of hope and freedom have long marked life in Viet Nam ever since its domination by China centuries earlier. As a result, the NLF and Democratic Republic of Viet Nam leadership was able to continue the revolution against the American-backed Southern regimes with stoic perseverance. Captain Stuart Herrington, a strong anti-Communist U.S. advisor who first visited Hau Nghia Province in 1971 to study the appeal and strength of the NLF, stated, "The obstacle of winning over the Vietnamese peasants was . . . not something that Americans could do. You couldn't manage this into happening. It was either going to happen by enlightened leadership and well managed programs by the Vietnamese themselves, or it wasn't going to happen. And it didn't happen."[17]

Although many Vietnamese turned against the revolution for various reasons and resented the terrorist tactics employed by PLA death squads, it was the failure of the South government to stop corruption, brutality, land policies that favored wealthy landlords, and intolerance of dissent that allowed the revolution to prosper. An alliance with the United States, whose soldiers, whether their behavior was better or worse, were generally not welcome, combined to almost guarantee victory for the NLF. The NLF, along with continuously increasing support from the North, led a revolution that, for the most part, proved effective in garnering the support needed to win.

THE IMPACT ON VIETNAMESE AND AMERICAN SOCIETY

For most Americans, the war began in the mid-1960s and lasted until the mid-1970s. For the Vietnamese, there was nearly constant warfare from the 1940s, with the intervention of the Japanese, until 1975, when PAVN and PLA troops wrested control of Saigon from the Government of Viet Nam. Both nations had dramatic changes occur to their cultures, with the United States undergoing psychological and emotional stress while the Vietnamese endured massive destruction of nearly their entire country. The consequences were great and varied, causing many to view the Viet Nam War as the "war without end."

In 1966, President Johnson pledged to push forward what he called a "social revolution" in Viet Nam, and American aid resulted in the shipment of an extraordinary amount of material goods to Viet Nam. This logistical "miracle" was praised by General William Westmoreland as the total tonnage of supplies sent to Viet Nam surpassed the amount sent overseas during all of World War II. The first American troops found few roads, one railroad, and inadequate sanitary, bridge, transport, and port facilities throughout Viet Nam, especially outside of Saigon. Large areas of Viet Nam had seen few cars or other modern amenities, and many people in the Central Highlands participated in hunting and gathering or slash-and-burn agriculture that had changed little in thousands of years. American crews built four major, and many more minor, deep water ports for unloading the massive influx of supplies and began paving roads wherever possible. Bridges were built or widened, huge air bases were built, and trucks and jeeps were introduced by the thousands.

This dramatically impacted Vietnamese society as streams of refugees from combat areas, pacification areas, free fire zones, or other disruptions to normal life headed for the cities. The giant post exchange (PX) stores had virtually any type or kind of consumer goods for the GIs to purchase, with much of it eventually ending up on the black market. The South economy suffered rampant inflation as GIs, loaded with extra combat pay, roamed the streets with American cash, with amounts spent in one night that might represent an entire month's or even year's salary for the average Vietnamese. Traditional Vietnamese morals quickly eroded as young women turned to working the bars, strip joints, and brothels, at least one of which, the so-called "Disneyland East," was built and run by the army at An Khe to keep GIs off the streets and control the massive increase in sexually transmitted diseases that spread across the land.

Everything was done to make the GIs feel at home. High percentages of GI meals were hot, including airlifted turkey meals on Thanksgiving and Christmas; cold Cokes and beers were available; and air-conditioned offices were built for officers and their staffs. TV shows were brought by the Armed Forces Television Network, and American-only bars and beaches were run for "R & R." Radio shows and even an air-conditioned bowling alley and swimming pool for those serving in the Saigon area were built. The PLA fighters in the jungles and swamps had little or none of these luxuries.

Cultural sensibilities were insulted as traditional Vietnamese viewed American tendencies both to hold hands and kiss in public, and also to demand copious luxuries only the wealthy elite in the South government could afford as taboo behaviors. Even a couple of hundred dollars per month pay for privates was rich by Vietnamese standards,

The graves of over 10,000 People's Liberation Army fighters neatly arrayed in a Buddhist cemetery near Cu Chi. Courtesy of Robert E. Vadas.

and many Vietnamese ended up filing complaints about how their young daughters would run away to stay with a GI.

The American effort also included money for schools and other facilities that provided jobs for many unemployed Vietnamese. This "false" economic buildup had tremendous impact when the Americans began pulling out and, after most had left in 1973, contributed to the social instability of the South government. But during the American presence, many children were vaccinated, schools generally remained open, and life, especially in Saigon, continued, although dramatically changed. Amid the overwhelming poverty of the urban Vietnamese grew a modest middle class, composed of those who, illegally or legally, benefited from the billions of U.S. dollars flowing into the city.

Many Buddhists came to resent the Americans' attempts to promote Christianity as Christian missionaries came along with the American troops. Few Buddhists were given high government positions. This source of cultural conflict had been brewing for centuries ever since the first Catholic missionaries arrived in Viet Nam in the 1600s.

Although conflict resulting from daily interactions between Vietnamese and foreigners was a source of constant tension and even violence, the greatest impact on Viet Nam during the war was the result of the many battles and violence associated with the years of warfare throughout the country. Overall, the conflict devastated Viet Nam and left nearly 3 million dead. General Vo Nguyen Giap has stated on numerous occasions that even the Vietnamese do not know how many of their soldiers died fighting the Americans. The best guess is around 2 million, mostly PAVN troops. Over 0.5 million civilians died during the conflict. The war produced over 9 million civilian refugees, of which over 200,000 eventually found their way to the United States by 1979.

Between 3 and 400,000 ARVN soldiers and their support organizations such as the Civilian Irregular Defense Group, Mike Force, a reserve militia of locals; and local militias were killed in battle, and tens of thousands more were left disabled or amputees. Over 8 million tons of bombs alone (2.5 times that dropped in World War II) was dropped by the Americans, which left over 100 million craters and displaced huge amounts of soil.[18] Entire regions were stripped of jungle from explosives, Rome plows, and defoliants, causing massive erosion, loss of fertility, and widespread damage to the environment. The loss of the mangroves along the riverways in the South resulted in severe erosion, and farmers were unable to grow healthy crops for years in areas of numerous sprayings. Local economies took years to recover as few nations were willing to import food produce from Viet Nam owing to fear of Agent Orange contamination. Deaths to humans from the chemicals in the defoliants were numerous and uncounted. Thousands of children were stillborn in the subsequent generation after the spraying was commenced and thousands more suffered a wide variety of mutations.

Nearly every bridge in the nation was destroyed, and the only railway, built by the French in the 1800s, was out of action for months after the end of hostilities in 1975. Virtually every family in Viet Nam, North and South, suffered losses to loved ones, and the social–cultural fabric of the entire nation was stressed to the breaking point. Nearly 300,000 Vietnamese soldiers and civilians remain listed as "missing in action" after twenty-five years of intensive searching.

The war was devastating to the Vietnamese family's social, cultural, economic, and environmental existence. The impact on Americans was significantly less dramatic, although the long years of fighting divided the nation and left deep psychological scars among its people and veterans. A total of 58,202 Americans lost their lives in Viet Nam, and another 150,000 were seriously wounded. Many thousands of returning veterans suffer from post-traumatic stress disorder, and initial divorce and suicide rates went up after the conflict's end (see Appendix D).

America during the war initially enjoyed economic prosperity as the military–industrial complex geared for a war economy. Jobs were plentiful during the 1960s, and the inflation that the war spawned did not begin to affect the country until the 1970s. The nation underwent a massive cultural change as the war divided young and old, veteran and nonveteran, hawks and doves, blacks and whites, and men and women.

An entire array of idiomatic expressions and words evolved from the Viet Nam era, including grunt, hippie, Earth Day, free love, shotgun, and numerous other expressions representing the "age of Aquarius." Many technological innovations used in Viet Nam have since gained common peacetime use, such as helicopters for "flight for life" emergency room trips. Politically, the 1973 War Powers Act passed by Congress represented a rethinking of when to use the military in global situations. When President George H.W. Bush announced at the end of the 1991 Gulf War that "we have finally gotten the monkey of Vietnam off our backs," he was referring to the low troop morale and antimilitary attitude that evolved as a result of the fiasco in Viet Nam. A general uneasiness about what directions to pursue in the international arena plagued the American psyche for years after the war in Viet Nam ended.

As a result of campus protests, a whole new era of student empowerment grew during the 1970s. Many previous policies were changed to give students a greater voice, and affirmative action laws and policies, designed to increase inclusion of women and minorities in government schools, the job market, changed the demographics of student populations nationwide. Prices were not the only things inflated as a result of Viet Nam: Many college professors now trace the current grade inflation to that which began in the 1960s when professors feared failing students lest they end up in Viet Nam.

Civil rights issues came to a crossroad during the war as black, Hispanic, and Native American veterans returned from the war unwilling to accept the prewar status of minorities. Viet Nam vets demanded changes in military policy, resulting in the end of the draft in 1973 and introduction of more humane treatment of recruits.

While most Americans rejected much of the youth movement antics during the Viet Nam era much of what the counterculture spoke of permeated the national consciousness. The alienation and verbal denunciations of American institutions that they represented struck harmonic chords with such issues as ecological concerns, alternative political views, and individual forms of expression. The 1970s witnessed, as a result, almost radical cultural changes as laws changed to address women's and minority rights and perspectives on traditional business and educational practice changed. The Supreme Court case of *Roe v. Wade* (1973) gave authority to states to legalize abortion, and some states or communities decriminalized the use of marijuana. Although the "Woodstock" generation has traditionally been stereotyped, in reality, great divisions within the generation existed. While many youths had faith in peace and nonviolence, other organizations such as the Students for a Democratic Society were more radical and confrontational. When Richard M. Nixon was elected in 1972 by a landslide, 48 percent of 18 to 24 year olds actually voted for Nixon, who represented conservative American values.

A steep rise in cynicism grew out of the Viet Nam War as an entire generation was battered by events like the assassinations of John and Robert Kennedy and Martin Luther King, My Lai, and urban riots, which made even the most optimistic wonder about the future. Dramatic drops in voter participation have occurred since the 1960s. By the mid-1970s, the nation was embroiled in political debate as President Nixon's illegal and unethical activities came to light in months of new disclosures during the Watergate crisis. Public support in American institutions fell even more as revelations about the Federal Bureau of Investigation (FBI) and Counter Intelligence Program, in which agents intentionally smeared the reputations of antiwar protesters and engaged in illegal wiretaps and other activities, came to light. By 1974, polls revealed that public faith in Congress, the presidency, and the FBI had dropped to record lows. By August 1974, President Nixon resigned in shame, a victim of his own paranoia, which originated in the activities of antiwar protestors.

The inflation that prospered while Nixon was in office, partly the result of President Johnson's "guns and butter" economic policies, was growing wildly in the 1970s and helped cause Republican Gerald R. Ford and Democrat Jimmy Carter to lose their respective fights for reelection.

At a speech to students at a graduation commencement during his term in office, President Ford told wildly applauding students that "our long national nightmare is finally over," after the war ended on April 30, 1975. The words were appropriate, but despite Ford's optimism, the nation fell into a state of denial, a denial that caused

Christian Science Monitor columnist Joseph Harsch to write: "Today, it is almost as though the war never happened. . . . Americans have somehow blocked it out of their consciousness."[19] The nation's public schools nearly entirely ignored the topic, protests vanished, writers went on to discuss other issues, and the media drew a large blank, focusing instead on the new trends of the day, such as disco music and "streaking." When Viet Nam was discussed, it was usually in reference to the plight of veterans, horrid tales of Agent Orange, or stories of Viet Nam vets involved in crime, suicide, and drug use. The pain surfaced, and resurfaced, contributing to the reputation of the "war that never ends."

NOTES

1. Martin Bolha, written personal communication (September 2000).

2. Ibid.

3. Todd Gitlin, *The Sixties: Years of Hope, Days of Rage* (New York: Bantam Press, 1987), 129.

4. Edward Doyle and Stephen Weiss, eds., *The Vietnam Experience: A Collision of Cultures* (Boston: Boston Publishing, 1984), 27.

5. John Lancaster, taped personal communication, transcribed by Adam Pallack (October 2000).

6. Doyle and Weiss, *Vietnam Experience*, 27.

7. History Channel, "The '50s, Road to the '60s" (April 25, 2001).

8. C. Kismaric, and M. Heiferman, *Growing Up with Dick and Jane: Learning and Living the American Dream* (San Francisco: Collins Publishers, 1996), preface.

9. Frontline, "Remembering My Lai" (1989).

10. Vietnamese Letters, Captured Vietnamese Documents. CDEC microfilm collection. Boston: William Joiner Center for the Study of War and Social Consequences, University of Massachusetts).

11. Frances Fitzgerald, *Fire in the Lake* (New York: Vintage Books, 1972), 173.

12. Ibid., 143.

13. Trinh Dai, taped personal communication, translated by Hanh Thi Ngoc Trinh-Vadas (January 2001).

14. Steve Hassna, written personal communication (October 2000).

15. Doyle and Weiss, *Vietnam Experience*, 41.

16. Harrison Salisbury, "Introduction," in *The Prison Diary of Ho Chi Minh* (New York: Bantam Books, 1971), 34.

17. Doyle and Weiss, *Vietnam Experience*, 111.

18. Jacques-Yves Cousteau and Staff of Cousteau Society, *The Cousteau Almanac* (New York: Dolphin Books, 1981), 28.

19. Edward Doyle and Terrence Maitland, eds., *The Vietnam Experience: The Aftermath* (Boston: Boston Publishing, 1985), 107.

PART II

DOCUMENTS

Chapter 3

The Cold War Comes to Indochina

THE VIETNAMESE ARE DIVIDED

The Geneva Accords of 1954 divided Viet Nam into two temporary "regroupment zones," with Ho Chi Minh's Viet Minh forces occupying the northern section and the French- and American-built government of Ngo Dinh Diem occupying the southern sections of Viet Nam. Ho Chi Minh was confident of winning the elections and ruling a unified, socialist Republic of Viet Nam. Diem, backed by American military and economic aid, struggled to consolidate power as ruler of a pro-Western, non-Communist nation in the South. Diem prohibited the elections in 1956, setting the stage for the Second Indochina War. Buddhists, Viet Minh cadres, and numerous civilian organizations in the South organized for resistance to what they called Diem's "puppet" regime, while Ho Chi Minh solidified his control in the North. Diem began the task of nation building with a government dominated by generals and politicians who were predominantly Catholic, anti-Communist, and intent upon retaining the capitalist business economy built by the French. The great majority of Vietnamese were called upon by both sides to resist the other, resulting in a firestorm in Viet Nam that was to last nineteen more years and cause the deaths of nearly 3 million Vietnamese and 60,000 Americans.

HUỸEN VĂN CHÌA JOINS THE REVOLUTION

Huỹen Văn Chìa (Huyen Van Chia), the oldest son of a farmer near the village of Cu Chi, was only 10 years old when he heard villagers talk about the French leaving after nearly 100 years of oppressive rule. Yet instead of celebrating this long awaited event, the entire community was in an uproar over the creation of a new government under Diem. There was now talk of government troops searching the villages and arresting supporters of Ho Chi Minh. Chia's farm lay on a flat, palm lined plain not far from the Saigon River, "Song Sai Gon," as it is affectionately called, nearly forty miles from the center of Saigon. The villagers of Cu Chi District, farmers and plantation workers alike, had fiercely resisted the French colonialists, suffering many dead. Sections of the Cu Chi District rose gently above the water level, allowing for tunnels and bunkers to be dug into the hard laterite clay. Some of the tunnels were already more than a decade old, and the villagers were talking about expanding them as a means to defend their farms against the new regime, armed and supported now by *Mỹ* (Me'ee), or the Americans.

A young Chia listened to his father's stories about the coming war, a war Chia was able to survive and relate, years later, to American students while sitting crossed legged in his shade house, not far from his rebuilt childhood farm:

I was born on the fifteenth day of September 1946 and remember sitting as I am on this day, listening to my father tell of our 2,000-year history of fighting for independence. Each generation of children sat like me now and heard the familiar stories of our great leaders, Tran Han Dao, Le Loi, and the Trungs, and how they opposed the Chinese and Mongols and found victory against great odds. My father had spent many years fighting the French and instilled in me the tradition of tranh *dau*.

We were very, very poor and had only our families, our land, and our ancestors with us. We sacrifice everything at all times to win our freedom. I hear Americans talk about the war starting in the 1960s, but let me tell you all now, our fight, the revolution, began here near these fields in the 1930s, the 1920s, even before that. We came to hate the French, who took everything from us and gave little in return. Some of us worked in their plantations, not far from where we sit now; it was there that the revolution started; it was in the way they treated our countrymen that began the war.

The revolution returned in 1959. We were called by some of the cadres,

Cu Chi villagers work in teams as they remove hard clay from a new tunnel complex. Over 150 miles of tunnels were dug in Cu Chi District alone. Courtesy of Duong Thanh Phong.

older Viet Minh, who gathered us near the river, over that way [pointing to the west], and spoke to all of us: men, women, children. We were told how the Americans, who we had begun to call "*đe quôc Mỹ*," were as the French and paid Diem's soldiers to hunt us down, to imprison those of us who sided with Bãc Ho. I wanted to do my part, to help my father and his friends, so I joined the front in 1959 and began working almost from the start in the tunnels. I was only thirteen, and because of my small size I could help only with the digging or with the carrying of supplies. We dug in teams of three or four using small spades with a curved blade. We had ropes and buckets, and we carried the dirt out that way. Sometimes, we would dig for hours all day long and gain only a few feet of tunnel. Most of the people of the district . . . pitched in. We worked in rotating teams, and other villagers would come with food and water to relieve us after so many hours underground. We then had to go and work our own fields for our food and then to take care of our animals. We had an entire secret life, right under the nose of Diem!

We took care to take into account all of the possibilities that we might face and designed our tunnels to counter them. We had numerous passageways and air holes that you could not see unless you climbed right on them. . . . We put pepper and other spices around these holes to chase away the American scout dogs; we built trap doors and booby-trapped many areas; we even had water traps in case of gas attacks. There were three layers. The top one, about three to five meters deep, was used mostly for fighting and travel. The middle tunnels were for our storerooms, arms caches, and meeting rooms. The deepest, about thirty meters deep in places, were used for wells and sleeping quarters. The American bombs could never penetrate our deepest layers. The top tunnels had also air raid shelters; we found that placing logs in a cone shaped arrangement made better shelters than the deeper ones. The cone allowed us to hear planes come from very far away and allowed us to stay close to the surface for immediate fighting once the bombardment stopped. The tunnels were narrow, so we had to walk like a duck through them. . . . They were too small for most of the Americans.

Our work was hard; it exhausted us nearly every night, but perseverance paid off, and after many months we had a system of many kilometers of tunnels and underground rooms for our men and women to hide and fight. At times, we had up to 5,000 guerrillas hiding and fighting from under the tunnels around Cu Chi.

I did this until I was finally old enough to fight myself. When I was seventeen, I became a guerrilla fighter for the front; I joined with a main force battalion in the Cu Chi District. I had been given training in the use of weapons and making traps and explosives off and on for those first three years. Some in the village had a job to make explosives and weapons in the underground factories; we made do with what we could. In the beginning, most of our weapons were homemade or stolen from the government. It was later that we had better guns like the AK-47.

Life in those tunnels was nearly unbearable, so at first, we went in only when we had to, during air raids or when government troops came through on sweeps. That was not often as the government [Army of the Republic of Vietnam; ARVN] soldiers were afraid of us back then and seldom came to us looking for trouble. That all changed when the Americans came. When they arrived, it was a different war. It became a very terrible time, but we never wavered in our determination—never. It is difficult to understand, I know, but you must understand, as Vietnamese, we cannot ever give in to foreigners—never.[1]

The Twenty-Fifth U.S. Army Division set up a large base near Cu Chi in 1966 with supporting firebases for artillery nearby. The existence of the tunnels was soon discovered, but the surrounding forests and fields around Cu Chi and the tunnels underneath were never entirely pacified during the war.

NGUYỄN DŨC ÁNH AVENGES HIS GRANDFATHER

The signing of the Geneva Accords started a migration of Vietnamese from the North to the South as well as from the South to the North. In this wave of refugees that streamed southward to lands outside of Saigon between 1954 and 1956 were members of the Nguyen family, who had lived for a century as large landowners and who fled for their lives on American ships waiting on the coast near the warm waters of the South China Sea.

The Nguyen odyssey begins in the coastal province of Thanh Hoa, about 200 kilometers south of Hanoi. Thanh Hoa lies between the sea and the Indochinese mountains running along the western border with Laos. Mostly fishers and farmers, the people of this part of Viet Nam resisted the French and, like most Vietnamese, supported Ho Chi Minh in his call for independence in 1946. The Nguyen family found themselves caught up in events after 1945. This is their story:

My name is Nguyễn Dũc Ánh (Nguyen Duc Ánh). I was born on 5 May 1953 in the hamlet of Phuc Dia, village of Tho Xuan, Thanh Hoa Province. Our hamlet has a high number of Catholics because of the arrival there of many missionaries in the 1880s. Our family, as a result of the missionaries, had a good education and a bit higher economic status. I am the oldest of eight children, six boys and two girls. My mother was Thi Hoi, my father Nguyen Quoc Cuong. My father, despite our economic status, joined with Ho Chi Minh in 1949 as everyone, even those who prospered under French rule, hated the French and dreamed of independence. My father rose to the rank of major in the Viet Minh and was held in high esteem by the revolution. My father, like all Vietnamese, was told of our history and of our sacred duty to fight foreigners; our province is the same as where our great hero, Le Loi, was born. My father was also influenced by Catholic Archbishop Thu who had urged resistance to the French and who had helped fight the Japanese during World War II. My mother joined the "Youth for Ho" organization, and so my parents helped the Communists during the war with France.

All of this was soon to change some time in late 1953. Those people under Viet Minh rule were forced to give up their lands and belongings to the revolution, and there were trials for large landowners who were accused of "stealing" from the poor. My grandfather was one such landlord; he was wealthy, one of the richest in the hamlet, and most of our lands were taken from him and he was put on trial in our village. He was just fifty-five at that time, and after his public trial, he was taken immediately out by Viet Minh guards and shot dead, right in front of the villagers, as a lesson for those who "stole" from the people.

My father protested this tragedy and was soon arrested and jailed. He lay in that jail for many months until some French troops, retreating after the defeat at Dien Bien Phu, passed through that area and released him from prison. We all then managed to escape together from the Viet Minh, my father's former organization. At Phat Diem, we boarded an American boat where we were taken south, to end up at Saigon Port.

After a while, we were given land by the Diem government near Xuan Loc. Many Catholics were given land in that area by Diem, although we found out later that that land was taken from other Vietnamese to give to us. . . . But my father was not a very good farmer, so he sold out again and got a position with the national police in 1957. His job took our family again to move to Tuy Hoa, near the coast at Nha Trang. Tuy Hoa was mostly a fishing village, and it was there that I went to school. I went to a Catholic school, and I remember one of our holidays in October of 1959. President Diem came to visit our school; he asked us how good of students we were. He then told us that someday we will grow big and serve our country. . . . I remember feeling very positive after that visit. Diem was, I believed, and still do today, a good man.

I met my first Americans then. Our house was next to missionaries who had two children our age. . . . At that time, only a few American advisors were in Viet Nam, so we didn't see them often. I liked them, though.

We moved again, this time to Nha Trang itself. It was late 1963, and we moved out of fear . . . after Diem was murdered. My father felt strongly that if Diem could be killed, then the South will fall to the Communists. My father feared for his safety because he was strongly connected to the national secret police . . . so he asked to get out of doing police work. . . . This was in 1968, after the Tet Offensive. My father got a better job working for the Americans outside Cam Ranh near the base. He was a driver, and the money was good. At that time, the Americans brought much money and offered people good jobs to raise their children.

Our family did OK in Nha Trang while my father worked at Cam Ranh.

The war was raging now everywhere, but until 1968 I didn't see much of it. My father taught us to hate the Communists for killing my grandfather so we lived in fear of their reprisal. Out of respect for my father, I listened to him.[2]

NGUYEN THI HANH* FLEES TO THE NORTH

Women have a storied and significant place in Vietnamese history, mythology, and legend. Confucian thought dictated the three sub-missions of women: submit and obey the father at home; obey the husband when leaving home; obey the first son when the husband dies. In addition, Confucian mandates suggested that women obey the four virtues: hard work, care for appearance, appropriate speech, and observe proper behavior. Resistance to this philosophy is as old as Confucius himself, as a plethora of ancient poetry denouncing the bondage of marriage and obedience to men has flourished to this day.

The tradition of women's high status is evident in the history of two Vietnamese sisters, collectively known as "Hai Trung." The elder, Trung Trac, whose husband was murdered by the Chinese for plotting a revolt, and her sister, Trung Nhi, led a group of nobles, nearly 2,000 years ago, to Lien Lau where they forced the Chinese authorities to flee. The Trung sisters then declared themselves queens of a new Vietnamese nation extending from Hue to southern China. The sisters ruled for a very short time, however, when in 43 A.D., their small army was overwhelmed by a new Chinese force. Facing defeat, Hai ba Trung killed themselves, forever endearing themselves to the hearts of all Vietnamese who learn of their exploits in every school in Viet Nam. The strength and perseverance exemplified by the Trung sisters are the basis for many legends, traditional songs, and poems.

Luc bình plants can be seen flowing gently atop rivers throughout Viet Nam, gliding along in both clumps and as individuals, either beautifully flowered or only as green leaves. Vietnamese lore ties this plant with the fate of women in traditional songs: Some will flower beautifully and thrive; others, less beautiful, will get caught upon the shore to wither; others will land in rich land, while others will mire

---

*Name changed to protect identity.

One of the more than 60,000 Vietnamese women who fought for the revolution. Courtesy of Duong Thanh Phong.

in mud; some will grow old and prosper, while others will wither at a young age; and a few will flow to the sea to thrive in distant lands.

The integration of legends, myths, and songs addresses the pain of separation and loss of true love that have accompanied the endless struggles and warfare that have been Viet Nam's destiny. This paradox of enduring pain while striving for victory is also exemplified in the heroic "Tales of Kieu," the poetic saga of a poor young woman who must endure great hardship to bring her parents out of debt while seeking solace of her own. The rise of a prostitute to a higher status typifies Vietnamese perceptions of suffering and perseverance within their culture. Throughout the Indochinese wars of the twentieth century, women played key roles in the resistance against the French and Americans, including 60,000 who fought as soldiers. Many thousands of women in the North helped build the Ho Chi Minh Trail. The suffering and exploits created legendary heroes like Ngo Thi Tuyen, who helped defend the famous Dragon's Jaw Bridge over the Ma River. This bridge was a key transportation link, and seventy-two American planes were shot down trying to destroy it. It held out almost mythically until a "smart" bomb finally brought it down in 1972.

The following is the story of Nguyen Thi Hanh, whose mother sat at the Paris Peace Talks in 1972 to 1973. Nguyen Thi Hanh told this story at the Southern Women's Museum in Ho Chi Minh City:

My name is Nguyen Thi Hanh, and I was born in Long My District, Can Tho Province. Both of my parents fought for Ho, and my father rose to high rank in the Viet Minh and later the NLF [National Liberation Front]. After the division between the North and the South, the revolution began again in 1959. When it became clear that Diem was attempting to kill all those who did not agree with his government, my parents thought that it was wise for me to be taken to safety, which meant, at that time, to the North. I was snuck out of the country, first to Phnom Penh in Campuchea, then thru Hong Hong, where I was taken through the mountains along the Chinese coast to Viet Nam. I was only seven years old and very frightened. I missed my parents terribly, only my younger brother came along as family because my parents remained behind to fight for the front. . . . When we reached the Viet Nam border, we got on a train to Hanoi. I had no idea at that time that it would be fifteen full years before I ever saw my mother and father again.

As the war expanded, I grew older and went to school. By 1969, I was a student in Hanoi, studying psychology and medicine. By 1971, I had decided to volunteer to fight for the revolution. At that time, I wanted to do anything to speed up the time when I could return home to see my parents. Word traveled slowly during the war; I seldom got news from my home. Life was very difficult. The Americans were bombing all over the countryside, almost every night, especially after 1964, when the Americans started coming over in great strength, we could see the flashes in the sky and hear the distant rumbling of the explosions. I wanted to help, so I joined the army. I remember my childhood schooling; I remember the stories about Hai Ba Trung and of the heroine Lady Trieu Thi Trinh and was inspired, as a woman, to give my life for my country.

I clearly remember today the feelings I had as a youth. I remember the anger. I asked myself, "Why do the Americans come here and bomb my homeland? Why?" I became so angry at the Americans for this war, a war that kept me and my younger brother so far from our home and family. When we first arrived, my brother was only three, so when the bombs began in earnest in 1964, he was but seven years old. He cried almost every night from the noise and from fear. It is hard to describe to you now, but there is nothing more frightful than a bombing raid from the air. It was at that time that I grew to love "*Bac Ho*" very much. He was an inspiration; his strength and nerve to resist such a power as the Americans gave us courage and the determination to continue no matter how difficult times were. Ho Chi Minh held great appeal to the women of Viet Nam because of his teachings of equality and of respect. Ho once wrote, "If women are not free, then the people are not free." When Ho set up the provisional revolutionary government, the first constitution gave women the right to vote and proclaimed economic and political equality for men and women.

Since those days, I live my life now without fear. I learned about life and death at that time, a time when fear came close to paralyzing one, a fear that grew with a rising sense of panic, to flee or run and hide.

So I joined the army and was ordered to work in the Third Division near Ninh Binh, to help out as a nurse and counselor for the many wounded *bo doi* (soldiers) that came back from the front, came back as shattered men, both physically and mentally. . . . I joined the revolution to fight for my home, to fight for the day when I could see my father and mother once again.[3]

TRÌNH QUẢNG DÁI IS DRAFTED INTO THE ARMY OF THE REPUBLIC OF VIET NAM

All males living in South Viet Nam had to report for military duty when they reached the age of eighteen, even sixteen in later years, unless given special waivers for study at a university as a result of bribes. At its apex of power in the early 1970s, the ARVN numbered over 600,000 men. Women were generally exempt from service. Having a large number of men in uniform, in a country with relatively low political and social support for the government, was difficult to accomplish. Morale and fighting spirit in the ARVN were poor throughout most of the war, with some notable exceptions. Leadership in the ARVN was obtained through loyalty to Diem or Thieu and generals who paid and took bribes regularly to appease countless requests for money, sex, transfers, and waivers from military obligation. Desertion in the ARVN ran high, averaging over 20 percent per year, with an estimated 30 to 40 percent of its membership loyal to Ho Chi Minh, many were agents for the NLF.

While many ARVN officers and men were highly motivated, such as Nguyen Duc Anh, the great majority were prone to desertion in the face of a pressed enemy attack. One such ARVN soldier that exemplifies this is Trinh Quang Dai:

My name is Trình Quáng Dái (Trinh Quang Dai). I was born in Binh Than District, near Saigon, on the seventh of June 1941. My father was born in Hanoi in 1904 and joined the resistance to French rule in the 1920s. He saw the revolution as the sole means by which Vietnamese people could be free. I grew up in and around Saigon, so, you see, I did not know at that time about my father's past. It was years later, during the war in the 1970s, that my mother finally talked to me about my father's activities with the Communists. . . . My parents moved to Saigon from the North around 1931 or 1932. They moved south because of the job opportunities near Saigon. It was better than in the North, also, because my father was an agent for the revolution against the French. He led a double life both as an agent, or spy, and as a head cook at a French restaurant in Saigon. I am told that my father made friends with many French and that they also liked him. After the war with the Japanese ended, my father became very active in assisting the Viet Minh around Saigon. Sometime in early 1943, my father was finally discovered by French agents working in counterintelligence. He was arrested one day; he simply did not return home from work one evening, without any word to my mother. At that time, people began to disappear all of the time . . . never to be seen again. He was taken to the Hoa Lo Prison, near Hanoi. There, he was beaten for many weeks, but it has been told to us that he never divulged information. The resistance members rarely talked, even under torture, because it was generally known that you might be killed anyway after talking, so what was the point?

My father's health weakened very fast under those conditions, and he became so sick that the French released him. He could not return home. He went to live with a relative inside the Cambodian border, maybe near the Dak To area. He died shortly after that, on August 19, 1943, from the beatings he took as a prisoner. Our relatives brought his death certificate to us after the war ended in 1975; that is how we know the exact date. I was told that he went to Cambodia to die to protect us, his wife, my mother, and myself. That way, my mother could not know if she was arrested and tortured where he was. I am an only child as my father died when I was only two or three years old.

I grew up in Saigon with my mother. I went to school, and as I got older, the war got bigger. I did not understand much of politics. My mother told me of Uncle Ho and of being Vietnamese, but at the same time the government told us every day on the radio that the Viet Cong [VC] were very bad and how we had to be strong to stay alive and fight the VC. . . . I believed what I was told.

Everyone had to join the army. . . . I did not want to fight—most men did not. Many tried to hide from the police or soldiers. . . . So when I turned eighteen, I left home and did not report to the government. One night, in 1965, I got very sick and went home to stay with my mother and to pray. I am Buddhist, and we always prayed during those times, when we got sick, or during the holidays, to talk to our ancestors, that is what we believe. . . . When I got there, the police were there and told me that I had to go to the army. I was sick; they could see that and gave me a date by which I better report. So I finally went into the service. . . . I spent six months training, first at Vung Tau, at the base there. I trained to be an MP, or military police. I also studied English because I had to interact with Americans on patrol all of the time. So after six months, I was ordered back to Saigon and reported to duty in District 5. I belonged to the sixth Battalion, security force, Saigon. Saigon was growing fast because of the people from the countryside. Living in Saigon in those years was OK. The war did not come often to the city, mostly in the countryside; you would hear stories. . . . The radio talked about the VC and how they would kill us all if they captured Saigon. We knew nothing else, for no one would talk much in those days. Everyone was afraid; we always heard about people vanishing, so we just tried to live our lives. . . . I was happy to be stationed in Saigon. My wife would come visit often, bringing food and small gifts. My wife got pregnant in early 1967, so I had work, our child was due, and the war was far away—so life was OK. I was not happy about working for the Americans . . . but they gave us jobs and there was money and food in Saigon, so what else was I to do? I managed to avoid combat back then; we usually just rounded up soldiers who had deserted or patrolled the streets and bar areas, usually at night, when the darkness seemed to bring forth more trouble. Drinking, fighting, hiding from the government, just like I used to do—that was most of what my job was about at that time, until the middle of 1967; then things changed.[4]

HOÀNG VĂN MỸ VOLUNTEERS TO GO SOUTH

Though conditions in the North were harsh and political dissent was eliminated, Ho was able to successfully appeal to traditional Vietnamese nationalism for his goal of reunification. His Viet Minh fighters, now a battle-hardened and increasingly better-equipped "People's Army" (PAVN) consolidated their forces and trained for the coming war. The soldiers of the PAVN were poor sons and daughters of farmers and fishers, mostly from the Red River or the South China Sea coastal regions. PAVN forces began moving south in large numbers in 1964 after the Americans began extensive bombing. After 1968, the PAVN bore the brunt of the fighting for the remainder of the war as the role of the People's Liberation Army diminished after the Tet Offensive. The PAVN soldiers were well trained and disciplined and fought well, earning the respect of nearly all of their American adversaries, with a reputation for "never quitting." They suffered devastating casualties—estimates run as high as 1.5 million men—yet their determination never wavered. The PAVN fought on, and volunteers kept filling their ranks, such as Hoàng Văn Mỹ, who volunteered in the summer of 1969. In an interview, he told of his harrowing weeks walking the Ho Chi Minh Trail and of the death and destruction he witnessed:

My name is Hoàng Văn Mỹ (Hoang Van My); yes, *Mỹ*, the same word as for "Americans." I was born in 1947 outside of Ninh Binh in Ninh Binh Province. I was born during the war with the French, a war with which my father fought and later died in. I was only five years old when my father was killed; he was in the Viet Minh and died outside Ha Nam, south of Hanoi, in 1952. He was killed fighting to cover our retreat from the French. I was raised by my mother and grandparents in a small fishing village where I went to school. I did well in school and went on to study history at the university in Hanoi. I got a job teaching when I was only twenty-one years old; I taught in Ninh Binh at a secondary school. In 1969 I joined the People's Army of Viet Nam. I volunteered. I wanted to help my countrymen in the South fight the Americans. We heard terrible stories of their suffering, and many of us volunteered from our district at the same time. I wanted also to honor my father who died for the revolution. But mainly, I fought for my fatherland, my country. . . .

I spent some training in the North, then was sent by train to the city of Vinh. From there, I walked to Saigon; yes, I walked. It took me more than three months—I walked the entire time. I had to walk across rivers, through high mountains, through jungles. There were soldiers along the way at stations. These stations were numbered; they were rest areas where we could get new supplies. The Americans bombed us many times, and violently. Most of the times the bombs missed, but we lost many men on that walk. The bombs killed many, but most died from disease, hunger, and weakness. . . . At that time, a lot of troubles occurred. I thought many times that I would die, never return, never return to my home. But I, we, were determined to continue, we must—we had no other choice. We knew we could never return home until peace came. . . . During those times, we had to encourage each other to continue, even the women—it was so difficult. Our goal was to advance the South into a unified whole country. We were told that the Southerners would greet us as liberators and that they suffered very much under the Americans. It was those thoughts that burned in us a desire to continue. Today, I am the happiest and luckiest soldier there is. You see, in 1969, there were over 400 of us walking the trail to free the South, over 400 men, like me. By 1975, when the peace came, of that 400 men, I am the only 1 left alive—yes, the only survivor. That is how terrible the war was at that time. But I would do it again, for that was my duty, my love for my country. I never, never once thought I should stop, never wavered. But in 1969, there was to be almost six years ahead for me of fighting. I got to the South in late 1969, near the Cambodian border, outside Tay Ninh City. I joined the Seventh PAVN Division and stayed with that unit for the entire war.[5]

AMERICAN MOTIVATIONS DIFFER AS THE WAR EXPANDS

JOHN LANCASTER JOINS THE U.S. MARINES

In March 1965, President Lyndon B. Johnson ordered the U.S. Marines to protect the air base near Da Nang. The young marines, mostly volunteers, were products of intensive physical and psychological training at Paris Island, South Carolina. They pledged to remain faithful to their fellow marines and to the Marine code, "*Semper Fidelis*" (Always Faithful), for life. During the war, about 0.5 million of the 2.7 million American men who served in Viet Nam were marines. The last two Americans to die in Viet Nam, on April 29, 1975, were also marines. The storied tradition of the U.S. Marine Corps along with a competitive recruitment theme were seductive forces for many American youths such as John Lancaster.

John recalled, in an interview years after the war, the political transition in the United States following the death of John F. Kennedy and the growing antiwar movement on many college campuses:

I'm originally from Hamburg, New York—a middle-class suburb of Buffalo. I'm a big-time Bills [football] fan! Still! My dad was an attorney. My mom was a homemaker. I have a brother and a sister, both younger. . . . My brother was fortunate enough not to have to serve in the war because

his lottery number was such that he . . . never got called. It was, like, 307—
he had a golden number.

I was born March 19, 1945. I went to public schools in Hamburg, graduated from Hamburg Central High School. I went off to the University of
Notre Dame on a naval (ROTC) [Reserve Officers' Training Corps] schol-
arship. I elected at the end of my junior year of college to take the Marine
Corps option . . . so I would get my commission in the Marine Corps as
opposed to the Navy. . . . So I took my commission out of the Naval ROTC
unit into the Marine Corps. After graduating with my bachelor of arts, I
got commissioned the day before I graduated. I went immediately to Quantico, Virginia, for the basic school for second lieutenants who had already
been through boot camp . . . and then . . . I was sent to a six-week intensive
Viet language course in Quantico, Va. . . .

Before I went, in my senior year at Notre Dame, the antiwar movement
had begun to kick up . . . even our conservative Catholic campus . . . and
there were demonstrations starting to go on against the ROTC units and
all that and having a good sense that I might be involved in this war one
way or another and really wanting to be a Marine Corps officer, I was paying
attention to what was going on in the war. . . . After I graduated, I kept
paying attention to it and watching the politics, and I sort of . . . was torn
about how I felt about the war—whether I wanted to go. When I was at
the basic school for second lieutenants, I met a woman that I'm still friends
with, we became real close, dated, and we even got engaged before I left
and were gonna get married, although we decided not to do that till I got
back from Vietnam—which was a good thing. She didn't want me to go at
all; she said she'd go to Canada with me if I wanted to bolt, and there was
a huge part of me that wanted to bolt, just to be with her . . . and . . . go
to Canada 'cause there was another huge part of me that thought this war
was totally wrong, the intellectual part of it. So I felt we had absolutely no
business being there. . . . I didn't believe in the domino theory or any of
that stuff at the time, and I thought that this was a bad war to be fighting.
. . . The other intellectual part . . . which I still feel very strongly about, is
that one thing that separates our country from Communist countries or
totalitarian governments or banana republics in Central America or South
America, some of these really hideous structures, is that the military truly is
controlled by, ultimately, us, the citizens through our politicians. . . . When
you choose to be in the armed services or get drafted . . . you do what you're
told to do; you don't get to question it. So I had that other intellectual
debate going on: this war right or wrong. . . . I've chosen a career here,
which I very much wanted—I wanted to be a marine. Whether I like this
war or not, this is one that been decided upon through our democratic
processes, and then we're there fighting it. I don't get to vote on whether
I'm going or not. I go, and that's the way it should be, because if it isn't
that way, what separates us from one of the other Tom, Dick, and Harry

countries where the military decides it's gonna take over the country or go start its own war without the people having any say in it whatsoever? . . . And then on the emotional level I had this being scared, being in love . . . not wanting to go. . . . The flip side of that was, you know, twenty-two-year-old testosterone-flowing guy who had been trained for four years to go fight war, that wanted to go do his trade, see how good he was at it, and get in there . . . and do this stuff. . . . That part of it was very exciting to me . . . and I really wanted to go do it.[6]

BILLY C. BRYELS BECOMES A "SCREAMING EAGLE"

Moving to suburbia and other pastoral facets of growing up in the 1950s do not reflect the reality of most African Americans coming of age throughout the United States. In 1954, the U.S. Supreme Court set in motion a series of events that, by the autumn of 1957, rocked the city of Little Rock, Arkansas, placing that community in the center of a national debate on race, equality, segregation, and civil rights. Nine young black high school students, hand picked for their academic excellence, entered Little Rock's Central High School in a test of the 1954 Supreme Court decision guaranteeing access to equal education in public schools. The event resulted in violence against the students and other blacks as white racists attempted to keep the students out of Central High. President Dwight D. Eisenhower ordered army units to stabilize the city, allowing for the first black student ever to graduate the following spring. Billy C. Bryels, an eleven-year-old student at an all-black elementary school at the time, recalled the events years later. His story is that of many black American men who wound up fighting in Viet Nam for a cause that they had reason to suspect from the beginning:

I think in terms of being African American, and one of our first challenges is survival, particularly being born in the South. . . . Fortunately, my parents were bright people and their attitude was we needed to go to school, we needed to respect our elders, we needed to go to church. In terms of developing a character, a personality, I think that it was very important: the church, the school, and certainly respecting our elders, which certainly included my parents and the neighborhood elders. . . . Hillary Clinton talks about it taking a village to raise the child; well, I've lived in a village. So I went to primary school and secondary school, started college in Little Rock, at an all-black college. At the time, we were just getting into the throes of the civil rights movement, so going to Little Rock University was not an option yet. I was a poor student. I was probably one of the most popular people on campus, though, but a poor student. I wish I could go back and do it over, but I can't. So, as it turned out, I was drafted out of college, if you will, and that was not a good day. . . . I called home one day from school and my mother answered the phone and said, "You have a letter from the president," and I said, "Now why would he want to write me?" And, of course, it was that famous greeting from Uncle Sam. I thought about it at the time: There were a number of people who were leaving the country, escaping to Canada, Mexico, where-have-you. That was not an option for me because, to be honest, I didn't think I'd be accepted any more there than I was in the United States. And having had my two older brothers in the military, my dad, his two brothers, most of the adult males in the community had served in the military, Korea; my dad was in World War II. So it was kind of an honorable thing to do, join the military . . . and it was one of the things that provided different opportunities to African Americans. In that light, I didn't think too harshly of it; I'm going to go to the military and to do the best I can. But I heard most African Americans were going to Viet Nam. . . . If we want to talk about my thoughts about Viet Nam, I didn't really have any, to be honest with you. I didn't even want to go; I had no quarrel with the Vietnamese—never even heard of Viet Nam until the war. It was not something we were taught in world history. We knew about China, but Viet Nam was not—something I knew about. Upon arriving there, it was interesting because they had a number of Vietnamese people on base at Cam Ranh Bay, where I initially entered the country. Beautiful place. I loved the scenery and beach and all those things. But it was interesting: They had a number of Vietnamese people doing the kinds of things I was accustomed to seeing African Americans do—laundry, sweeping, cleaning, garbage details, and those kinds of things. The thought occurred to me, which was later made very popular by Richard Pryor: They were the new "niggers." In fact, living in San Jose today, it is very, very prevalent: They have all the lowest jobs. That was one of my first thoughts on arriving in Viet Nam, having my first encounters with Vietnamese—they were servants. They were not people of authority.

About 1957 . . . that was a time of bigotry, to a large extent, because there were things flashing in the news—lynchings in Mississippi and Alabama, flare-ups in Tennessee, all around Arkansas. So to have these folks defy the governor, the ultimate of authority in the state, and say we were going to school no matter what was frightening! One of my thoughts was "They're going to be killed." . . .

To leave, literally, a place where education was something that was doled out as white folks saw fit—and certainly they did not see us as intelligent and deserving of higher education, by any stretch—and we go to the military . . . and somehow expect to compete as something other than a servant.

And that is basically what we were—we were cannon fodder; we were servants again. It's consistent, though, with everything I know from my childhood. There were certain places we could not go, and we had to learn that—had to learn from childhood. One, of course, was how white folks think and act and then how black folks think and act and be able to differentiate between the two at the drop of a hat.

Communism? That's a good question in terms of where I come from. In Little Rock in the late 1950s and early 1960s, the whole thing about Communism: . . . We were about to be bombed, atomic bombs being dropped on us and all. A number of folk around the Little Rock area were buying bomb shelters. They were these big tanks, with stairs; you dig a hole and buy it and now you're protected from nuclear attack even. Well, the reality was this wasn't about to happen; that was Cold War rhetoric, bullshit, if you will pardon the expression. So communism was not something you actually lived in—the kind of Communist environment black folk did because everything we did was dictated—where we lived, what kind of job we have, where we go to school. I was born in the colored section of the hospital. That sounds like apartheid, that sounds like South Africa, but it actually was Little Rock, Arkansas. What you have read about, the different drinking fountains—that happened. I experienced that inside the state capitol. In 1965 we're marching on the state capitol . . . of Arkansas, rather, which is in Little Rock, and they had those signs up in the basement cafeteria. They had two drinking fountains: One was colored, the other was white. The same at the hospital—you could not have my mother delivering in the next room to a white woman, could you? If we can't go to school together, we damn sure can't be born together . . . in a clean environment like a hospital, together. That was the idea: We were not clean, we were not—we didn't deserve it. . . . My dad worked for a heavy equipment company. . . . He knew more about their heavy equipment than they did. But he was not treated as a manager. He actually taught people how to do the job. That made him appear as a superior "nigger," if you will. It was very unusual. I was their butler, yard boy, chauffeur, jack of all trades, and the trade-off was they would help finance my college tuition. So I went in the Army. . . . We had a number of African American drill sergeants. I respected it. I really did. I can recall one of my motivations was to not embarrass them. To be the best I could be . . . I worked hard at being a good soldier. I was motivated. I was motivated to be a good soldier. I was not motivated to go to Viet Nam . . . but going airborne—guaranteed that I'd go there.[7]

STEVE HASSNA GOES TO WAR

"Honor's a fine imaginary notion that draws in raw and unex-
perienced men to real mischiefs, while hunting a shadow."
Joseph Addison[8]

History is replete with calls to young men to war for honor and
glory, for country, for nation, for vengeance, for family, to sacrifice
for a cause good or bad. Viet Nam, of course, was no different. American politics of the 1950s forged a generation of Cold War "warriors"
who viewed communism as America's enemy and, without much
thought, were willing to fight in that distant land for "God, country,
honor."

Inspired by boyhood heroes, both real and imaginary, many young
American men went looking for adventure. Products of the postwar
baby boom, they were influenced by the restless nature of motorcycle-
riding actor Marlon Brando in *The Wild One* (1953) as much as by
the patriotic zeal of movie star John Wayne fighting the Japanese in
The Sands of Iwo Jima (1956). This duality in inspiration was fertile
ground for changes in heart in many American GIs: They arrived in
Viet Nam patriotic and dedicated, but, after living through a year of
experiences that reflected a reality they had not envisioned, came back
from Viet Nam changed, wondering if they really had been that imaginary "guy in the white hat" portrayed by the heroes in their childhood. One such man is Steve Hassna, a Californian who volunteered
for service and found himself in the jungles of Binh Dinh Province
as a paratrooper in the 2nd Battalion, 327th Infantry, 1st Brigade of
the 101st Airborne Division. This is his story, most of which can be
found in his book, *Short Timers Journal: Soldiering in Viet Nam*.[9]

I entered the Army to be a paratrooper and make it a career. I was nineteen and did not really understand just what that meant. It was all God,
country, and all that. I thought I understood the politics of the time. I was
a child of the post–World War II baby boom and had been raised from the
start of the Cold War. In fact, I was born the year the Cold War started
(November 1946). It was John Wayne in *The Big Picture*, *War in Korea*,
and *The Sands of Iwo Jima*. Stop the Commies, nuclear destruction, the
whole nine yards!

I was from an Irish–Syrian working class background, brought up Catholic, and by nineteen was ready to stop the "yellow peril," even though I

Steve Hassna of the 101st Airborne takes time off at his
base camp in Bo Loc, November, 1967. Courtesy of
Steve Hassna.

didn't have a clue what the world political scene really was. I also wanted
out of Oakland, California, and thought this adventure would be the best
way. . . . Both sides of my family came to the United States in the teens and
twenties of this century. Hard work, Catholic Church, patriotism—these
were the values I grew up with, a good background to get your ass shot
off, in a war you think you understand when you're twenty years old!

By June of 1966, the United States had gotten itself into a real shoot-
'em-up in Nam and the country, and everyone where I lived knew it. We
also had the 1964 Civil Rights Act, the Watts riots in Los Angeles, and
unrest in other parts of the country. I think most people were on edge and
didn't quite know what to make of it all. Thirty-five young men from my

high school graduating class enlisted, myself included. There were also signs of nonsupport for the war, in a very visual and vocal way. This was a first and followed on the heels of the free speech movement that started in Berkeley. We had everything from that free speech movement to Hells Angels [motorcycle organization] beating up the Vietnam Day committee members in 1965.

I was raised with the red scare . . . and all the other indoctrination that was deliberately created to get me to go to war. It worked: I tried to enlist in the Marine Corps when I was a junior in high school. . . . I was ripe. I went in with a gung-ho kill-a-Commie-for-mommy attitude. I wanted to be an infantry paratrooper, period!

When the military knew that they were going to get a lot of people into combat arms, they knew that they were going to have to have their elite units at full strength. These units are the 173rd Airborne, the 101st Airborne, Special Forces, and the 1st Air Cavalry. So they started training en masse. I went to Airborne infantry training, not ordinary infantry training; from there, I had orders to Jump School at Fort Benning.

I became a trained paratrooper. It was leave time after jump school—the lull before the storm. I went home and kicked around; I was so psyched that I wore my uniform around the house, out on the street. Then, a symbolic thing happened to me when I was on leave when I went to the San Leandro Roller Arena to see a live band. This was March 1967, and I am standing there, and who should start playing but the Buffalo Springfield [band], and they are playing "For What It's Worth," and I am hearing Stephen Stills and Neil Young and others singing and I am just thinking, "What are they saying?"

About four months later, I understood exactly what they were singing—but it was too late.[10]

KEN CUSHNER JOINS CAMPUS PROTESTS

During the early years of U.S. involvement in Viet Nam, from 1950 to 1964, few Americans protested. As the war expanded into the mid-1960s, rising resistance to the war grew significantly from the ranks of young men who were exposed to the possibility of the draft. The great majority of antiwar protesters in the late 1960s had been brought up patriotic and filled with the notion that communism was a great "evil." The metamorphosis from "patriotic" conformist American to the rebellious "antiwar" protester was an individualistic occurrence that millions of Americans experienced at various times during the Viet Nam War. As politicians struggled to define the purpose of the war, many returning veterans articulated a different reality concerning Viet Nam, and resistance to the draft increased dramatically. By the war's end, over 500,000 men had avoided the draft by refusing to register or by going to Canada. Others, some 8,700, fought the draft in courts and were sentenced to prison terms of up to five years. Another 170,000 men were given I-0 status as conscientious objectors who were unwilling to fight on religious grounds.

Tens of thousands of others, a sizable majority of those who protested the Viet Nam War and who were not drafted, protested the war for political, moral, or religious reasons. Ken Cushner, one of those men, grew up on the east side of Cleveland, Ohio, at a time when the war began to divide the American populace. Growing up in predominantly working and middle class sections, Ken knew of brothers of friends who were sent to fight in Viet Nam, a few who were wounded. Race riots in 1966 and 1968 on Cleveland's predominantly black east side brought the Cushner family to within a short distance of the anger and violence that marked the late 1960s.

In the spring of 1969, Ken decided to go to college and enrolled at Kent State University in nearby Kent, Ohio. Years later, Ken Cushner wrote his reflections on the antiwar movement and of the killings at Kent State on May 4, 1970:

I grew up in a middle class Jewish family, moving between three suburbs of Cleveland, Ohio. Our family identified as Jews, both religiously as well as culturally, although that was always in flux. In my early years, I grew up as part of a small Jewish community, one of just two Jewish families in my elementary school. . . . I really did not identify with the other Jewish kid in my class. . . . I struggled to identify with the local "cool" group, which pulled me even further from my Jewish heritage and my parents' wishes. At the same time, my parents were moving away from their religious identification with Judaism to a more secular orientation. . . . Once my siblings and I reached confirmation, my parents dropped their affiliation with any organized synagogue.

Cleveland Heights/University Heights (where our family settled) was much more politically and socially conscious as a whole than I was when I was growing up. To be perfectly honest, throughout high school, I was struggling with my own identity. I was oblivious to the growing drug culture and the antiwar movement. More of my peers in high school, I would say in retrospect, at least on the outside, were supportive of the war effort. But I do not believe this was due to any political motivation, but driven more by a perceived need to identify with a "macho" adolescent male identity. I do recall some close friends in my junior and senior years (1968 to

1969) talking about enlisting in the army as well as challenging the "hippies" seen occasionally outside . . . protesting the war. I suppose my involvement with a rock-and-roll band kept me quite busy on weekends with little time to search for confrontations. A few of my friends' older brothers went to Viet Nam, but most, if not all, of my friends were college bound and were able to avoid the draft.

My eyes were opened in the summer of 1969. After graduation, a couple of friends and I converted a Volkswagen minibus and went off on a three-week venture around the eastern United States and Canada. We literally stumbled upon Woodstock in upstate New York the very week of the famed concert. I was quickly introduced to a counterculture and the growing social movements of the decade. Welcome to reality! It was here that I began to rethink, or, rather, think about, my attitude toward the war effort.[11]

LARRY SEEGER FIGHTS THE "NOBLE CAUSE"

Despite efforts by American politicians to correct the flawed system to determine who went to Viet Nam, a sizable percentage of those who fought in Viet Nam came from working and lower middle class economic backgrounds. Most of these men, at least for the greater part of the Viet Nam War, had retained the stoic work ethic endowed upon them by their depression and World War II–era parents. They grew up on farms and in small towns where military service was highly revered, as well as inner cities. Many did not take to antiwar protesters and considered many of those protesting on campuses as "spoiled" kids who were shirking their responsibilities to their nation. They did not, typically, take drugs, nor did they often have the luxury to hitch-hike around the country to "find themselves," although many of them had hard lives, with divorce, alcoholism, or other maladies to deal with as a child. They represented what President Richard M. Nixon called the great "silent majority" of Americans who, though upset by a war they did not understand, served with distinction, many times volunteering for another tour of duty in Viet Nam. One such man is Lawrence C. (Larry) Seeger. Writing his reflections years later, he had this to say about his experiences during the war:

I was born in Oak Park, Illinois, on 29 May 1942. I had one sibling, a brother who was a year and a half older. My parents divorced when I was about two years old. My father didn't serve in World War II. My mother remarried, and we moved to a rural area near a small town in northern

Larry Seeger, of the Twenty-Third Infantry Division, next to a Chinook helicopter near the demilitarized zone. Courtesy of Larry Seeger.

Illinois. My stepfather was from an Irish family in a poor neighborhood in Chicago. He worked intermittently at various manufacturing jobs but was plagued by lifelong alcoholism. My mother worked her whole life in banking as a teller, cashier, and loan officer. Our economic status was lower middle class. I wore a lot of hand-me-down clothes, and I remember my parents frequently arguing over money. We moved to California after I finished the ninth grade, and I was an above-average student in high school. My brother attended the U.S. Military Academy at West Point for one year, and I studied architecture at the University of California at Berkeley [CAL].

At that time, CAL was a hotbed of social unrest and student protests. The invigorating environment of open discussion on campus was the best part of my education. I learned to distrust academic credentials and authority by observing leaders purposely distorting or omitting facts in order to gain converts to their point of view. And I watched hundreds of supposedly bright young students blindly follow a charismatic protest leader named Mario Savio like sheep over a cliff during what is called the "free speech movement." I was devoted to the writings of Ayn Rand; and the life of General Douglas MacArthur and his "Duty, Honor, Country" speech in 1962 were influential to me. I worked at a half a dozen different jobs during summers and when I was in college, and in June 1966, I enlisted in the army at Oakland, California. After advanced infantry training at Fort Ord, California, I was selected for officer candidate school and was commissioned a second lieutenant in field artillery at Fort Sill, Oklahoma, in June 1967.

In the early 1960s, the Vietnam War was still in its infancy and not very controversial, and I didn't really have strong opinions about U.S. involvement in Southeast Asia, although my inclination was to be patriotic and to support and identify with our country's policies. I served both of my tours in the Republic of Viet Nam in "I" Corps, the northernmost part of the country. I arrived in country the first time just prior to the Tet Offensive of 1968 and spent that year as an artillery officer in support of the First Marine Division. I went to flight school between tours and spent my second tour flying Chinook helicopters for the Twenty-Third Infantry Division out of Chu Lai and Phu Bai.[12]

GREG GIBBONS: NAVY CORPSMAN

Some, like Steve Hassna, went to war with patriotic zeal only to return disillusioned by what they saw in Viet Nam, while others, like Larry Seeger, returned home with their patriotism and belief in the righteousness of the war relatively untouched. The majority of Americans who fought in Viet Nam, however, returned with less precise perceptions of the war, generally believing that they had done something of value while at the same time questioning much of what went on over there. Some may have been occasional participants in antiwar protests, while others returned with strong feelings against the antiwar movement.

Fate had more to do with which Americans ended up fighting in Viet Nam than any other variable. Those Americans who did not volunteer had to, by law, register with their local selective service board at the time of their eighteenth birthday. Upon registration, they were eventually assigned a specific classification status that determined their eligibility for conscription. Those classified I-A would be eligible for conscription, although they had the option of entering college to get a II-S deferment. Greg Gibbons related this story in writing:

I grew up in a small Wisconsin city, south of Madison. My parents were basically middle class, and my dad owned his own dry-cleaning business. I am the oldest of six children and attended Catholic grade school and public high school. Upon high school graduation, I attended the University of Wisconsin–Whitewater pretty much at the insistence of my parents even though I would have preferred to complete my military obligation before going to school. . . . I was not a very serious student, at that time.

I joined the Navy Reserve in 1965, as Vietnam was just heating up, basically to stay out of the marines and the army. . . . Naval Reserve had a two-year active duty commitment, unlike most other reserve components. I trained initially as a radar operator while going to school at UW–Whitewater. When my grades didn't hold up (too much time partying!), I needed to fulfill my active duty commitment. Radar school wasn't open, so, for some reason unknown to myself to this day, I put down hospital corpsman as one of my "dream sheet" selections, and because they needed corpsmen in Vietnam, that is where I ended up. So much for my original notion about serving out the war on a ship!

I was generally a supporter of the war effort. I grew up in the shadow of World War II (the "good" war), believed in the "rightness" of America's cause and the duty to serve my country and accept and support its decisions. . . . So, by and large, if my government said it was important for us to be in Vietnam and defend them against communism, I was willing to accept and support that stand. I was also willing to serve since I saw that as my duty.

At the time I went on active duty (1968), public attitudes toward the war had begun to turn negative. The big Tet Offensive had just occurred, and people realized that, despite the government's assertions to the contrary, there was no "light at the end of the tunnel." However, that change had really not yet filtered down to midwestern Monroe, Wisconsin. As I recall, there was still rather widespread support for the war effort at the time I went on active duty. Certainly, this feeling was not unanimous, but it never was anywhere that I know of. In fact, during my time at UW–Whitewater, there had been a couple of student antiwar protests and marches. I had participated in a couple, not out of any antiwar fervor, but more for something to do. Initially with [the] Twenty-Sixth Marines, I served as a corpsman (medic) for a "grunt" infantry platoon. We certainly did not participate in any battles that anyone would recognize the names of (such as Tet Offensive or the battle for Hue). We were somewhat unique in that 1/26 was serving as an amphibious unit at this time. Basically, this meant that our rear area was on U.S. Navy ships stationed off the coast. We conducted "search-and-destroy" missions; we would end up making contact with the enemy (whether NVA [North Vietnamese Army] or VC) only in small units. However, in truth, I treated more casualties from booby traps than direct contact during this time. As a corpsman, I moved right along with the marines, went out on patrols and ambushes with them, and basically did whatever they did—until the "shit hit the fan." Then my role became different from theirs.[13]

BYRON JAMES LEAVES THE SACRED MOUNTAINS

To the Diné, commonly called Navajo, their ancient lands within the protection of their four sacred mountains, on land known today as the Four Corners region of the desert Southwest, is called Diné Bikéyah. During the 1940s, in an effort to develop an unbreakable communication code to fight the Japanese in World War II, the U.S. Marine Corps created the secret 382nd Communications Platoon. With a strength of over 300 Diné men, the 382nd was created to utilize the significantly complex Navajo language in the Pacific theater of war. The years after World War II left the Navajo with a great sense of pride and patriotism that spilled over into the Viet Nam War years. Byron James is a Navajo from the remote lands near Round Rock, Arizona. Growing up the traditional way, Byron was raised within a large extended family that spent its summers in the high country in the Lukachukai Mountains, lands marked with towering pines and clear water spilling over into countless waterfalls that eventually evaporate into the dry washes in the desert lands below. His uncle was a code talker and he, and his father, also a World War II–era veteran, inspired him with a sense of duty that, when mixed with a traditional sense of the obligations of the Navajo warrior, led him to enter the army in 1970, even as protests raged around the nation against a war Byron knew little about. His story adds a Native American perspective to the Viet Nam story:

I was born November 12, 1949, at a community down the road, Ganado. I was born there; I am from around here but I was born there in the hospital. I went to school at Chinle High School . . . graduated in 1969, and . . . I let them draft me into the army. I didn't have any money to go to college or anything, like you had a lotta assistance and all that nowadays but back then they didn't have anything for us. . . . I went from the BIA [Bureau of Indian Affairs] elementary here, to Chinle High school, and that was it. So what I planned to do is let them draft me, do my two years, use my GI bill to go to school. I kinda got sidetracked. I joined in Albuquerque. . . . I entered March 21, 1970; four of us Navajos got on a bus to Albuquerque, we did all our basics, we were processed . . . then I went to Fort Sam Houston for medical training. I became a medic. . . .

By 1970, well, before I went over to Viet Nam, when I was in high school, I didn't think about it too much—the war. I heard about it, you had to. There were peace talks going on in Paris . . . and the teachers kept saying, "You guys are not going . . . the peace talks are in progress. . . . The war is going to end soon." And so we had this idea that the time we left school, the war was going to be over. And that's all I remember thinking about; and after I got medical training, but before I went home, someone over in personnel called us over: . . . They needed helicopter pilots over in Viet Nam. The requirement to be a pilot then was college . . . but because they were losing so many pilots, they dropped the requirements down to high school with a high GQ test score. I was a graduate with a GQ score over 100, so they called me over to personnel and said, "You're qualified. If you want, you can go to Fort Rutgers, Alabama, after basic to flight school." They say it's a six-year active commitment. I said, "No way. I came here for two years—that's it." So I turned it down. . . . I had the high score, and could do anything.

They gave you thirty-day leaves, if you are going that way, to Nam. My grandmother was in bad shape; we visited her, in the hospital, every day for a week. . . . For us Navajo, taking care of family is very important. Then I went to Fort Lewis, Washington. Some guys were of legal drinking age, and we got pretty drunk. We were like, "Uncle Ho, Grandpa Ho, count your days—your days are numbered! Give me three months. We'll stop the war!" Our morale was very high—we were wide-eyed and didn't know what to expect!

The next day we stopped in Anchorage, Alaska, refueled there, and continued on. . . . The next morning they woke us up; . . . they were going into the air base outside of Tokyo. Still, I couldn't believe it. I was really—huh— going to Viet Nam! About half way there, it hit us! It really is unbelievable; it really is!

Well, we stopped and changed planes, and there were some guys returning this way. They got on our plane, for a while, everybody was quiet—no one talked while these guys were talking to us. . . . Oh yeah, we got a different story now. It was really, really bad there! The infantry guys would tell us, "Don't do this, don't do that." It finally got into our heads where we are going—what's really going on there. I guess there was nothing happening in Paris. . . . They were saying they are having problems about the shape of the table—nothing going on there—they should stop the war. That's what these guys were telling us. It made us think again. The bravado from the night before was over.

We finally landed, about 10 A.M. or so. You land and you see parking lots and buildings. We landed at Cam Ranh Bay. What we saw was concertina wires, machine gun bunkers. "Where the hell is this?" We wanted off the plane! We taxied, and before we stopped, the pilot says, "See you in about a year." "What?" I said, "Oh my god, one year in this place?" It was real now.[14]

NOTES

1. Huyen Van Chia, personal communication (January 1998); and videotaped personal communication, Cu Chi, Viet Nam (January 11, 2001).

2. Nguyen Duc Anh, written personal communication (October 2000).

3. Nguyen Thi Hanh, taped personal communication, Ho Chi Minh City, translated by Hanh Thi Ngoc Trinh-Vadas (January 20, 2001).

4. Trinh Quang Dai, written and taped personal communication, Ho Chi Minh City (January 25, 2000, and January 26, 2001).

5. Hoang Van My, taped personal communication (January 11, 1998) and interview (January 9, 2001), translated by Hanh Thi Ngoc Trinh-Vadas.

6. John Lancaster, taped personal communication, transcribed by Adam Pallack (October 2000).

7. Billy C. Bryels, taped personal communication, transcribed by Ann Thomas (April 2001).

8. Ottenheimer Publisher's Editor, *Book of Familiar Quotations* (New York: Crown Publishers, 1955), 143.

9. Steve Hassna, *The Short Timers Journal: Soldiering in Vietnam.* Winter Soldier Archive No. 1 & No. 2.

10. Steve Hassna, written personal communication (October 2000).

11. Ken Cushner, written personal communication (October 2000).

12. Larry Seeger, written personal communication (February 15, 2001).

13. Greg Gibbons, written personal communication (February 10, 2001).

14. Byron James, taped personal communication, transcribed by Robert E. Vadas (May 25, 2001).

Chapter 4

Americans and Vietnamese Fight Their Wars

American troop levels in Viet Nam climbed over 0.5 million by 1969. As the tempo and destruction of the war reached a feverish pitch, increasing amounts of victories devastated People's Army of Viet Nam (PAVN) and People's Liberation Army (PLA) forces. Yet these revolutionary forces received a steadily increasing number of men and supplies sent south along the Ho Chi Minh Trail. Victory eluded American forces so long as PAVN supply lines remained open and fighting morale remained high. For the most part, morale remained relatively high for both sides, but as time wore on, a sense of despair began to develop and America's soldiers began to note this in letters sent home.

AMERICANS IN VIET NAM: THE EARLY YEARS

Jack S. Swender arrived in Viet Nam in July of 1965. Assigned to Second Battalion, Seventh Regiment, First Marine Division, the twenty-two-year-old lance corporal from Kansas City describes why he was fighting in Viet Nam:

20 September 1965
Dear Uncle and Aunt,
. . . Some people wonder why Americans are in Vietnam. The way I see the situation, I would rather fight to stop communism in South Vietnam

than in Kincaid, Humbolt, Blue Mound, or Kansas City, and that is just about what it would end up being. Except for the fact that by that time, I would be old and gray and my children would be fighting the war. The price for victory is high when life cannot be replaced, but I think it is far better to fight and die for freedom than to live under oppression and fear.

Living in a country where communism thrives on illiterate people, I look to the many teachers I have for relatives and I know in the long run that victory will truly be theirs—for communism cannot thrive in a society of people who know the whole truth. This war is not going to be won in a day or even a year. This war and others like it will only be won when the children of that nation are educated and grow in freedom to rule themselves. Last year alone, 4,700 teachers and priests in South Vietnam were killed. This we are trying to stop—this is our objective.

Well enough soothing my own conscience and guilt,

Your nephew,

Jack[1]

Jack was killed on December 18, 1965.

On February 2, 1967, twenty-year-old Private First Class John Dabonka was killed in action near the Mekong Delta city of My Tho, a few weeks after he wrote the following letter:

December 23, 1966

Dear Mom and Dad,

Everything is just fine—in fact it's better than I thought It would be. They have us in a big base camp. We're going to be staying here for a month, This area is perfectly safe. While we're in base camp, we aren't allowed to carry ammo or even keep it in our tents. . . . Besides the platoon leader, I'm the next most important man in the platoon. All the talk I hear from the guys who have been here awhile make it sound pretty easy over here. We eat three hot meals a day. I heard when we go to the field, they fly hot meals to us in the morning and night, and for lunch you eat C-rations, and you're allowed two canteens of water a day. When you're in home base, you drink all you want, plus while you're in the field you get a beer and soda free every other day.

Last night I had a little trouble falling asleep because of the artillery rounds going off. It's a 175 [mm gun], and it has a range of miles, but when it goes off it sounds like a firecracker going off in your ear. All in all things look pretty good. They have PX's where you can buy whatever you want or need, which is doing me no good because I'm broke. Don't send me money because it's no good here. We use scrip for money which looks like a Sweepstakes ticket, and besides I'll be getting paid in a few days. You should be receiving $150 in about a week. If you need it, you can use it, but if you don't, then put it in a bank, OK?

The people live like pigs. They don't know how to use soap. When they have to go to the bathroom, they go wherever they're standing, they don't care who is looking. Kids not even six [years old] run up to you and ask for a cig[arette]. The houses they live in are like rundown shacks. You can see everything—they have no doors, curtains. I'm real glad I have what I have. It seems poor to you maybe, and you want new things because you think our house doesn't look good, but after seeing the way these people live, there's no comparison. We are more than millionaires to these people—they have nothing. I can't see how people can live like this. It seems funny, in one of your letters you write about the TV going on the blink. At the same time, I almost had to laugh. These people don't even have the slightest idea what a TV is even. Right now our big guns are going off and it sounds good knowing it's yours and they don't have any.

It takes me a day to write one letter, and every chance I have I'd rather write to you than anyone else. Tell Susan I'm sorry, but I just don't have the time to write as much as I would like to. . . . Mom, the least of my problems now are girls. That's one of the things I don't have time to worry about.

One thing I don't do is worry—it doesn't pay. If I worried about everything over here that there is to worry about, I'd have a nervous breakdown. . . . Also I'm fortunate because my platoon leader, Lt. Sanderson, also keeps a cool head. This man is really sharp when it comes to this stuff. I have already learned a lot about human nature from this man. He's only 23 years old, but his knowledge is really something. A person can't go wrong following his example.

Well, it's about time. I thought you would never send those onions. I can't wait for them to arrive. . . . For sure, now, I'm going to close this short novel.

With all my love,
Your grateful son, Johnny[2]

Lieutenant Marion Lee (Sandy) Kempner was a platoon leader in 3/7th Regiment First Marine Division. He wrote this letter to his grandparents:

August 9, 1966
Dear Mummum and Muggins,

Muggins, I am told that, to put it mildly, you have some reservations about this war and its effect upon the American psychosis. You, of course, are not alone in these feelings, but a couple of points should be made.

Our claim to legality is that we were invited to come here by the Vietnam government and, however flimsy that legality is, such is the peg upon which we hang our hat, and it is a lot stronger than many we have hung it on before, such as the Spanish–American War, a host of expeditions against South American sovereignties, or, for that matter, our declaration of war against Germany in World War I. But the legality or lack of it is really of no importance because our friends on the other side are not bothered by such trivialities and if we are, then we can primly say that we have followed the legal and narrow trail and lost the battle to an opponent who is not playing by our rules. We are here because we think this is where we must fight to stop a communist threat. But not having gained momentum in conquering this country could bowl us out of Asia altogether—and perhaps out of existence. [If] this makes us the policemen of the world, then so be it. Surely this is no more of a burden than the British accepted from 1815 until 1915, and we have a good deal more reason to adopt it since at no time was Britain threatened during this period with total annihilation or subjection which, make no mistake about it, we are.

This is not the place we would prefer to make this stand. Thailand is a great deal more stable. We have backing in the Philippines, and Pakistan and India would be [a] better environment to utilize our standard armaments in which we have invested so much. But we were given no choice and we must fight where the confrontation is, despite its cost, unfeasibility, and possible illegality, and physical and mental toll upon the participants.

As to the effect of this war upon the people, who can tell? All of our wars have had some effect, usually for the better, increasing our sense of internationalism in [the] Korean War and World War II and showing us that war is not all glory as we discovered in World War I. While the war—for that matter the civil rights movement—may be responsible for pushing a few deranged minds over the brink of sanity, there is no guarantee that something else would not have done it later. Certainly our churches and laws are strong enough to withstand any feeling of the populace that murder and lawlessness are acceptable ways to deal with problems. I think that the human being has a stronger sense of right and wrong than that.

   Love,
   Sandy

Sandy was wounded in September of 1966 and wrote home about it for the first time:

September 16, 1966
Dear Mom and Dad, doting father-to-be, Peach and Fuzzy:
As I suppose you can see by my new stationery, this is not my normal letter. While walking down the road one day, in the merry, merry month of September, my squad got into a helluva fray, and lost (momentarily) one member.

ME!

I am all right, I am all right, I am all right, etc.

A carbine round hit me where it would do the most good, right in the butt, the left buttock to be exact, exiting from the upper thigh. It hit no bones, blood vessels, nerves, or anything else of importance except my pride. It was, however, a little bit closer to my pecker than was comfortable. But that is as good as ever, although it is now going through a year's hibernation.

I am writing this letter in the hospital less than one hour after I got hit, so please don't worry—by the time you get this letter and can answer it, I will probably be back on my hill.

Please, now, I am all right. The only thing that bothers me is the "indignity" of it, as Jose would say and Dad would feel, and disappointment that the wound ain't serious enough to warrant taking me out on the Repose where it is air-conditioned and there are nurses.

P.S. I am all right!!

Sandy recovered from that wound but was killed on November 11, 1966. An excerpt from one of his final letters poetically describes the surreality of Viet Nam:

October 20, 1966
Dear Aunt Frannie,
    . . . The plant, and the hill upon which it grew, was also representative of Vietnam. It is a country of thorns and cuts, of guns and marauding, of little hope and of great failure. Yet in the midst of it all, a beautiful thought, gesture, and even person can arise among it waving bravely at the death that pours down upon it. Some day this hill will be burned by napalm, and the red flower will crackle up and die among the thorns.
    Love,
    Sandy[3]

VIETNAMESE IN THE PEOPLE'S ARMY OF VIET NAM AND PEOPLE'S LIBERATION ARMY WRITE HOME

Vietnamese culture places a high value on family relationships, and separation was one of the greatest challenges facing the young fighters of the PAVN and PLA. The pain of separation and the legitimacy of their fight against the Americans are reflected in most of their letters. Members of Long Range Reconnaissance Patrol Third/Twenty-Fifth, Infantry Division, found the following letters on May 27, 1967, after

an operation in Quang Ngai Province. The first is written to a PAVN
soldier from his older brother, a teacher in Hanoi:

Hanoi, August 16, 1966
Dear younger brother,
   I am writing a letter to you, younger brother, telling you that I graduated
from engineering school and now I am teaching economics at the university.
Did you receive the last letter I sent? At that time I sent a letter I sent
another on the same day! Now, what are you doing? Our Aunt Thi got
married! Have you gotten other letters from any one else? How is Aunt De?
How is Uncle and Aunt Nuoi? How is Uncle Dum? What grade level is
Uncle Dum studying? He is trying to become the best student! I received
a letter from Mom by the way of Liem who went to Hanoi. Mom has not
written to our brother in a while.
   Dear brother, I miss you very much. If I visit home I wouldn't miss your
face anymore. I remember how you looked as a young boy at home. Please
take a photo of yourself now if you can and send it to me. I bet you look
very different now. Our aunt and uncle also cannot recall your face, as if
you have disappeared. It is strange, I know. How is the situation now for
your sister? I am waiting for you and our sister very much, because the
Americans are very, very bad, causing us to be apart all of these eleven years.
The Americans are fighting against all Vietnamese bringing more and more
terrible weapons. We must keep fighting and we must win decisively; north
and south can never be separated. You and I will meet again in happiness
at that time, forever, right? I know 100% that *de quoc My* [imperialist Amer-
ica] will lose and finally go away.
   Buddha has helped me which is why my health is very very good; I have
not gotten sick. Sometime I cry alot because I miss you young brother, my
blood, so I must stop now. Best regard to you and family and I will see you
in the next letter. I must go now.
   I am always waiting for a letter from you, good luck, good health
   Nguyen Van Quang
   P.S. I sent best regards to Tu our neighbor at home[4]

   The next three letters, written to Huynh Trong An, Huynh Viet's
mother, and from Nguyen Vach to an unnamed love, represent the
common form of Vietnamese letter writing, a poetic style, to express
deep emotions:

March 10, 1967
Dear Mom!!!
I left home! Mom . . . I have left!!!!
I said goodbye to go with the army.

Two People's Army of Viet Nam regulars take time out to read a letter. Note the barren tree limbs killed by Agent Orange spraying. Courtesy of Duong Thanh Phong.

Dearest Mom! My heart now feels a vast loneliness.
I'm living far from you, mother, my heart feels so very sad.
Mom . . . Mom! America's soldiers step on us, invade our lands.
Now I cannot sit around
I hold my gun in my arms to fight with this enemy
I have gone far away!
Mom, since I left home I can only wish you happiness.
I had to go because duty was waiting
I keep forever my Mother's image
Mom . . . from now on Mom from now on . . .
I still have Mother's image in my heart!
From morning 'till appears the darkness
I miss Mom, living far away,
My heart over flows with love, Mom

The winter nights bring cold, strong winds,
Yet, Mother is always waiting for me to return home,
Oh, oh my Mom! My Mom!
I had to go, I had to go
Until our family again feels the happy warmth of reunion
And my country hears the laughter of many again
and then, Mother I will return home.
    Viet

19 January 1966
Dear Darling!!!
Darling! do not cry more! You should go back home
Why are you crying? Do you know if you cry, it will be miserable?
Your tears are worth ten thousand words, enough for one poem
    being exhausted!
If you love me, please listen to what I would like to tell you
Stop crying! do not cry anymore! Darling!!!
When I hear that you cried, the words stuck in my throat,
I miss you so much, comply with my wish a little!
Do not cry anymore, please! Only happiness again!
Why cry? Crying brings only misery in life
Why cry? Apply rouge to cover your tears! There is more to worry
    about!
Our nation is being oppressed!
I have been missing you so much till now, I understood,
It is your heart, they are tears of melancholy
It is the night's cold, strong wind
Enjoy yourself, always wait for the future!
Your tears have been since you were born . . .
There is a dream when we meet each other . . .
We are living far away, there is poem in our path . . .
Please!!! Darling you should return home
Return home!!! Darling return home
You keep your promise to me, love me forever
Remember! Always wait for me!!!
    Nguyen Vach

Nguyen Vach had many letters on him when he was killed. Sometimes it took as long as eighteen months for a letter to reach a loved one. He tries to comfort his mother with a poem he never was able to send:

March 13, 1964
Dear Mom!!!

Tonight! I could not sleep well!
I am alone! I wonder myself
Mom! Mom, what are you thinking about me!
Because I have revolutionary will?
That is why I had chosen this hard life,
Really, I do not wish for pity,
My actions are not corrupt, I do not deny the interests of our
   people!
From time to time I work very hard,
I study, do my duty, I complete my obligations satisfactorily,
Therefore all the Americans want to kill me
Dear Mom!!! Any way, 'till the sea is dry, and rocks worn away,
In my heart, very faithfully,
I destroy every thing indignant from far away,
I kept my promise to fight America, and to
obey my Mother, who taught me,
to fight the Americans when they invaded our country!!
   Nguyen Vach[5]

AMERICANS IN VIET NAM: EXPECTATIONS MEET REALITY

Similar emotions and concerns were common with American soldiers fighting in Viet Nam, although many began noting differences between what they had expected prior to their arrival in Viet Nam and what Viet Nam was in reality.

JOHN LANCASTER (LIEUTENANT, FIRST MARINES DIVISION, 1967 TO 1968)

I did infantry [training] and then I got orders for the language school, and then after language school, I had to report to Traverse Air Force Base where I got on a charter flight on January 4, for a, well, they flew us first to a week's worth of briefing and precountry indoctrination in Okinawa [Japan]. I was then flown into Da Nang. This is a funny story. . . . We landed in the middle of the Tet Offensive in Da Nang, got off this, I forget what kind of aircraft it was, they start mortaring the damn airfield, we didn't get all our equipment or anything. No one was there to greet us—never been there before—didn't have a clue where to go, didn't know where the bunkers were, didn't know where anything was—we got out and started hunting around. Ok, where do we go? Where do we get some gear? We asked some guy if he knew where the HQ [headquarters] was for the First Marine Division. . . . He said no, but the officers' club is over there. . . . So we went down there and actually proceeded to drink beer for the next two days . . . and then we figured we better show up. So we went out finally and commandeered a marine corporal who had a jeep, so we asked him if he knew where the HQ was for First Marine Div. We drove to headquarters, which were sort of dug into the side of Marble Mountain outside of Da Nang at the time. So we went in there and we showed up, and I'll never forget we went into this dugout and there was this typical old government-issue gray metal desk sitting there with a corporal behind it—just files and files piled everywhere. He could barely peer out from between these things. We gave him copies of our orders and said ok, we're reporting for this thing here. He looked at our orders and said, "Yeah I think I've heard of you guys. You're somewhere in here, the O-club. Go down there, walk down the hill a little bit, it's right over there. Go have a beer; I'll give you a call."

So three days later—by this time we've been mortared and wondered where to go, and were so drunk we hardly knew who we were, sleeping on the ground on our bags—and we got called back up in before some general and he said, "I'm assigning you all to the First Battalion Twenty-Seventh Marines," and he said they're at sea now, "and they'll be off-loaded the day after tomorrow, and by the way, none of these guys are really ready for this." They were on a goodwill trip to South Korea and Australia, they were going to be doing winter operations in South Korea, they have all their winter gear with them . . . and . . . they're still carrying M-14s . . . so you'll have to collect their M-14s [standard U.S. military rifle before 1967]. Issue them jungle gear, issue 'em M-16s, train 'em how to use the M-16s" and da da da da da. "And you also need to know that most of the guys you'll be dealing with are on their second tour over there and have not had a full year plus back in the states. So they're gonna be a little cranky, and uh," he said, "good luck."

I'm there with my mouth dropped down 'bout to my ankles, and I'm saying well, fine. He then said, "Oh, by the way, they're gonna have some Ontos [a 6-barreled self-propelled gun] besides their winter gear, they'll have this that and the other thing and you're going to have to figure out where to stow everything."

So, I'm like, well, where is 2, 3? Do you have any maps? How am I going to get these folks there? Is it far away, is it close, they walking? Or we doing trucks? Helicopters?

And he says, "Oh, those are details you're just going to have to figure out. But I've got help for you. Here's first sergeant—oh, I forgot his name now—this first sergeant, he'll help you out."

Well, of course, he [first sergeant] knew absolutely everything, and the general was jerking my chain a little bit! So I was assigned the Second Platoon of Delta Company in the First Battalion Twenty-seventh Marines for about the first month I was there. We operated down around south of Da Nang. After about a month, we moved north to the Hue, Phu Bai area. . . .

It all eventually shifted for me, particularly when I ran into some of the problems I ran into with my platoon and saw and heard what they'd been through their first tour of duty. And here I was, trying to tell them what to do on their second tour of duty; the whole battalion was like that, not just my platoon. They had no clue why we were fighting this war. They didn't understand what are we doing in this war and asked, "What's this really about?" They didn't agree with the way it was being fought, and neither did I. It was really stupid stuff; for example, my platoon was given an assignment once, when we got up around Hue, of protecting a pipeline that went from the sea into the Phu Bai airstrip, an aboveground pipeline, jet fuel. Get the picture? Exposed, totally exposed, the bad guys would come up, put a satchel charge on it, blow a hole in it, and all the jet fuel would fall onto the ground. No brains! And they were supposed to walk back and forth along the thing . . . tell them to keep moving up and down the pipeline, and one of the bad guys would, they'd wait until they walked by, got good and far away, then they'd run out, place a satchel charge on it, blow a hole, and run away. . . . That's just one incredibly stupid example.

I have been using the words "bad guys" [for Vietnamese]. I didn't really feel they were bad guys at some point when I was over there. It became clear to me that these guys were fighting because they wanted a better way of life for their wives and children 'cause they wanted a unified country and they had a charismatic leader and a tremendous commitment. This was their country and they wanted it back. . . . They wanted to rid themselves of Americans and Europeans and have their county back and have it whole. That was real clear to me. I mean that was the way they talked about it . . . and I was involved in some interrogations of some guys we captured, and it was real obvious to me why they were fighting this war. They weren't bad people. . . . They were highly motivated people who wanted their country whole and wanted a better life for their families. Their fighting quality was excellent. They were very tenacious fighters . . . and when they decided to give up, they disappeared like you wouldn't believe. They knew when to quit, and it wasn't like they were quitting and giving up, it was like stop fighting now and come back later.

[About Vietnamese culture] . . . the things I do remember from being over there that amazed me was how hard working they are—hard working people—and how entrepreneurial they are and Buddhism in their culture. I had some sense of it. . . . You'd see it in the peacefulness of these villages . . . villages where these people would just try to keep on farming and not be involved in the war one way or another and were constantly just being sucked into it. . . . They seemed to have more of a sense, particularly on the side we were fighting—maybe it was because it was their country—of a will to win, do what it would take to win. One way or another, we didn't seem to have that will; maybe we did down on the unit level, although I'm not sure we even did there. It was hard for me—I started even wondering, "What are we really doin' here?" This little two-bit Communist country is not going to be attacking California at any point in my lifetime. What is this really about? Domino theory? Why are we really here?[6]

BILLY C. BRYELS (101ST ARMY AIRBORNE DIVISION, 1967 TO 1968)

My initial contact was surreal to me. Two weeks earlier, I was in Oakland, California, and now I'm in Viet Nam and I'm in a firefight. People were shooting, and I had to be reminded to get down and take shelter. Take cover, if you will, from all the chaos. Talk about communism—what is communism? To me it was a big word not unlike what I had experienced all my life. I didn't see it particularly as threatening. Communism was just a big, ugly word that made no sense to me as a threat because I had lived apartheid. . . . I was nineteen when I went into the military . . . so communism can't affect me that bad, not important to me at all.

I'm in Viet Nam, and I start to bond with some of my fellow soldiers. Black or white. Mostly black, I have to admit. We had a little clique—we're starting to bond with other soldiers and now we're starting to see people shot. I'm seeing people killed that I know! And they're not shot and being killed by police in Biloxi, Mississippi, but by somebody, an anonymous person in the bushes—the Communists, the Viet Cong. So now we start to develop an attitude. I think to this day part of my attitude had nothing to do with their communism or ethnicity or any of that. It was the fact that they were trying to kill us. Trying to kill me. It became very personal in that light. . . . I have since come to understand the Vietnamese—I was actually invading their homes. I was in their yard. They had every right to shoot me. But during the war, I thought I had every right to shoot him. He was the problem. I wasn't. And it's mixed emotions: At the same time I wanted to go home. I had no stake in Viet Nam.

There were several times when it just didn't make sense, but there was nothing that we would realize from a firefight, bombing, what-have-you, that would give me any satisfaction. If I talked to my fellow soldiers, you know, we weren't gaining anything. I mean, we were given orders to go out and search and destroy. We did that every week. We burned down peoples' homes, killed their cattle, and this guy's not a real threat to me. We killed people who were not a threat to us. I mean point-blank-shoot-somebody-in-the-head because he's Vietnamese. And I'm saying there's no point to this. To this day I've no clue. There's no point to it. It made no sense.

The guys in my unit—they were afraid of communism so typically we didn't talk about communism. If anything, we were trying to figure out how to get another marijuana cigarette, listen to some good rhythm and blues from home, or write a letter or something of that nature—we were not concerned about communism. Staying alive, absolutely. Again, we had this conditioning of a kind of communism that said that's the way we live so we didn't feel threatened by some Communist in Viet Nam, China, or someplace, or Russia; that's a joke. We're not really threatened—that was the bottom line. I was more threatened by Sergeant Burrows who was the platoon sergeant, E-6. He would do more harm to me than any Communist. And that's the truth. He had a control over me. He actually volunteered me once to go into a special group that was really, I found out later, they were going to try to rescue some POWs [prisoners of war] and it was an actual volunteer to be a part of this strike group that was going to go into North Viet Nam. It was quite risky. I did not volunteer, so as I get to the station where they were interviewing these volunteers, the guy says, "You do know why you're here." And I say, "No, I don't." He says, "Nobody told you?" No. He started to tell me, "They didn't tell you this?" and I said, "No." He says it's "strictly volunteer—you don't want to, you don't have to go." And to Sergeant Burrows's surprise, I ended up back in the platoon. He never said a word, and I never said anything to him.[7]

LARRY SEEGER (TWENTY-THIRD ARMY INFANTRY DIVISION, 1969 TO 1971)

I learned a great deal from my two years in Vietnam, but I don't think my attitude towards the war was changed significantly by my experiences there. During my first tour of duty, I was assigned as a searchlight platoon commander providing support for the 11th Marine Regiment in the vicinity of Da Nang. My troops and equipment were deployed in widespread locations that required me to regularly travel from place to place. I had lots of opportunities to meet and become friends with Vietnamese. One particular family that I regularly visited with lived in a village near the base of a series of rock formations called Marble Mountain. Two children of this family were teenage girls who had jobs working in the U.S. military installations, and the cash they brought home was particularly useful to the family's well being. There was an unscrupulous local leader who tried to force the family to give him a significant part of the girls' earnings, but the father refused to deal with him. For revenge, the girls were falsely reported to be Viet

Cong sympathizers, and the local police, called "white mice" because of their dress white uniform shirts, had picked them up and were interrogating them in jail. When I came to visit, the mother and father were distraught over the girls' possible mistreatment there; but when I asked if I could try to help, they were terrified. Not only were the parents reluctant to inquire about the children for fear of reprisals against them, but the interference of U.S. military there would have been resented. I finally was able to get the U.S. military advisor to the national police to inquire on their behalf, and the girls were eventually released, but not without some disagreeable handling. The impression I came away with was of the powerlessness of ordinary citizens to be treated fairly and justly by those in authority. I think that Americans don't realize the level of bribery and corruption that permeates whole societies in most parts of the world. Our highly publicized crimes by a few government officials pale in comparison.[8]

STEVE HASSNA (101ST ARMY AIRBORNE DIVISION, 1967 TO 1968)

I arrived in Vietnam on March 21, 1967, at Bien Hoa Air Force Base. Coming off the plane, you have a tendency to go into total shock. You don't know what to expect. You're not ready for the heat and the chaos of all these people running around. You walk down the ramp and across the concrete pad to a big open hangar. There are no walls, just uprights and cross beams, and, underneath, all these benches. The area is about the size of two tennis courts with different sections set up for in-country and out-country processing and guys returning from the hospital. There are lotsa people laying around, trying to keep out of site. Some people might be AWOL [absent without leave] as it was a good place to hang around for a day or so. There would be Vietnamese and American concession stands with Cokes, sandwiches, and stuff like that. Some guys there were "ghosting," which is when a guy would cut loose on a Monday from, say, the hospital, but he don't get back to his unit until Friday.

The newbee [new body] really feels helpless when he gets to Vietnam. He walks off the plane from the States into all this chaos. Yet, to everybody around him, there's no chaos at all. The NCO [noncommissioned officer] or officer sitting on top of this little platform in the middle of this scene, shuffling his papers; everything is perfectly normal. He knows that there are approximately so many AWOLs out there, that there are so many people leaving country or going here and there in-country. All kinds of things are going on underneath that hangar roof. Everything! The newbee thinks, "What's happening?"

So they throw the newbees on buses. I remember that the bus had chicken wire around the windows, like being in a cage. I was under the impression when I was sent to Vietnam that it was to help the Vietnamese people. But the sergeant told us that the wire was to keep the grenades and rocks and bottles out of the bus, and I was thinking, "Why would they want to blow me up if I'm here to help them?" Well, it was too early then to register that idea—for I was still saying, "Oh! Looka that! Dirt, potholes. Guns. Poverty." There ain't no poverty in the States like that . . . there just ain't. And among the houses we went by, there was an air of oppression, of total surrender. From one day to the next, the family didn't know if they'd be sleeping there or five miles down the road, while the U.S. or the North Vietnamese or whoever felt like it shelled their house. . . . The people went about doing their business, but they seemed to be looking over their shoulders the whole time. And I got to doing that—it was a very strange feeling. After 3 months in-country, I was looking over my shoulder and trying to look straight ahead at the same time. You didn't know when you were going to get fired at, from where, by whom, and for what reason . . . and that's what the Vietnamese walked around with. To be as patient and as strong as they were really blows me away; anyway, that first bus ride warned me to keep looking over my shoulder.

Then they assign you to a unit. This is done according to what strength is needed . . . so when they told me, "You are going to the 101st," I went, "Aw, wow! All right! 101st! Hard core!" Hard core means cold blooded. I kinda wanted to go to the 173rd because we heard that they were getting in all the shit. You see, the army really had me! They had me out there bringing God and Christianity and democracy to the Vietnamese people, whether they liked it or not. I was going out there to stop the Commies. I was going to kick ass and take names. See, it was a shot of pride. There's an exhilaration in the fact that this kid is going to a very old, established airborne combat unit.

Well, it didn't work out quite as well as we planned.[9]

GREG GIBBONS (U.S. CORPSMAN, U.S. NAVY, 1969 TO 1970)

I was transferred to the 13th Marines, which was an artillery unit. Initially, the battery I was assigned to was supporting the infantry battalion I had left, so the only difference was I no longer had to go out on patrols. Later the unit was at artillery bases a few kilometers west (Six Shooter) and northwest (Northern Artillery Cantonment) of Da Nang. Contact with the enemy consisted of mortar or rocket attacks and an infrequent attempt by sappers to penetrate our perimeter. Far more fulfilling to me at this point, however, was the opportunity to go out on MedCaps [providing medical care to

Vietnamese]. . . . Generally, this entailed my going out, with a squad of marines as an escort, and providing what treatment I could to them. Particularly fascinating were the little kids; they were very open and, like little kids, playful and fun to be around. They were too young for the war to have become personally relevant to them. The adults, . . . on the other hand, were much more reserved and hidden in their interactions with us. In both cases, however, it was wonderful to see what even a limited amount of medical care could do. Very rewarding!

I'm not sure I had any real feelings about my "enemy." They were the enemy and, to an extent, I guess I depersonalized them. I guess this could be considered a defensive mechanism to make the possibility of taking human life more palatable. While I indicated that my role was to save lives rather than take them, I realized it was a possibility that I would need to do [that] later. I was as prepared for that eventually as I could make myself. Certainly, during my tour, I treated a number of them. However, I'm not sure I can say I did it with the same vigor as with our own troops.[10]

BYRON JAMES (FOURTH ARMY INFANTRY DIVISION, 1970 TO 1971)

Initially, I was assigned to a hospital, but I never liked hospitals. As a Navajo, I am an outdoors person . . . and I got with my boss and said, "I do not like this place, get me somewhere, out in the boonies . . . somewhere, some job in supply."

It's not that I can't handle it—I just do not like hospitals. So they transferred me to an infantry unit, east of Pleiku. I stayed with them, it was a small platoon positioned forward, away from the coast. I never even saw my own company commander!

The First Cav[alry] was further west in the Central Highlands. I never got that far, Kontum, Dak To. I was with the First Brigade in the Fourth Division. They were scattered: The First was right in that area—the Third was up north—the Second along Quang Tri—along the coast, they were split—not like other units. . . . And mostly what I did, as a junior medic— I was an E-3—is that I went on patrols and carried stuff for senior medics, IV [intravenous] bottles, etc. I could patch some myself though; the senior medics said, "Do a good job for these guys, they will treat you like kings." I learned that once the guys called you "Doc," you had it made.

After I left the hospital, with my infantry unit . . . some of the guys asked me, "How'd you get here, Byron?" And I said I volunteered for the bush. They laughed at me: "What? You left an easy job to do this?" They couldn't believe it. They did give me a lot of respect though; they protected me, carried my stuff for me, stuff like that.

In turn, I'd get back on patrol and volunteer to go on duty, stand night watch with one or more of them. Respect goes both ways. There were lots of good soldiers, most—but some had an attitude problem, with authority, or lazy. But most were good people I served with. I always see these movies where they put down our people—I say, "That's bull." There were a lot of good soldiers. Just a very few that were bad, some white, some Native American, who defied orders. It took all kinds. . . .

I respected them [the Vietnamese]. They were just soldiers like us, just soldiers. They were young like we were; they had families just like we did. When we picked up their dead . . . we would find their family pictures on them. So we knew they had families . . . girlfriends and stuff, so you knew it was just—ah . . . can't really say I hate them . . . can't say that. Their country sent them down, just like our country sent us over there.[11]

THE VIETNAMESE FIGHT ON

NGUYEN DUC ANH (ARMY OF THE REPUBLIC OF VIET NAM)

It was during the Tet Offensive that I personally witnessed the terrible effects of war for the first time. I was in the tenth grade at school. The VC [Viet Cong] with some Northerners attacked Nha Trang at several parts of the city. Overall it was a failure, but at first they attacked and occupied the post office in the north part of Nha Trang. The ARVN [Army of the Republic of Viet Nam] counterattacked with American help and retook the areas in Nha Trang that the Communists had occupied. When the battle ended and after the smoke had cleared somewhat, I cautiously ventured out into the streets. I saw many, many dead all over the place. I went up close to some NVA [North Vietnamese Army] dead; I looked carefully and on some of their arms were tattoos. The same tattoo on all their arms: It read "*Sanh Bac Tu Nam*." It meant "Born in the North to die in the South." North and South language is little bit different. In South, we say, "*sinh*." In North, they say "*sanh*." I was very awed by this, by these men, the NVA: They had determination to fight—they had their reasons to fight and it impressed me. I thought about what I knew then and came to know later in the war when I was an officer myself in the ARVN: that many, if not most, of the ARVN soldiers did not have the same determination to fight, the determination that the Communists had.

It was a few years later, in 1972, before I joined the ARVN to fight for the South. I was in school before then and graduated in 1970. I was sent to Saigon in 1971 to study at the Culture University in Saigon. I went to study history and English. I did not really want to join to fight that much,

Some Army of the Republic of Viet Nam troops, like these rangers near
the demilitarized zone in 1969, fought well. Most, however, lacked the
motivation and resolve of their People's Army of Viet Nam adversaries.
Courtesy of Larry Seeger.

but I had no choice really. It was the law at that time. It was 1972 and the
Easter Offensive was raging, May of 1972, and so I joined.

I did my basic training at Thu Duc Academy for Officer Training, about
thirty miles from Saigon. I graduated as a warrant officer and was sent north,
to Quang Nam Province, as a platoon leader with the 101st battalion, 2nd
Company, ARVN Provincial Militia. Most of us, in my family, felt that the
South was doomed. We felt that way all the years after 1963 because we
felt that Diem was the only hope for building a nation free from the Communists. We liked Diem—he was a good man. He had helped create an
alternative perspective to communism in the South. Later, by the time I
joined, I knew that we had no hope. I saw the determination of the NVA
and VC and knew we would lose the war. But we fought on anyway . . . we
had no choice. Nguyen Thieu was president at that time and I did not like
him. He was corrupt. He was detached from the people, and only his relatives could get good jobs. He ran a corrupt government. Vietnamese society under Thieu remained a "tiered" society, and I knew that we could
not win the support of the people with him as president. I knew then that
our cause was doomed.

I fought in many battles. I have killed many people, many times, even
civilians. One time I had to toss a grenade in a house where civilians were

talking—women and children, they were supporters of the VC, so I did my job, and they were killed. We did not allow civilians to be neutral. We would seek them all out and ask them: "Us or them? Which side are you on?"

As long as we had U.S. air support, we would win battles, but by then, most U.S. soldiers were gone from Viet Nam. The South did not fight well in that war. For example, one time, we were ordered to go on a mission. My platoon, which I was leader of, assembled to prepare to go. Out of my unit of thirty-two men, only fifteen or sixteen bothered to show up. The rest, they were home or hiding; they had no will to fight. So it was for the South at that time. How can you win if your own soldiers are corrupt? It was 1973 when most of the Americans left; Nixon withdrew U.S. forces from Viet Nam. Do not get me wrong. I still like Nixon. Nixon was a politician—he did what he had to do. Still, if Nixon did not resign, I believe that he would have helped us again in the end. Thieu was stupid to trust Nixon like that. . . . He had no knowledge of the Americans and how they were. Thieu was Vietnamese, and a Vietnamese is faithful to his friends, no matter what. So Thieu was shocked when Nixon abandoned us in 1975. But at first, after the U.S. left, we trusted the Americans, so we kept fighting.[12]

TRINH QUANG DAI (ARMY OF THE REPUBLIC OF VIET NAM)

I was working out of our base in District 5 Saigon, for several years. Mostly on patrol as an MP [military policeman], as I have said, and I managed to avoid most of the fighting during those years. By 1967, however, the war was expanding and the Thieu government did not have much support of the Vietnamese people. Vietnamese fighting Vietnamese—this is not good, and most of us had no heart to do this. But we obeyed our orders and tried to live life the best we could. We looked suspiciously upon the Americans; most of us knew that they were foreigners trying to control us Vietnamese, and that's not good. But what else could we do? The radio blasted on about fighting the Communists and how they would kill us all if they won the war. I had no idea about politics at that time, especially in the beginning, but that changed in the summer 1967.

I was told to report to my commanding officer at our base. So I drove a jeep there from my patrol area. . . . When I arrived, I walked into the building; suddenly, I was surrounded by three men in uniform. I was told to follow them and was nearly dragged out of the building and taken in handcuffs to the security prison in District 5. It was there that the police took VC suspects. I knew a bit about it so when I arrived, I became quite scared! I was taken inside and placed on a table. I was strapped onto this table. I was told that I was "VC." I had no idea what they meant! I didn't know anything! I was scared, and they began to beat me. It hurt very much! They got a belt of leather, sometimes, a stick as well. They hit me on the back and on the back of my legs. I was told that someone had given my name as helping the VC. I did not know about my father's true identity at that time, so I had no idea what they wanted or why they thought I was VC. No matter how much they beat me, it didn't matter—I had nothing to tell. I found out later that one of my very good friends in the army, a man who I had worked with many times as an MP, had traveled to Can Tho region, which is south of Saigon. He went there to visit his family. By chance he had lost his wallet, and by chance a CIA [Central Intelligence Agency] operative found it—and found it in VC territory. They took my friend the next day to the security prison and tortured him until he was broken and bleeding. He was not VC—we all knew him, so he had nothing to tell. But after a while, most men will break down when tortured, and so he became desperate and shouted a few names that he knew. My name came from his lips, so the police came after me. That is how it worked back then—fear ruled everyone in Viet Nam. Only the very rich and the powerful could escape the police if they thought you were VC.

I spent three full months in that prison. I was beaten almost every day. I lost weight. I became weak from the pain. I was in misery! But I did not tell any names, because I did not know any VC at the time. I was not a VC. At least at that time!

My wife was pregnant with our first child, and she came to visit. She was allowed a few minutes each week for a visit. She was scared: There she was, pregnant, and her husband is in prison. It was a terrible time. It was like that for three months. Then one day a group of our neighbors collected some money. They went to see the police official in charge and told of my wife's condition; they told that I was not VC. But most importantly, they had money for the bribe. In Viet Nam during the war, money could always get you things that otherwise you could not. So one day in October 1967, I was released. I was sent home and ordered to report to duty the next day. I was warned to never talk to the VC or tell about my experience. I went home and reported like I was told.

The week before, on 23 October 1967, our first child was born, a daughter, Thi Ngoc Hanh. I was in prison the day she was born.

For most of the rest of the war, I was sent all over the country wherever they needed us. I spent over one year in the Can Tho District, near Vinh Long. I then was sent to Kieu Giang Island, which was a POW camp at the time. There were Americans there, as advisors, but most of the guards were ARVN, like myself. For the most part, the Americans tried to make sure that the prisoners were treated well. The ARVN guards were different. Many of them were very mean, and we sometimes heard the screams of those being beaten. But the Americans were OK. We were kept apart from the prisoners so they could not talk to us. I just kept my mouth quiet! I did my job and prayed every night to Buddha for my safety and for the protection of my new daughter. She was at home with her mother and grandmother. I got letters sometimes, not often.

After my own stay in the prison for those three months, my views on everything changed. I hated the government, but what could I do? I was frightened for my family. Do you understand what that means?

I had a family in 1972, and I wanted to just live in peace. I avoided combat whenever I could. I had no reason to fight other than fear of the government. . . . Most of the guys in my unit felt the same. Some of the officers—they were serious—they hated the VC. But not us—we just wanted peace.[13]

On December 26, 1972, tremendous explosions rocked a usually quiet residential neighborhood of Hanoi. Known as the "Christmas Bombings," the attacks were designed by President Richard M. Nixon to break the will of the North. While most attacks were precise, a miscalculation that Monday night let loose thousands of tons of bombs from a B-52 barrage on a residential district. The bombing of Kham Thien Street left 283 people in all dead and another 266 seriously injured. A total of 543 homes were completely destroyed and hundreds more damaged.[14] A young Vietnamese army nurse witnessed the bombings from afar and was one of the first sent into the horror of the aftermath less than an hour after the last bombs went off:

NGUYEN THI HANH (NURSE, PEOPLE'S ARMY OF VIET NAM)

After I joined the PAVN in 1971, I spent some time training in nursing and psychology. I was attached to the Third PAVN Army Hospital Division, which would travel many places both to avoid being detected by the American bombers and to provide relief to the areas that were being bombed. When I was stationed near a hospital one time, I can clearly remember the *bo doi* [soldiers] in the rooms. What I remember most is how young they were, maybe eighteen or nineteen. They had no time to live their life, to marry, to have children, to live in peace; they had to give all to their country. Many of the wounded died in the hospital, but most were there to be nursed back to health, to be sent again back to the front. My job, as I had said, was usually to help them in their mental state, the psychology of recovering. . . . For many months, I would do my duty like this, witnessing many bombings in the North, but always I was lucky and was never hurt myself. The closest I came to the bombs was that terrible night during the 1972 raids on Hanoi. It was the worst of the entire war. . . . I was stationed just south of the city when we awoke to the distant thunder of many bombs going off in the direction of Hanoi. Before the bombers had even left the skies, we were ordered north to the city to assist with what we could. I was one of the first to pull up to that neighborhood in a Russian army truck. I got out and stumbled among the debris toward where the fires were burning and met people streaming away. The damage was unbelievable! I will never forget that night: The survivors were coming toward us in shock, dazed, with incomprehensible fear in their eyes. Some were quiet, others were screaming as loud as they could. I was terrified, but my sense of duty took over and I did what I could to help. We saved some from the rubble, but many had died. Some [were] buried for days, even weeks before we could clear the debris from the buildings. I was so angry that I cannot even to this day articulate well. I was sad and angry at the same time. I became furious at the Americans for bombing the poor people in those homes, the children! I cannot forget the dead—the crying—the screaming! I cannot ever forget.[15]

HOANG VAN MY (PEOPLE'S ARMY OF VIET NAM)

I endured many hardships walking down the Ho Chi Minh Road. It was a terrible time, of course, but we had to fight, to repatriate our brothers and sisters in the South. We are all Vietnamese. I know that Americans think that we invaded the South. We must laugh a little at that thought! Imagine, invading our own country! It was not ever like that. We were all Vietnamese, so we went south to fight and die for our country.

I went first to the border region in Tay Ninh Province with the Seventh Division. I was with that unit until the end of the war on April 30, 1975. The entire time I fought in the South in that area except on two occasions. The first was during the battle in Laos in 1971. I was there, at Tchepone, and it was a terrible fight. But we won that battle, and the South government soldiers retreated in panic. It was a great victory, although we lost many of our soldiers. We had them trapped in a narrow valley. They came on the ground and with American helicopters. But we shot down many, many copters and so they fled in fear. After that time, we were never bothered in that area again—we were too strong.

It was our usual tactic to avoid a fight when we could. Our role was to engage, then retreat to fight again. Survival was most important. . . . But at Tchepone, we had to fight to save our supplies on the Ho Chi Minh Road. So we gathered in great strength and stood our ground. It was the first time we had such a great victory over the South and Americans, after so many years of hardships. It was a needed moral victory. The second time our unit left Tay Ninh was near the end of the war, on April 30, 1975; I was north of Cu Chi at that time. So, most of the war I spent in the Tay Ninh region.

During the war, we fought many battles and I lost many of my friends. The weapons that the Americans used were very destructive, and we had many, many killed. To survive, we had to hug close to the Americans or South soldiers and keep in contact with them wherever they went. Sometimes less than fifteen meters separated us in our holes from the enemy. That way, we could avoid their bombs from the air. They did not want to risk killing their own men, so if we held close to the Americans, then we had a better chance to—to survive. The B-52 bombers were a terrible weapon. We feared them—no warning. Suddenly the ground would just begin to lift up from the earth with tremendous force. The roar was so loud. It is hard to imagine that. I still cannot describe it properly. It was terrible. But it never shook our resolve. We had no choice. I never once considered giving up the fight, never once. I was wounded three times, only once seriously. I received a bullet here [pointing to his left side] and it is still inside me—they never got it out. I was OK and a few weeks later was back in the front line around Nui Ba Den. When I was wounded, I went to Kampuchea to heal.

The second strategy during the war that we had to utilize was to make friends with the local people, like the saying "Become fish in the sea." The people were the sea, we the fish—we cannot live without them. They were our strength, our intelligence, our food source, our moral support to stay alive. If we did not get along with the people, then our fight to save the South would wither like a vine cut from a tree. We had two parts of our unit: one to teach the soldiers and encourage us to fight, the other to talk to the villagers, to encourage them to support the revolution. Both parts, the soldiers and the people, made our revolution.

The Americans, of course, tried to separate the villagers and the Vietnamese soldiers. It was very dangerous for the villagers to assist us. If they are caught, then they will get tortured and maybe killed by the government and the Americans. So we devised plans with great care and met with only some of them in secret places. We usually avoided the villages themselves but would send out men nearby, and the people would make like they are going fishing in the canal or going to tend the fields. . . . Then we would meet and they would give us information and food. We could not have lived without their help. We spent our time near the border area in the forests. At night, we could breathe a little easier—the Americans never liked the nighttime. They would always come out of their bases in the day, roaring down the roads in their vehicles, making sweeps against us; then, as the evening approached, they would retreat and return to their bases for protection. I was the son of a fisherman . . . and a teacher—I did not grow up living in the jungle. So I had also to adjust and learn to live in the forest. It was very difficult, of course, but it was a better place than the tunnels.

Most of the time I fought, in my six years of war, I only fought against American soldiers a few times. In the beginning, it was usually against the South government troops that I fought. . . . So I did not see Americans often, but I heard once of some in my division taking two Americans prisoners. One was a black man. They were captured near Nui Ba Den, and it was a funny story they told us, our men. They said that the Americans, who usually rode all around in trucks and tanks, could not walk far, they are not in condition like us. So on their way to Kampuchea one of the men, the black man I think, could not walk anymore. So four of our men had to carry him through the hills and jungles, four men! He was a big guy! And also, we had to feed them, but they wanted so much food, because of their size, of course. Sometimes we had to steal food, like a chicken or something, from the government zone to feed our prisoners. It was dangerous, but we did it. I do not know what happened to the fate of those two men. But I, myself, never saw them and never saw American prisoners.[16]

HUYEN VAN CHIA (PEOPLE'S LIBERATION ARMY)

It was sometime before the Tet celebrations in 1960, seven [weeks], I believe, that the war came to our homes and fields in earnest. It was, I believe, called [Operation] "Cedar Falls." The Americans came in full force, with tanks, many men, planes, helicopters, and they surrounded and destroyed the village of Ben Suc. Ben Suc is over there, across the river. They destroyed the village and took all the people away, closer to Saigon, so the government could keep an eye on them. It was an attempt to destroy the connection between the front fighters and the people. It did not work. In reality, it made everyone so very angry. Why do these Americans come here and kill our family? Kill our neighbors? Burn our homes and plow away the forests? How can they believe that by doing this, that we would then wish to support their cause and the South government? What were they thinking?

By then, we were driven underground for nearly all the time for many years. At one point—this is true—I was living underground in the tunnels for five straight months. I cannot remember even a very few times that I came up above ground except to fight in battles. Who can understand so much misery? The smells, the death, but it was our sworn duty. We never, never thought about giving up. You may ask, "How can you stay in those terrible holes in the ground for so long?" The answer is simple: We had no choice. If you went outside, death waited for everyone. So, given the choice, life or death, you see, it is an easy choice.

I continued fighting the Americans from the tunnels. The tunnels allowed us to keep many fighters in the field close to Saigon. Despite our casualties, despite the hardships, we were in a strategic locale, being less than fifty kilometers from Saigon, so we clung to the lands around here, the Cu Chi District, Ben Suc, and the areas around the plantations. One time I had to escape because Americans had found one of our entrances. They sent soldiers down into the tunnels, which was very frightening. At times there would be total darkness—you had to feel your way along the walls, and so it gave us the advantage because we were so familiar with the maze. . . . So I went toward the river; not far from where the memorial now stands to the fighters was an escape entry under water. Yes, it curled under the bank and allowed for a few of us to slip away into the blackness of the water and swim to safety.

By the summer, the Americans, they would fly over every day and bomb, many times, just at random. A few bombs here, some artillery there. It was more of a nuisance than a tactical effect on the situation. Other times they would bomb with the B-52s. You can still see the craters from the B-52s. Their power is unbelievable. Sometimes, when they attacked, our men would die in the tunnels from near misses without any scratch on them. Just from the concussion—the lungs, they would explode from the pressure. It was a terrible way to die. We would bury them right inside the tunnels, in the walls—we had no choice. To go outside to bury our comrades would risk death. I am a Buddhist, so those things were difficult for me especially.

One time in November, yes—November 1, I believe, 1967—the Americans had sent an armored force to sweep near Ben Suc, maybe a kilometer from the river. We knew of their plans and came out of the tunnels to wait for them. We set up an ambush. I had, at the time, an RPG [rifle propelled grenade]. I was with two others; we formed a cadre. We always fought in threes—we would take care of ourselves that way. The tension was intense! We [were] so afraid, but we didn't dare move. The tanks got closer, rumbling, shaking the earth, as [the enemy] crawled slowly toward our right. We waited for what seemed like hours! They were firing their weapons, here and there, randomly, to suppress any ambush. There were tanks and three of their APCs. I was behind a ditch, with some cover which made up a small bunker for us that we had built previously outside of our tunnel entrances. There were only a few small bushes for cover as most of the trees were gone. The bombs and the Agent Orange killed all of the trees in the forests for many kilometers. It is said that you could see all the way to Saigon because all of the trees had been killed by the Americans! I will take this image to my grave, with the smell, the noise, the smoke rising above the broken fields—we all felt deep in our hearts that we would never see another day. Suddenly, as the first tank swept on with its side exposed to my sights, not more than ten meters away, it was time: So I twisted a bit while I swung myself up with the rocket on my right shoulder. I was exposed a little then and fired directly into the side of the tank. It was so close, I could not miss! It went up in a fire! It hit hard on the side, and the tank came to a jerky stop. Then we tried to—to reload, and then it hit. A tremendous explosion, and then all went blank.

I awoke many hours later in a field hospital outside Tay Ninh. There they treated me for my wounds. The second tank had killed my two cadre companions. It also took from me my right arm, as you can see. Someone had crawled to me, under fire, and pulled me to safety, and I was sent across the river toward Tay Ninh. Behind Nui Ba Den was a dressing station underground. From there I was sent to the rear inside Kampuchea. I was there, in a hospital, to heal for many months. I lost most of my eyesight here [right eye] and my arm. It was a terrible wound but after time I recovered enough to move on my own. That day was November 1, 1967. It was my last day as a front fighter, but not my last in helping the revolution.[17]

COMBAT EXPERIENCES FORGE LASTING OPINIONS ON THE WAR

As the antiwar movement grew in the United States as well as globally, the war continued unabated in the beleaguered provinces throughout Viet Nam. The soldiers on all sides continued fighting despite great variance in motivations, morale, and commitment to victory. Here are more stories:

LARRY SEEGER (TWENTY-THIRD INFANTRY DIVISION, 1969 TO 1971)

Probably the most significant combat operation I was involved in was called "Lam Son 719," which was an incursion into Laos in February 1971 by mostly ARVN troops with U.S. air support. The purpose of this operation was to physically interdict the Ho Chi Minh Trial at Tchepone (Laos). The overall goal was supposed to be to deny Viet Cong forces in the South the supplies necessary to conduct major offenses, while ARVN units gradually supplanted the American units that were being withdrawn. The mission was a technical success, in that Tchepone was occupied for a time and war material was found and destroyed. But the Ho Chi Minh Trail was not just one highway. It was a porous network of trails that could expand to avoid obstructions as necessary, and the NVA was nothing if not innovative in adjusting to temporary setbacks. The end result was that the ground was typically relinquished after a short time, and the ARVN returned with some marginally increased confidence in their combat capabilities. I was a CH-47

(Chinook) cargo helicopter pilot serving my second tour. The operation was the first time I had been in combat outside of the Republic of Viet Nam, against regular North Vietnamese Army forces equipped with USSR tanks and true antiaircraft weapons. My Chinook was shot down while trying to resupply Landing Zone 30, and I was slightly wounded in the crash. Nearly one hundred helicopters were lost during the operation, including 2 other Chinooks.[18]

BETH MARIE MURPHY (R.N., HOSPITAL SHIP U.S.S. *SANCTUARY*, 1969 TO 1970)

In a short while I was seeing the face of the war in many seriously injured young men, most younger than I was at that time (I was twenty-two). Slowly, the war did not make sense. I would talk with the men and hear how they would take a certain hill where many were injured, and the next day, they would leave the hill only to retake it later and lose more lives and sustain more injuries. Also, the reports we were hearing in the news media about how well the war was going did not match with what we were receiving in casualties. It seemed as if there was no real plan. It was supposedly a war of attrition with body counts of the enemy. However, it was, in reality, the body counts of our young men that were being counted. How can you win a war when there is no front line—only jungle encounters? Over the year I was there, I became angry with the U.S. government who was obviously lying to Americans and those of us serving in Vietnam. Yet I was also committed to the men who were there fighting. It was very confusing to someone who had no political savvy.[19]

STEVE HASSNA (101ST ARMY AIRBORNE DIVISION, 1967 TO 1968)

I had nothing but respect for, and fear of, the NVA. They were well organized, well equipped, and highly motivated. Hard fighters that didn't back up. But so were we, so I think the feeling was mutual. During an operation in Chu Lai, my platoon was sent to recon an abandoned NVA base camp. I was on "R & R" at the time, and I was told about what happened next by the survivors of my platoon. Lucky me!

There would be storage sheds and hooches [huts] used by the farmers. My platoon was sent to check out one of these mounds. . . . My platoon just walked into it as if on a Sunday stroll. Then realized it was occupied;

in fact it was an NVA Regimental C.P. [Command Post]. Everyone was totally surprised! NVA troops in hammocks writing letters or cooking chow—both sides just stared at each other—then all hell broke loose!

What was left of my company made it back across the paddies and into a creek for protection. Nineteen hours later, with the rest of our company and battalion coming to the rescue, they were extricated. Of the twenty-six that went into the C.P., twelve were still walking. . . . My platoon was gone.

. . . Things happened that reinforce how stupid the whole thing was. On two separate nights, platoons from my company got overrun by animals! The first night, an elephant walked into our night perimeter—they had set up the perimeter across a trail. This elephant walks right down the trail, nudges a sergeant who was sleeping, who starts screaming, the elephant also starts screaming, or whatever (noise) they do . . . and both the elephant and the sergeant take off in opposite directions.

Then, a tiger tripped one of our devices (claymore trip wire) in the middle of the night, and killed it. The next morning, the platoon lieutenant and two others go out to check. They forgot to check for other trip wires, and after they found the tiger, he tripped another wire and [the lieutenant] lost both his legs at the knee. The other two were killed instantly.

Then there were the monkeys—this is right out of a silent movie gag: A platoon is in its night perimeter, which is darker than a black hole in space, when out of nowhere, this whole group of monkeys overrun the perimeter. It's dark, troops are yelling and screaming, the monkeys are doing the same, and trip flares are going off all over the place. The rest of the night, the platoon is staring into the dark wondering what the f—— had just happened.[20]

NGUYEN HUONG KY (PEOPLE'S LIBERATION ARMY)

I was a front fighter for many years. I am from Saigon and joined in 1966. During the Tet Offensive, I was part of a blocking force that was sent toward the Hoc Mon Road just west of Than Son Nhut Airport. Another company attacked the airport through the walls—on the west side, while we waited near the textile factory in ambush. We waited for maybe one hour or so. Then, as we anticipated, the Americans came storming down the road in their tanks and APCs. They were sent to rescue the garrison at the airport. We opened up from two sides. . . . I remember tanks beginning to burn— we destroyed the entire column. We had them pinned down near the road embankment for what seemed like many hours . . . but probably only about one or two. Finally, after a while, they sent reinforcements, more tanks on the road, and helicopters overhead. We could not defend against helicopters so it was time to withdraw. We left many dead heroes on the battlefield that day—it was very hard—but for a while there, on the road outside the air-port, we stood up to, and beat, the Americans.[21]

PHAN VAN HOANG (PEOPLE'S LIBERATION ARMY)

I was a student in Hue in 1968. . . . I had been supportive of the revo-lution, but only in my heart—Ho Chi Minh was a symbol of strength and determination for me at that time. I did not fight, though. I was more against Thieu than for the Communists. But that changed in 1968. I was in the student resistance at the university. I took part in the student revolt in 1967 in Hue. I was born in 1945, and in 1968 I was at the university. One night, the police came for me and arrested me. I was taken to the CIA building, where an agent, his name was Robert, that is all I can remember, was beginning to interrogate me. But there was some kind of distraction. Robert had to leave, there was confusion, and I saw my chance: I turned and fled. I managed to escape from a window left unguarded. . . . Because I had just been brought in from my home, I was not yet processed and was left unshackled. I was lucky—I managed to find my way to freedom. That is when I joined the PLA. I had been a student activist before that time, not a guerrilla. But then my experience with the Americans changed all that. I was captured as part of the Phoenix Program that the CIA was running. They tortured and killed many suspects, innocent or not. I was very lucky, but my days as a student were over. I joined the local PLA unit and was sent to the South. I trained in the delta region, near Ben Tre. I joined an elite sapper unit. . . . and later was in intelligence. Many times, I was in and out of Saigon, I had many disguises, and was never caught again. The first time I was captured put a scare into me—it was enough! I fought with the PLA until the end of the war.

On April 30, 1975, I was already in Saigon with others, long before the main battle formations entered the city. We helped by destroying commu-nications and equipment of the ARVN.[22]

NOTES

1. Bernard Edelman, ed., *Dear America: Letters Home from Vietnam* (New York: Pocket Books, 1985), 205.

2. Ibid., 55.

3. Ibid., 206.

4. Vietnamese Letters, Captured Vietnamese Documents, translated by Hanh Thi Ngoc Trinh-Vadas. CDEC microfilm collection. Boston: William Joiner Center for the Study of War and Social Consequences, University of Massachusetts.

5. Ibid.

6. John Lancaster, taped personal communication, transcribed by Adam Pallack (October 2000).

7. Billy C. Bryels, taped personal communication, transcribed by Ann Thomas (March 2001).

8. Larry Seeger, written personal communication (February 2001).

9. Steve Hassna, written personal communication (October 2000).

10. Greg Gibbons, written personal communication (March 2001).

11. Byron James, taped personal communication, transcribed by Robert E. Vadas (May 2001).

12. Nguyen Duc Anh, written personal communication (November 2000).

13. Trinh Quang Dai, taped personal communication, translated by Hanh Thi Ngoc Trinh-Vadas (January 2001).

14. Tri Binh, "A Bustling Testament to Courage and Solidarity," *Viet Nam News*, 28 (December 2000): 5.

15. Nguyen Thi Hanh, personal communication, Viet Nam, translated by Hanh Thi Ngoc Trinh-Vadas (January 2001).

16. Huong Van My, taped personal communication, Viet Nam, translated by Hanh Thi Ngoc Trinh-Vadas (January 1998).

17. Huyen Van Chia, taped personal communication, Cu Chi, Viet Nam, translated by Hanh Thi Ngoc Trinh-Vadas (January 2001).

18. Seeger.

19. Beth Marie Murphy, written personal communication (October 2000).

20. Hassna.

21. Nguyen Huong Ky, personal communication, translated by Hanh Thi Ngoc Trinh-Vadas (January 2001).

22. Phan Van Hoang, written personal communication (January 2000).

Chapter 5

Stalemate Tests the Will of Fighters and Civilians Alike

Victory remained elusive for both sides in Viet Nam as the costs in human, environmental, cultural, economic, and political terms rose dramatically. The Tet battles subsided after significant casualties to both sides, while the political situation in the United States became volatile. The antiwar movement grew as opinion polls registered a majority of Americans opposed to the continuation of the war by the summer of 1968. In Viet Nam, many soldiers doing the fighting began to lose heart and wondered themselves about the legitimacy of their fight. Morale sagged, and some units began to rebel in the field.

Those supporting the revolution resolved to continue in the face of massive casualties and with the death of Ho Chi Minh in September 1969. By the spring of 1970, tensions in America reached a boiling point as President Richard M. Nixon ordered the invasion of Cambodia and student protests exploded across the land.

DESPITE HARDSHIP, THE REVOLUTION CONTINUES

In the 1960s, the revolutionaries fighting the Southern government and their American allies generally retained high morale and resolve. Some members did rally to the South government, bringing tales of hardship and terror caused by the massive firepower of the

American troops. Some letters written then describe the sorrows, de-
sires, and motivations of the People's Liberation Army (PLA). The
first is an undated poem from the notebook of Nguyen Van "Be
Danh" of a Demolition Platoon of the 514th Battalion (PLA):

> Autumn passes away, winter comes, and then spring returns.
> I am as always enraptured by my mission.
> Before me, flowers bloom in brilliant colors in front of someone's
>   house,
> A bamboo branch sways gracefully, reminding me of the native
>   village I love.
> Our unit stops to rest in an isolated area.
> My shoes are still covered with dust gathered during the march.
> I hurriedly compose this letter to you
> and send you all my love.[1]

An older sister wrote back to him from Be Danh's home village, Hau
My:

Hau My, May 30, 1966
Dear Em Danh,
    I found out your address from the letter you wrote to Chi Tam, and so
I hurry and dash off a few lines to inquire about your health. Dear Danh,
have there been any changes in your health since the day you left Hau My,
your native village? How have you been doing in your mission? I am sure
you are well and I am sure that you are making good progress in your work.
    Hau My, our native village, is no longer as happy as before—it's become
very desolate. The Americans pour their bombs and shells on the village
every day without stopping. But the people in Hau My still maintain their
revolutionary tradition and still cling to their rice fields and orchards. They
devote themselves to the production task in order to contribute large quan-
tities of resources to the Revolution. But in the last sweep operation, many
people in Hau My were shot dead by the enemy. The older sisters and I
and our families fortunately escaped unhurt. The father of Nam Rang was
seriously wounded but his condition has improved. Be Danh, don't be pes-
simistic when you read this letter. Instead, you should intensify your hatred.
The front line and the rear areas should join hands to increase our strength
to fight harder and avenge the people of South Viet Nam in general and
the people of Hau My in particular.
    Life in the army must be very gay. Has it ever happened that this gay life
makes you forget about Hau My, your desolate native village? If you have,
just tell the truth. As for myself, I am fine and doing well in my mission,
just like the rest of the girls—Rang, Xoai, Anh, La, and Banh. They send
you their best regards. This is just a short note to ask about your health;

I'll write at greater length in my next letter. I wish you good health and continuous progress in your mission.

Love,

Your older sister: Chin Thuan

P.S. If you receive this letter, please write. Give my best regards to the other people in your unit. I agree with you, and I think that you should go ahead with your marriage announcement. What do you think?[2]

Long An Province, south of Saigon, was an area of significant revolutionary activity. Because of the proximity to their home villages, the PLA fighters had contact with one another more frequently than those soldiers fighting in the People's Army of Viet Nam (PAVN). Letters from this region attest to the concern with one another's health and friendships, with words of encouragement to keep fighting:

Dear Muoi Thoi:

I was very happy when I got your letter. We got to know each other through our work for the Revolution, and we've come to understand each other well in spite of the fact that I am with the Province Unit and you work in the village.

How have you been and how have you been doing in your mission? What is the situation in the village now? Is it shelled and bombed heavily by the enemy? Has the revolutionary movement in the village expanded? As for me, my health is just as good as it used to be.

Oh, let me tell you about our attack on the Americans in the Truog Ga settlement. It was our first fight with the Americans. They lost 150 dead and wounded. I myself participated in this attack, which took place on the 25th of July. The rainy season will come soon, right? If you receive this letter, please let me know. I received your letter on April 14, 1967, but I was busy and couldn't write back, so don't be mad at me. Please give my best regards to your parents, to Mrs. Ba, Uncle and Aunt Tam, and Hay. Vinh was wounded in the left arm; he was hit by aircraft fire. He's all right now, but his arm is slightly paralyzed. Please give my regards to Aunt Bay. I want to say much more, but I'm going to save it for my next letter. Since I've written you, you should write back. I'm anxious to hear from you.

Let's fight against the Americans.

Le Hoang Luong

C646B Unit, 4th Platoon

May 12, 1967.[3]

Morale among the PLA fighters was high until the American military pressed assaults on their own territory. While those who continued to fight did so under nearly unbearable hardship, morale sagged and some began to go over to the other side. A typical interview of one such "rallier" is quoted that some of the men were complaining about the lack of success and benefits to their families in joining the front:

They [PLA] continued to fight with determination because they were forced to do so. In the front's battalions, the privates always live under constant pressure which is maintained through the three man cell system. They controlled one another and therefore each man is always watched over constantly. If you don't fight well, your comrades in the cell will notice it and you will be criticized violently in "*Kiem thao*" sessions.[4]

To exploit this morale drop, much of which was caused by the massive damage that American bombs and shells had wrought upon the villages and countryside, American officials were urged to increase the "psywar" operations of the Central Intelligence Agency. To support their premise, a Rand report quoted a PLA fighter who rallied in late 1966:

I certainly am not flattering the GVN [Government of Viet Nam] . . . with what I am going to say, but the truth is that the majority of the people living there . . . think that the GVN will win this war. . . . The people have never witnessed any of their victories. The only thing the people have ever grasped is the increase of shellings and of their hardships. As a result, they are thinking the front just lies and that it would never be able to defeat the GVN.[5]

The following poem is not dated, although it came from a group of letters from the Ben Tre area dated in 1967. It is written to a man named Vach, from an unknown friend:

Dear friend!
What are you living for Vach?
Is there trying conditions? If the rain is very heavy,
    when the snows cover every where.
As time has passed, we had many years living together, more and
    more close
        we grew in friendship.
Now, is our life changed into a new future?
Dear Vach!

The war of resistance is about to be victorious, so that we should
  withstand all types
of difficulty, American bombs, bad weather, poor food!!!!
Dear Vach!
It is said that: desperate disease must bring desperate remedies!!!!
We always wait for any duties, we made hard choices for a coming
  victory!
After that, we will meet each other on the way to the new glory of
  the revolution![6]

Members of the National Liberation Front spent significant
amounts of time encouraging each other to continue the fight as
times were hard, and letters of encouragement often came from the
front fighter committees to the population committees. The following excerpt of a letter from the Liberation Front Committee, Ben Tre
Province, Giong Trom District, refers to the dropping of Agent Orange and contains exaggerated accounts of victory to bolster morale:

July 5, 1967
Dear population, managerial cadre, freedom fighter!!!
During the dry season 1966–1967, our civilian and military forces defeated all enemies, the second time against the global counter strategy of
America's soldiers. We killed 185 American soldiers. With 8,500 American
soldiers wounded. Our country is cheering a victory! We will continue fighting enemies. . . . We had beaten America's plan. . . . Our troops managed
to escape to safety. From June 16 until the 20th, America's soldiers gave
10 helicopters, many trucks, and two times, dropped toxic chemicals on
some areas: Phong My, Chau Hoa Chau Binh, and Binh Thanh. After that,
thousands of people were made sick or dead by the poisoning; sad to report
that two babies died of this as well. For a long time, America's soldiers tried
to change Balai River side into a desert!!!!!! Nobody lives there now, no
animals, no green trees. We . . . decided never to submit to our enemies.
We have to help each other, love each other, we have a block of great unity;
our rice and clothes we divide equally. . . . We have been willing to fight
America's soldiers to contribute to victory. America's soldiers fought stub-
bornly again; they paved toxic chemicals on our forests and the fields of Ba
Chau. We feel like we are in a desperate situation; we lack rice, lack medical
supplies. But we kept our heart. We had to fight America, face to face. We
would rather die than lose our country.[7]

During the war, it was common for family members to be fighting
in the same unit. The following is a letter from a PLA fighter to his
wife, in which he tries to soothe her concerns about their son who

is a member of his own unit. The letter was found in a hut. No explanation of the whereabouts of the man who wrote it, or his or his son's fate, accompanied the unit report:

June 6, 1967
Dear Cuc, the loving mother of Trieu:
Since that day our son and I left the house, it has been almost a month. I know that for that whole month Cuc has been burning with impatience more than anyone else, because in previous business trips it has been only me who has left you, but this time both me and our son are leaving you. To be good wife, a sweet mother, it is natural that you must be burning with impatience. I am sure it is true, isn't it, Cuc?

I would like to inform you, Cuc, that up to this time our son and I are still safe and healthy. One day, after going for two days, I saw Trieu looked tired; I stopped for one day to let him rest. After that we had to go for two more days before we arrived at the area that I had to work. Trieu rested for four days, then we had to continue our trip for three more days. Now Trieu is resting at a place with some elderly soldiers whom I met while arranging some work for Trieu. After about five to seven days I will come back to pick up our son and take him to where I am working.

That first evening, about 4 P.M., we came to the rest area. That night, I tore the khaki hammock into half to make for our son a rucksack like mine. This means our son has all necessary things. Trieu has a covered nylon hammock which was made by his 3rd sister (Dao). I gave Trieu my yellow hammock, which was made from a parachute, for his blanket. I also gave Trieu a pair of socks to keep his feet warm at night. So Trieu's clothes are temporarily enough. The last few weeks, Trieu has taken medicine to prevent malaria, so his health is fine. The peanuts that I carried with me were roasted with salt for Trieu, but our son said that "I do not like salt." On the road, we caught a big fish, but Trieu said he was fed up with this. I had to buy a piece of pork to supplement his diet with dehydrated foods. On that same day, Trieu attended a festive party of the army and had pork. So I still save some salted peanut, pickled fish, shrimp paste, one can of condensed milk, and one bag of candy.

The first time we entered the forest, when Trieu saw straight trees, he kept marveling and said he wants to make handles for hammers from these trees and to make handles for hoes. Seeing canes, he wanted to bring some home to decorate the house; seeing straight trees about the size of your thigh, Trieu said that these trees were good to make underground shelters, etc. Trieu said, "Whenever I can go home, I will bring some canes for the 2nd uncle to make some nets and some hammer's handles as well."

. . . Trieu asked about anything he saw; sometime it was so naive that I had to laugh at him. Our son is very well behaved. Although he misses our family, because he is with me, he is not very sad. After a while, he will get used to it, then everything will be normal. So Cuc, can you put your mind at rest and let our son stay here with me?

Love

Giao[8]

STALEMATE TAKES ITS TOLL ON AMERICAN MORALE

Lieutenant Junior Grade Edward Vick, Jr., served in Viet Nam with the Navy's River Patrol Flotilla 5, Riverine Division 534 and 551, which operated in the Mekong Delta. The controversial strategy of serving one year only was good for individual morale as the time neared to be sent home but had negative impact on unit effectiveness since by the time a soldier had gained valuable combat experience, a new recruit took his place, who had to learn everything from scratch:

October 6, 1969

Hi—

Three days from now I'll be all through playing this silly game. Three more patrols and I'll be off the river and have nothing to do but pack up for Hong Kong. Following that I'll have nothing to do but get ready to depart beautiful Vietnam.

With every week this thing gets more ridiculous. With the force nearly half turned over this month, they are starting a new operation in the U Minh Forest areas of the Ca Mau Peninsula in the southern delta. It has been a VC [Viet Cong] base area since before the French were here, when they were the Viet Minh. The U.S. has never before been there except for air strikes. No one is there now except for 10 PBRs (patrol boat recon), [which] began patrolling two days ago and have already lost two boats and one killed and ten wounded. At this stage it's just insane—it's suicidal for the boats and can never be pacified by 10 little boats. The Army won't touch it. I'm glad I'm through with it all. . . .

The rain's beginning to slack off and should be stopped altogether by the latter half of October. With any luck I'll be home for Thanksgiving!

Carolina [a college sports team] won yesterday—how about that miracle!

Love, Ed[9]

The nature of the war elicited mixed emotions from most Americans. Patriotism, cynicism, camaraderie with their friends, and the politics of the war all could lead to a sense of confusion. Allen Paul was with Second Battalion, Fifth Cavalry, First Cavalry Division (Air Mobile). In a letter to his love, he tries to describe the confusion and emotions that the war elicited:

May 8, 1968

My Dearest Bev,

For the last week we have been waiting for an attack, and last night it came in full force. Honey, I was never so scared in my life. We got hit by 12 mortars and rockets, and some even hit our ammo dumps, which really hurt the battery. A mortar landed about 30 feet from me and I was lucky enough to have my head down, but the sergeant next to me didn't, and we think he lost an eye. We got three men seriously hurt and four others shaken up by the blast. This was my first real look at war, and it sure was an ugly sight. I helped carry some of the wounded away, and boy, I sure hope I don't have to do that again. It was an experience you can never explain in a million words.

The noise from shooting is enough to drive a person crazy. Even after the attack last night, we had to stay up and wait for a ground attack which, lucky for us, never came. We expect to catch a lot of hell through May because it seems that the VC are really putting a big push on.

Bev, I was so surprised last night to see that the men here were willing to risk their own lives to save a buddy's. It really makes you have faith in people again, but I hope I don't have to go through what we did last night in a long time (like never!).

I take your picture out quite often and just look at it, because it's such a relief from this pitiful place to see such a beautiful being. I am thinking of you always.

All my love,

Al[10]

Great effort was made to create physical comfort for GIs in Viet Nam. The result was an eerie sense of unreality as one moment a soldier was in mud and the chaos of battle, then an hour later he might be heli-lifted to base where he could listen to Jimi Hendrix (a rock-and-roll-singer) and drink a cold Coke or beer. Soldiers often wrote to describe this. Written by First Lieutenant Robert Salerni of the 554th Engineer Battalion, 79th Engineer Group, 20th Engineer Brigade, based at Cu Chi and Nui Ba Den:

Nui Ba Den, March 12, 1969 Wednesday 2005 hrs

Dear Mom, Dad & Tom,

. . . There are a lot of inconsistencies about this war—a lot of things seem unreal. At times you wouldn't even think a war is on. You're watching movies on television. Or you're listening to the radio, and getting the same disc jockeys and the same predominantly rock 'n' roll music [that] you'd get on an American station. However, instead of commercials or public-service announcements, you get reminded to drive carefully or to keep your weapon clean or to be constantly vigilant, etc., and then back to the music. Yet at other times, you are aware that a war is on. This is a war of contrasts in a land of contrasts . . .

I hope you all are well.

Love,

Bobby[11]

Most soldiers spent much time writing home about everyday issues to connect with their loved ones and families. Private First Class Bernard Robinson, assigned to the 3rd Marine Division's Civil Action Program 357 in I Corps between June 1969 and July 1970, got the news of the birth of his daughter in the states:

November 27 [1969]

Thursday

Hi Sweet Thing,

Yesterday I can say it was one of the happiest days in my life. Hearing about the baby. It is one of the best things a man over here can be told. I wish you could have seen the way me and my friends were acting after we heard about it. We were shooting our rifles and making all kinds of noise. The people in the village thought we were going crazy. It was really something to see. I wanted to be home so bad.

Denise, how has the baby been feeling? Is she getting used to being in the world? Does she seem to be happy? How are you feeling after having her? How many times do you have to see the doctor a month? What did the doctor say about your and her health?

Today is Thanksgiving, and I have a lot to be thankful for—a wonderful wife and being able to have a child of ours. I'm thankful to be a father.

All my love,

Bernie

Father of one girl[12]

Despite the occasional reassurances from home, many Americans' sense of purpose was lost, sometimes within weeks of arriving in Viet Nam. Some turned to drugs or became isolated and pensive.

Sp/4 (Specialist 4th class) William J. Kalwas of Rochester, New York, went to Viet Nam in June 1970 where he was assigned to the Army Engineer Command at Long Binh. His loss of purpose is clearly noted in this letter he sent to his family:

September 12, 1970

Dear Dad, Bob & Jean,

I received your letter of September 7 on the 12th, a Sunday. It really seems funny that the summer is already over in the World. Seems like only yesterday that I was going down to the lake and freezing, waiting for it to warm up so I could go skiing. Damn this Army anyhow.

I can just picture looking back on this time period in a few years and suddenly jumping to a tropical environment, blanking out my familiar life patterns for 18 months. Before I get off on an anti-Army kick, I'll end this train of thought, because in my mood right now I could get really violent on paper. And after all I'm over here because the gooks "want" us here. I'm really serving an important purpose over here, allowing the lifers to sock away beaucoup money at my expense and that's about it. Vietnam wants to be free. Look, they even have elections. What a fine democratic country. Maybe they'll remember us after we've pulled out . . . at least until we stop giving them everything they want.

Well, I didn't suppress all my feelings, because after a while it becomes impossible and they just have to spill out. I don't expect you to swallow everything because you haven't been over here to see the people in action: hooch mates ripping off GIs' clothes and other belongings; ARVN [Army of the Republic of Viet Nam] troops refusing to take used serviceable equipment yet demanding new pieces (and getting them); government officials charging the American command for using the land and its resources. . . . This is why people get disgusted with Vietnam.

The Vietnamese don't want us over here. All they want is our money. Many of us who see all this can't do anything about it because those higher up are too intent on hauling in more money than they could amass anywhere else in the world for doing as little as they do. After a while, all I see just catches up with me and I begin to realize the futility of it all. I really don't want any part of it, so I participate as little as possible in all things Army. I just try to enjoy living with the GIs I'm here with and learn what I can from them. Eventually my tour will be over, and I'll be able to come back to the U.S. . . .

One thing I'll applaud [is] the sincerity and openness of the American enlisted GIs around me. Something in Vietnam releases all the restraints in our people, and you can talk and act freely without fear of retribution. Don't get me wrong. I'd never dream of staying here. But this similarity of situations among most the GIs is really a unique, moving experience. I will miss this part of Nam. But that's about it.

Peace & Love

Bill[13]

Few battles during the war better exemplify the tactics, and consequential frustration of the troops, than does the battle for Hill 875, a lonely jungle-covered piece of land jutting above the triple-canopy valleys near the Laotian border. One can clearly see the metamorphosis in American troop attitude from determined persistence to capture the hill to cynical frustration after the hill was abandoned just days after its capture. The spirit of the troops to then assault once again is best spoken by Trooper Fred Shipman who stated that we had to "look inside our soul . . . to know that we're going to make it." Such courage quickly turned to despair when the same soldiers left the hill and reviewed the hundreds of empty boots lined up on the Dak To airstrip in a solemn ceremony to remember the fallen. "I couldn't understand why we made this sacrifice, then just left it," said Fred Shipman. Mike Pfohl added, "I wanted to break ranks and walk away. I was angry. I was angry. It was for show. It wasn't necessary."[14]

THE WAR DIVIDES SOLDIERS AND CIVILIANS ALIKE

The Tet battles in the spring of 1968 deeply divided the general population as well as American soldiers in the field. The following stories and letters reflect these divisions. The first is from Private First Class Stephen W. Pickett, of Jackson Heights, New York, who served with Fourth Battalion, Twenty-Third Infantry (Mechanized), Twenty-Fifth Infantry Division, based in Dong Zu outside of Cu Chi Village:

Tuesday
November 14, 1967
7:00 P.M.
Dear Mom, Dad, Chris and Vicki,
We were well informed here about the demonstrations by both sides. Even though I'm here, I still have an open mind—realizing, of course, that an immediate pullout or anything of the sort is out of the question. It would degrade the heroic deaths of those who never returned because it would mean going back on everything that we have done. There are many here who feel as I do, but we will continue to fight for the country in which we believe.
Saul Alinsky, the social agitator, once said that no matter how much he criticizes his government, once he has left the United States he suddenly can't find a nasty thing to say about it.
I am sure that that is what the most sincere people feel, whether liberal or conservative. That is one of the very essences of our nation.
Take care of yourselves and keep writing. Vicki, thanks for the turkey. . . .
Love,
Your son and brother,
Stephen[15]

Stephen was just twenty years old when he was killed on a search-and-destroy mission exactly one month after he wrote this letter.

While some GIs joined antiwar protests in Viet Nam and others were angered by the demonstrators back home, a great many agonized about how the war was dividing the nation. The following letter from Sp/4 Howard Goldberg, assigned to Headquarters and Headquarters Company, Eleventh Light Infantry Brigade, Americal Division, exemplifies this concern. Howard was stationed at Duc Pho and survived the war:

November 13, 1968
Dear Mom,
How are you? I received the food package that you sent. It was luscious, and I really appreciated it. Thank you. Happiness is a warm stomach.
I hope you are feeling well. I realize that the wedding is taking much work and expense to prepare for it. I'm already so excited about coming home that I've been having trouble getting to sleep at night. So I had to go to the medics to get some sleeping pills. I'm a light sleeper and a heavy thinker, I guess, and there are so many things that I have to get done and we're needed in so many places that it drags me down sometimes.
This may sound strange, Mom, but I worry more about the war back home than I do about my own life over here. What good is the peace that we accomplish here if we don't have peace in our own backyard? If you only knew the horrors that arguments and hate can bear upon people as I've seen here. We can't hate righteously, we can only try to understand—to work with people rather than to destroy. Darwin's eat or be eaten works well with animals, but what are we? Do we speak of God and hate the "ungodly"? Are our brothers just the next-door neighbors or all of humanity? Or is the alien who walks from his flying saucer shot before he speaks because he doesn't look like us? You may not know it, but you taught me the answers. But, Mom, have you forgotten?
I'll have to sign off now. A special "Take Care" to Grampa, Al, Elaine, Jeff, Auntie Riva and Family from me. Only 31 days left to go. Miss you.
Love, your son,
Howie[16]

When Nixon began withdrawing troops from Viet Nam, lower morale and increased frustration and anger among the men resulted. The following letter reflects this attitude, which was exacerbated by the poor fighting quality and corruption that permeated most ARVN units. Sp/4 George Ewing, Jr., served in Vietnam with 299th Engineer Battalion and was stationed near the Laos–Viet Nam border in the Central Highlands:

July 7, 1969
Dear Mom & Dad,
They think the enemy went back into Cambodia to get resupplied and that he's on his way back. There's talk of the 299th moving again, but they've been talking about it for a couple of months now. The politics behind all the monkey business around here is insane. This gradual withdrawal is going to cause more damage than good. As there become less and less GIs over here, it means that the guys still here will have to depend on the ARVNs. I would not want to have to depend on an ARVN for anything. I don't see how we ever won a war if we are fighting the same way as they fought in WW II. Maybe we will leave soon after all.
George[17]

The protests and violence associated with the antiwar movement reached their zenith in the spring of 1970 after President Nixon sent American troops across the border into Cambodia. At Jackson State College in Mississippi, two students were shot dead by state troopers on May 14, 1970, and at Kent State University in Ohio, four students were killed by Ohio National Guardsmen on May 4. Within days of the Kent State killings, 1,350 protests on university and college campuses alone broke out, involving over 4,350,000 people.[18] Ken Cushner, who was a student at Kent State University then, reflected on that day:

I never really have supported war as a resolution to conflict. While I understand and accept conflict as part of our existence, I do believe that alternatives to violence do exist and should be pursued at every level. . . . I was a freshman and in the crowd of students who were fired upon on May 4, 1970. I saw things happen on that day and on the campus that should not have happened under any circumstances. I saw four young people killed and nine students wounded who were exercising their constitutional right to protest a war in which they did not believe. Their rights to free speech were halted with their lives.
. . . Tension between students, the Guard, and the campus administration had heightened. Larry took me to the commons area where the ROTC [Reserve Officers' Training Corps] building had been burned the previous night to show me what had happened over the weekend. Hundreds of students were gathering at the time chanting antiwar chants and circling the remains of the building. Larry and I somehow found ourselves marching in front of this group. When we turned left, hundreds behind us turned left, when we turned right, hundreds of students turned right. . . . This was my introduction to mob or group psychology—how a leaderless and unfocused group can become dangerous and poorly focused. Numerous confrontations occurred that night between the National Guard and students. Students

were being sprayed with pepper gas; were chased across campus by guards-men who ended up bayoneting a few students; helicopters kept groups of students in their searchlights; and face-to-face confrontations on the streets with Guardsmen and local law enforcement officials escalated. In a final confrontation that evening, unprepared students made unrealistic demands of campus administrators that could not have been realized.

Students had been encouraged to gather on the Commons the next day (Monday, May 4) to protest the presence of the National Guard. About noon, perhaps up to a thousand students were gathered. A face off was developing with students on one side and Guardsmen on the other. There were instances of students chanting anti-war slogans with Guardsmen driving by in Jeeps stating that the gathering was unlawful and demanding that the students leave the area. Tear gas fired by Guardsmen attempting to disperse the crowd was returned by students. In addition, a number of students were actively throwing rocks at the Guard.

What I witnessed next is still, in many ways, in dispute. I recall the Guard wearing gas masks and carrying bayonet-equipped rifles moving in formation up a hill, chasing a group of us into a parking lot. In a sense, the Guard boxed themselves in at that point. There were students to the left side chanting antiwar slogans with a few throwing rocks and a fenced area in front and to their right side. The Guardsmen had no option at this point but to turn and retreat. At this point, students felt rather empowered, believing they had chased the Guard away. While students were well aware that the Guard were carrying bayonet-mounted rifles, the word going out among the students was that their rifles were not loaded. Many wrongly believed that the Guard had not used live ammunition in the urban riots the previous summer and that there was no way they would have done so with an un-armed group of students. How wrong we were!

Suddenly, and I would say without provocation, this group of about 20 Guardsmen stopped, turned back toward the group of students, the front line knelt, and fired more than 60 shots within 13 seconds. In the aftermath of the shooting, 4 students lay dead, and 9 were wounded. . . . The car I was hiding behind had its windows shot out. I can still feel the emotion of the day—the fear, the uncertainty, the horror and the loss—students lying face down in pools of blood, others angry or crying in disbelief.

The students, in response and in their anger, re-formed and confronted the Guard on the Commons. Again, warning came that they would continue their assault on us. Students stood their ground, in a sense, challenging the Guard. I attribute the saving of many students' lives, including my own, to one very special professor, Dr. Glenn Frank, who approached the Guard asking for a few minutes with the students. Persuading, and in fact crying, he pleaded with the students to leave, saying that what we had just witnessed would be repeated. Thankfully, we obliged and left. . . .

The Guard saw the confrontation quite differently. There were stories circulating that a sniper fired a shot from the roof of a nearby building, or that a student fired off the first shot into the crowd. Neither of these to this day has ever been substantiated.[19]

The commander of the Ohio National Guard Unit at Kent State on May 4, 1970, was Lieutenant Colonel Charles Fassinger. Fassinger, a Korean War veteran, had brought his unit to Kent directly from several days of maintaining order in a truckers' strike throughout the northeastern Ohio region. His perspective of the Kent killings were related years later:

The issue that . . . has been misunderstood is that the events began three days earlier in the town of Kent. The . . . Guard was called in by the mayor of Kent to assist the city in controlling the disturbances downtown . . . by moving the students back to the campus. Then, there was the burning of the ROTC building by students, still antigovernment, anti-Vietnam issues. On Monday morning the 4th, the rally on campus was now more anti-Guard than antiwar. . . . The focus was: Get the Guard off campus. The meeting with local law enforcement agencies, Campus officials, and the Guard established the need for a prohibition of rallies because of the events of the previous nights, such as the ROTC burning. It was well advertised that rallies were prohibited . . . but around 10:30 or 11:00, students began gathering at the victory bell. . . . Over a period of roughly an hour or so, more and more students joined the rally. They became boisterous and started throwing rocks and objects at the Guard. At that time the Riot Act was read and the crowd ordered to disperse. The order was ignored. . . . It was obvious that it wasn't going away, the crowd was turning into a mob mentality. . . . So at the request of Campus officials, the Riot Act was read again and the students ordered to disperse. The students responded with rocks at the officer in the Jeep reading the Act. . . . In an attempt to disperse the crowd, tear gas was fired into it, many of which were returned by students at the Guard. The decision was made to align and move the crowd. Two sections of troops moved around Taylor Hall and down onto the practice field in which they were then stopped by a construction fence. We had thought we had accomplished our mission—to move the crowd, but they renewed their efforts and gathered around us to throw more rocks. We then decided to return to our departure site near the hill, and on the way, at the Pagoda, the shooting took place.

I myself was right under the Pagoda. . . . We ordered a cease-fire! We had to grab some to get their attention, but the firing immediately stopped.

The incident since—well, it doesn't ever go away—two things have gone through my mind in the 30 years since: Could we have done anything different under the conditions that existed? There really isn't, given the exact conditions that we were under at the time. . . . The second is that it was a terrible tragedy, and finding fault doesn't change anything. The Guardsmen on that day were in civilian clothes themselves 5 days earlier . . . some going to school, some did not want to go to Vietnam either. They have all had to live with what happened all these years as well.[20]

ALAN CANFORA (KENT STATE UNIVERSITY STUDENT, SHOT MAY 4, 1970)

Alan, one of thirteen students shot by National Guardsmen at Kent State, grew up in working class Barberton, Ohio. His father lost an eye during World War II, and a best friend died in Viet Nam one month before the Kent State tragedy. Several of his boyhood friends had fought in and returned from Viet Nam, speaking of the senselessness of the war. This added to his growing antiwar perspective at Kent, where he was a student. Now the director of the Kent State University May 4 Center, he wrote the following:

It was shocking to see the armed, uniformed Guardsmen suddenly all turn together and start to shoot a powerful 13-second barrage of 67 shots into our crowd of unarmed students. For a brief moment, I assumed they were firing blanks because there was no reason whatsoever to fire live ammunition as they seemed to be retreating over the hilltop. At the moment the massacre occurred, as I stood and watched carefully, I saw several of my fellow students run away and "hit the dirt." As the bullets began to fly, my survival instinct caused me to . . . dash behind an oak tree a few feet away—the only tree in the direct line of fire.

Just as I reached safety, kneeling behind that beautiful tree during the first seconds of gunfire, I felt a sharp pain in my right wrist when an M-1 bullet passed through my arm. With shock and utter disbelief, I immediately thought to myself: "I've been shot! It seems like a nightmare, but this is real. I've really been shot!" My pain was great during that unique moment of unprecedented anguish, but I had another serious concern: The bullets were continuing to rain in my direction for another 11 or 12 seconds.[21]

Shortly after the Kent State shootings, many tens of thousands of disillusioned young people ran away from home, dropped out of school, or joined radical organizations. The majority of Americans, however, remained aloof from the antiwar movement, retained conservative perspectives about their country, and openly derided student protesters. Unable to comprehend the seething tensions that were boiling into the streets, they reacted many times with intolerance and anger. President Nixon energized this sentiment with several inflammatory remarks that added to the tension:

You know, you see these bums, you know, blowin' up the campuses. Listen, the boys that are on the college campuses are the luckiest people in the world, going to the greatest universities, and here they are, burnin' up the books, I mean stormin' about this issue, I mean you name it—get rid of the war, there'll be another one.[22]

Public opinion polls around the nation after the Kent State and Jackson State killings revealed a majority of Americans felt the students killed "got what they deserved."

Jeff Miller, from New York, was one of the four students killed at Kent State on May 4, 1970. The photo of him lying with his blood streaming to a curb and a terrified young woman kneeling over his body has come to represent the anguish of the antiwar movement. Jeff had attended the Woodstock festival the previous summer, played drums, and exemplified the great majority of student protesters: casually involved in politics, cynical about the system, idealistic about life, and against the war in Viet Nam. In the following excerpts from a poem written on February 14, 1966, Jeff expresses this passion against the war:

The strife and fighting continue into the night.
Mechanical birds sound of death as they buzz overhead,
Spitting fire into doomed towns where the women
and children run and hide in the bushes and ask why—
Why are we not left to live our own lives?

In the pastures converted into battlefields
The small pellets speed through the air,
Pausing occasionally to claim another victim.
A teenager from a small Ohio farm clutches his side in pain,
And as he feels his life ebbing away, he, too, asks why—
Why is he dying here, thousands of miles from home,
Giving his life for those who did not even ask for his help?

The war without a purpose marches on relentlessly,
Not stopping to mourn for its dead,
Content to wait for its end.

But all the frightened parents who still have their sons
Fear that the end is not in sight.[23]

The following statements from various soldiers who fought in Viet
Nam continue the antiwar debates.

LARRY SEEGER (TWENTY-THIRD ARMY INFANTRY DIVISION, 1968 TO 1971)

I do harbor resentment against Americans who evaded service in the military under the convenient premise that they were morally opposed to that particular conflict. I think that those who claim that prerogative are of weak character who failed to live up to their responsibilities as citizens. The men and women who served honorably, who sacrificed their youth and vitality trying to accomplish what was asked of them, were the true patriots. The dilemma of our republic is that we idealize individual liberty but require compliance with laws in exchange for the privilege of living in a just and secure society. The price that citizens pay to exercise civil disobedience is supposed to be the penalty prescribed for violating the law that is broken. But the draft dodgers were pardoned by [President] Jimmy Carter, and their apologists continue to try to elevate their cowardice and honor them with a mostly nonexistent high moral purpose. They ran and they hid from their country's call, and for every runner a faithful citizen stepped into his place to serve, to suffer, and perhaps be maimed or killed. I will agree that it may have been imprudent for the United States to engage in a guerrilla war in Vietnam and that the civilian and higher military command was faulty. But I will never accept the premise that America's overall purpose in being there was immoral, or that the vast majority of servicemen & women conducted themselves in any other manner than with honor and distinction. I found it outrageous that they were in large measure ignored, or worse, scorned upon their return home.

I hold little animosity towards those who lawfully protested the Vietnam War. There is lots of room to argue that it was a bad idea, that our goals were unachievable, that it wasn't worth the expenditure of our national treasure, or that the Vietnamese should have been left to their own fate. We still argue similar issues. Are we the world's policemen? What responsibility do we have to ensure that other peoples have a chance at the same liberties we enjoy? Which genocide, which famine, which gross violation of human rights deserves our commitment? Is it Somalia, or Cambodia, or Kuwait, or Bosnia? Reasonable men still argue the virtues of our proper role and response to these issues and others and may loudly protest if troops are deployed, or not deployed, to suit their views. But protests cross a boundary of decency when honorable service is mischaracterized as evil, or aid and support for the enemy is given.[24]

JOHN ZUTZ (585TH ENGINEERING COMPANY, 1969 TO 1970)

I grew up in Madison, WI—a center of antiwar protest. There were weeks and months when the city was awash in tear gas. After high school I attended a few protests just to see what it was all about. I was drafted into the army in June '69, arrived in Vietnam in early December '69. I was assigned as a truck driver to the 585th Engr. Company. . . . I was home on leave on my way to Vietnam when the news broke about My Lai. I was in Vietnam when the students were shot at Kent State and when Stirling Hall in Madison was bombed.

Let's get it straight, finally. The antiwar movement wanted to end the war and bring the troops home immediately. At some point the majority of our citizens agreed with that view. Still our government leaders continued to throw more money, arms, and bodies into a black hole. As one who was on the ground in Vietnam and also participated in the antiwar movement, I view Richard Nixon as a traitor for lying about his secret plan to end the war and for ordering the FBI [Federal Bureau of Investigation] and others to infiltrate and disrupt legitimate political processes. I view [Secretary of Defense] Robert McNamara as a traitor for pushing the war when he knew at the time it was wrong—as he admits in his book. I view Gen. [William] Westmoreland and his whole chain of command as traitors for fudging the numbers to make it look like we were winning. And don't forget the others who prolonged the war—[Lyndon B.] Johnson, [Henry] Kissinger, [Melvin] Laird [then secretary of state], Abrams, and all the senators and congressmen who worried more about appearances than what was right. Certainly Kent State was a tragedy, and probably a crime, but it seems insignificant compared to the crime committed against 58,000 American boys and girls and 3 million Vietnamese.

Fighting with "one arm behind our backs" happened. But if Washington had freed that other arm, how could it be effectively used? Yes, we could have won . . . if we killed every single Vietnamese.[25]

GREG GIBBONS (CORPSMAN, U.S. NAVY, 1969 TO 1970)

My first experience with the antiwar movement was more of a "lark" than any intentioned activity. While in Vietnam, like most troops, I had a very

negative perception of the antiwar movement in general. The personaliza-
tion of the antiwar activists against soldiers in Vietnam (such as signs identifying us as "baby killers" and so forth) probably contributed significantly.
And even more horrendous were the activities of certain antiwar Americans
in support of the North Vietnamese. This, in our view, was without prec-
edent and, if not there, certainly close to treason!

The other significant fact of the antiwar movement's impact is the manner
in which we, as Vietnam veterans, were treated when we returned to the
"good old USA." It was not a pleasant welcome home, as the stories of
many will attest. The transference of disagreement with and hatred of the
war to the soldiers who served there, many of whom even agreed with the
movement's views on the war itself, I found to be extremely hurtful. This
transference even extended into other groups, such as the traditional veterans organizations, where we as Vietnam veterans were not welcomed, even
in our hometowns. This was completely shocking to me, as a person who
grew up in a generally patriotic environment and had been imbued with the
concept that it was my duty to serve my country. No one had told me that
this didn't apply to Vietnam! Since the war's end, some of my personal views
have changed significantly with regard to the antiwar protesters. In fact, they
have changed more than my views regarding some of the more traditional
organizations in our society. I acknowledge the right of these antiwar protesters to express their views. In fact, in some ways, that was one of the
rights we were fighting to protect. In a few instances, I have actually grown
to admire the stand of a couple of them, such as [boxer] Mohammed Ali.
They believed in a point of view and had the courage to stand up for that
view, but they did it in what I would call an acceptable way. They accepted
the negative repercussions of taking that stand. On the other hand, some
others [views] have not changed. In fact, they have hardened. To cite a
single (rather well known) example, I cannot accept the actions of Jane
Fonda both in going to Hanoi and during her visit there. [Jane Fonda, a
well known actress, protested the war and went to Hanoi, where she was
photographed on a PAVN antiaircraft weapon. She later apologized to outraged veterans.] I do believe these were treasonous acts! And, as a result,
my family knows that nothing with her name on it, other than the occasional
derogatory item, enters my house—ever!

I can't believe that this country, which I love, let her get away with what
she did—however earnestly she may have believed in her cause. I guess the
"who you are and who you know" view wins out again.[26]

LEO T. PROFILET (CAPTAIN, U.S. NAVY, PRISONER OF WAR, HANOI, 1967 TO 1973)

There were two parts to that movement. One consisted of citizens exercising their constitutional right to protest their government's actions. Unfortunately, the North Vietnamese were greatly encouraged in their war efforts by this movement. They made no bones about their belief that "we will win the war in the streets of America." In my view, the movement lengthened the war instead of shortening it as they claimed.

The other part of the movement consisted of citizens who went to Hanoi, the capital city of our wartime enemy, and took active parts in their psychological war (propaganda) by broadcasts to the POWs and the troops in South Vietnam urging the recognition of the United States as the "enemy of mankind" and calling on them to cease resisting and fighting. After WWII, "Axis Sally" and "Tokyo Rose" [American slang for two American women who used their radio shows to induce GIs to stop fighting during World War II] were charged with treason for doing the same thing. The most prominent members of this part of the movement were three who, arguably, had benefited most from life in the United States: a movie starlet, her husband, and an ex-attorney general of the U.S.[27]

BETH MARIE MURPHY (R.N., HOSPITAL SHIP U.S.S. *SANCTUARY*, 1969 TO 1970)

I have learned, in the past 7 or 8 years, how politics was the driving force of the war in those days. I read McNamara's book and was *so* angry so many lives had been lost for nothing. All this has made me very cynical about politics and the governing of the U.S. There is politics everywhere, but even more so in a nation that sees itself as the world leader. I think this has been some of the reason I have stayed here in Canada. I think the conduct of the war was immoral. There really was no plan, just body counts. I believe from early on those in power realized the war could not be won, but it was pride and arrogance that prevented the U.S. from pulling out and saying it was impossible to win. The U.S. had never lost a war and wasn't going to admit defeat to an insignificant country like N. Vietnam. Yet, even in spite of this knowledge, Nixon and all the other politicians poured many more troops and money into an impossible war. I was, however, very angry at the antiwar movement at home as in the beginning I believed we should be there to help a small country. As that changed, I became even angrier at the antiwar movement, not because they were protesting the war, but because of the treatment the troops would receive when they got home. Those who fought in Vietnam were mostly drafted and most of the others went because of a sense of patriotism and it was the right thing to do (I include myself in this group). These people did not go to kill people but to fight for the interests of the U.S., including those of the protesters. While I was in Vietnam there were sort of antiwar protests, some troops wore black armbands with their fatigues.

When I got home and went to visit my sister at Duke University in North Carolina, I did not get an immediate hug from her—no!—because I had my uniform on. She said something to the effect like "Get that uniform off before we are killed here!" A great welcome home![28]

BILLY C. BRYELS (101ST ARMY AIRBORNE DIVISION, 1967 TO 1968)

I thought it [antiwar movement] was a good thing because I certainly didn't support the war. I had no reason to support the war. Again if there was going to be a fight or battle, we needed to do that in Little Rock or Biloxi or Birmingham. You know what I'm saying? For me to suggest that I should be angry at the Vietnamese. Even then, more than I realized it at the time, I had no quarrel with them. Communism was again something way out in the distance. It didn't offer no immediate threat to me. So to persecute Jane Fonda for advocating the end of the war to me was ridiculous. That didn't make sense. We had that whole thing of hawks and doves. I was probably a dove. As a soldier, in a combat environment, I had to do what I had to do. And that was fight. You know you can't just stand there and hope that they were going to go away because they weren't going to go away. So . . . I felt the antiwar movement was justified.

After I went home, in 1968, I was trying to recover from my injuries for the most part and look for gainful employment. I had a wife and child. Antiwar movement was not something I was interested in actively participating in, but I remember the killings at Kent State. My first thought was a kind of fear thing again. Somebody had this kind of power at home and abroad. There is no justification for shooting unarmed students. So to this day, nobody was prosecuted for the Jackson State or the Kent State shootings. It was justified. They were defying, so again it's a kind of conditioning. Psychological conditioning. Shortly after shooting the students at Kent State they stopped protesting at Kent State. You would too. Again, now, you have to put this in its proper context, the time, the 60s. I mean we have a major revolution going on at home. The civil rights thing was as hot as it

Billy C. Bryels, 101st Airborne, 1967, Viet Nam. Courtesy of Billy C. Bryels.

was ever going to be. We heard very little of it [while in Viet Nam]. There was no medium to really hear about it. I mean the armed forces newspaper that we got occasionally was not going to report that black folk were being lynched in America while we were in Viet Nam lynching other folks. There were some reports coming. My wife at the time would send newspaper articles, but she was not very political at the time herself. Again, we were all kind of victims of this apartheid that we'd been conditioned to. The righteous anger comes from realizing we're not going any place here. We'll just kill for killing's sake. There's no reward. We do the deed and then we stop and have lunch. What was that about? There was no reward—I can't think of a better word. Gain. To this day, in hindsight, we didn't gain.[29]

RICHARD BATES (U.S. NAVY, 1971 TO 1973)

Few civilian age-mates that I came into contact with were actually politically aware. They opposed the war because it was behavior that was expected by their peer group. There was no discussion about the immorality of Vietnam. They were protesting because they needed to fit in. By 1971, young people were jaded. They were seduced by all of the byproducts of the protest movement, the residue: experimenting with drugs, enjoying the new music of the youth culture, and taking advantage of relaxed norms about sex. This was the post–political consciousness era where protesting the war was a vehicle for getting high.[30]

TRAN DZOAN TOI (CAPTAIN, PEOPLE'S ARMY OF VIET NAM)

Dzoan was a captain in the PAVN and a veteran of the French war. He retired as a colonel in 1991.

Yes, we had up-to-date news all the time during the war; we knew of the support we had around the world. The antiwar activities in the United States were well known to us. We always had the understanding, and we taught this to our soldiers, that the American people were never our enemy—it was the American government who waged war against our people. That was our enemy. So it was not a surprise to hear of the support we received from the honest people in the United States. But, of course, it did not really matter to us as far as our military situation. Our revolution had the support of Vietnamese people, and that is how and why we won the war against the Americans. I have now, 25 years after the war, nothing but respect for the American people, the same as when we were at war with the American armed forces. We knew most of their soldiers were here against their will, but we hated the American imperialism. That was different—we knew that men like Nixon were politicians out to control our destiny. We stood up to them, and that is why we won.[31]

STEVE HASSNA (101ST ARMY AIRBORNE DIVISION, 1967 TO 1968)

Combat taught me that war is not all it's cracked up to be, and I had a feeling in my gut that something wasn't right about the war in Viet Nam. No real political understanding, just something chewing at my gut. After a year of being a drill sgt. I was burnt out. Again, no politics, I just wanted away from the madness. I was getting trainees from universities, grad students that had lost their deferments, people with degrees in political science, history, and English. These young men would ask some very pointed questions which I felt compelled to answer as best I could.

So I left the Army disgusted and confused. After a couple months, I thought about reenlisting because being back home in the San Francisco

Bay area was even more confusing and f——— up! At least in the Army you knew how the game worked. But I didn't reenlist.

Then in May 1970, it all came crashing down. The Cambodian invasion and President Nixon saying [on April 30, 1970, President Nixon spoke to a national audience on television to announce his decision to invade Cambodia. Nixon falsely claimed that night that the United States had always respected Cambodian neutrality before] that it was the "first time ever that U.S. troops were in Cambodia." I told my wife, "That was a lie!"

The 1st Brigade of the 101st Airborne Division had been in Cambodia in 1967, from December until the start of Tet in Jan. 1968. We were operating west of Song Be, and if you spit west of Song Be you hit Cambodia! So when I heard Nixon lie on TV, I lost it.

Then, four days later, troops fire on students at Kent State and I just lost it. I quit my job, lost my wife & family, and went off to try and stop that f———ing war!

That's when I finally met and hooked up with the VVAW [Vietnam Veterans against the War]. During the time I was in Viet Nam, I didn't pay much attention to the antiwar folks. I was a soldier and could have cared less. No, I was not spit on when I returned home. . . . In fact, I have not met a single soldier that was; I think that [the spitting-on-vets issue] was propaganda to discredit the folks against the war. I did not see any actual incidents [antiwar activities] while in Viet Nam, but I heard grumblings . . . but grunts grumble about everything, it's all we can do. Grumbling about the hill as you assault it to take out an NVA [North Vietnamese Army] unit, you are grumbling about them shooting at you, or the rain, the mud, officers, leeches, everything! But you continue to fight on. I did hear a lot of complaints about racial injustice. Black troops were getting letters from home about what was happening and guys got real pissed when Detroit went up in flames [during the 1967 race riots]. . . . Geronimo Pratt, for example, was a member of the 101st Airborne before he became a Black Panther.

One thing that is not talked about is the GI movement and resistance to the war. There were GIs organizing all over the U.S. and Europe, with newspapers and coffee houses outside military bases. Many called for direct sabotage and the killing of officers and NCOs [noncommissioned officers] which I do know was going on in Nam and elsewhere. As a drill sgt. I would find GI resistance newspapers in our barracks and wondered how they got there. One company of troops in Viet Nam refused orders to leave a firebase, etc., etc.; this is a side to the war that needs to be talked about. There were lots of protests by students and civilians, but also of active duty military personnel during the Viet Nam War. In fact, the U.S. military, towards the end of the war, was in chaos from within: race, antiwar, you name it—the military was in bad shape.

Initially, one of the things I did feel was that even if I did not agree with the antiwar people, under the Constitution, it is the right of citizens to express disagreement with the government, and that's what I was fighting for, now, wasn't it? In 1972 I joined their ranks and have been at it ever since.[32]

JOHN LANCASTER (LIEUTENANT FIRST MARINE DIVISION, 1967 TO 1968)

I talked to them [his men] all the time . . . and I'll never forget one of the worst times of the war for me within my platoon was when Martin Luther King, Jr., was assassinated. I didn't have many African Americans in the platoon, only a couple . . . but there were some Hispanics and Native Americans who thought highly of him, and white guys that did . . . and they were getting news from home and people were starting to riot—this great man had been assassinated. There was just a lot of people that were very conflicted. They'd ask me, "Why are we here, Lieutenant? Why are we doing this, really, why?" They'd been told why, sort of officially . . . but they weren't buying it.

. . . What I used to say is that our primary job here is to keep all of us alive. Let's all get back alive. If we can do what we're told to do in the process of doing, that's fine. If not, our number one mission is to stay alive. I used to say that if we stay together as a unit, fight well as a team, do what we need to do, and keep our heads down, we'll do ok here—and that worked until that night [the night his unit was overrun]. I'd say we got along very well together . . . and there was a lot of respect at least in the company level within our company . . . of the enlisted men for the officers, so we did not have those types of problems and I never felt threatened by any one of my troops.[33]

MICHAEL RUSH (CAPTAIN, FIRST CAVALRY DIVISION, 1969 TO 1970)

Anger and confusion exemplified the strongest two emotions during the heyday of the antiwar movement in May 1970. The following letter, from a young man to his wife, sums this up: While many Americans sided with either the antiwar "doves" or the prowar "hawks," most soldiers in Viet Nam were just confused.

May 15, 1970
Dear Joanie,

I am in the recovery land of penicillin and bandages, but I am a lucky one. I was dusted off by helicopter to the 93rd Evacuation Hospital for a liver infection. The water has gotten to me. Sorry I have not written, but the times have been a bit slow. I passed out during my first blood test— real cute, I am better and ready to leave by Tuesday of next week. I guess I haven't written in a few days.

Mike Bradley writes about how bad the colleges are. He is very bitter in his letter and is outspoken against the Army. This war has split the country— even I don't know where to stand. We have to clean out Cambodia, yet we are doing other people's jobs for them. Why fight if the GI will do it? Then the campus deaths—what is happening, Joanie? I am really confused about everything. Where does man find the hatred to do the things he does? And many over here do not even care. Where is the life we wanted and talked about? Will we be able to find the pieces?

Please don't worry.

Love,

Mike[34]

The Vietnamese fighters facing the Americans continued the war with an enduring persistence. The fighting did, however, force many to reflect on their sacrifice. Be Danh took it upon himself to write to a group of mothers of front fighters:

Dear Mothers,

Tonight I cannot sleep. I think of one thing and another. . . . I'm lost in thought under the moonlit sky. While all the others are sleeping peacefully, your son is clutching a carbine and looking out at the enemy. I think of before, each time flowers bloomed indicating spring was near, everyone was excited and thrilled to welcome a beautiful spring. This spring, how can we be happy? With the Americans sowing sorrow and misery, when tons of bombs fall on the fatherland, . . . when the country is plunged into a sea of fire, what else can we do but turn our hatred into action. . . .

This spring your children on the front line have only this letter, sent over long distances . . . to inquire about our mothers and to wish them good health . . .

Be Danh, December 1966[35]

BYRON JAMES (FOURTH ARMY INFANTRY DIVISION, 1970 TO 1971)

Byron, the Navajo from Round Rock, Arizona, also had conflicting emotions concerning the war and the antiwar activities. He stated, years later, his feelings of how the war was a mistake, but he also had a deep sense of duty as an American and a Navajo warrior:

I heard about the antiwar protests, but no way, not for me. This is my country. I am not going to run away from my country. I had an uncle in the code talkers . . . the Marines in WW II. My dad had also been a Second War veteran; he did talk to me about being careful, about making friends, do not get too friendly because something will happen to him and it will be hard. My uncle, he didn't say too much. I had two uncles fight in the Pacific in WW II, one a code talker. . . .

. . . What they told us is that the Vietnamese people wanted us there. . . . They need us there. They wanted our help, and when I got there, the peasants, the farmers, they didn't care; they just wanted to be left alone. They didn't care; they just wanted to be left by themselves. It was eye opening for me. It was different from what I had been told about fighting communism. . . . They didn't want us there. Nothing to do with the Americans. It gave me mixed feelings. I thought we were there to help. . . . I felt used there. We didn't belong there—we should never had gone there. You mentioned the riots and the protests here. At that time I didn't understand why they are protesting, but after three or four months, in Viet Nam, it made better sense, why they were protesting. . . .

Some people were angry about it. They said, "These protesters should come over here—see the atrocities of the war." I personally saw all kinds of things: The Viet Cong started to do these things, the atrocities; then the U.S. started doing it. Both sides. And they would say, "Why not come over here and not hide behind Uncle Sam's coattails?" I just couldn't understand a lot of things then. It makes you think. Then there was Jane Fonda, and she called us, what? American pigs? It really burned everyone up pretty much. A lot of guys I went to basic with, and I met over there, in Nam— we all had basically the same views: Our government lied to us!

One of my classmates—usually Navajo do not do this—but he put his finger in front of his M-16 rifle and pulled the trigger, just to get out of combat. He got court martialed for that—reduced rank. Took away his medals, awards, and gave him a dishonorable [discharge]. . . . Navajos do not do that! He disgraced the tribe, not only himself, his family, the tribe. It's not the Diné way.[36]

NOTES

    1. David W.P. Elliot, and Elliot Mai, "Documents on Elite Viet Cong Delta Unit. Memorandum." 5852-ISA/ARPA (Santa Monica: Rand Corp., 1969), 7.
    2. Ibid., 23.
    3. Ibid., 58.

4. Melvin Gurtov, "The War in Delta: Views from Three Viet Cong Battalions. Memorandum," 5353-1-ISA/ARPA (Santa Monica: Rand Corp., 1967), 33.

5. Ibid., 53.

6. Vietnamese Letters, Captured Vietnamese Documents, translated by Hanh Thi Ngoc Trinh-Vadas. CDEC microfilm collection. (Boston: William Joiner Center for the Study of War and Social Consequences, University of Massachusetts.)

7. Ibid.

8. Ibid.

9. Bernard Edelman, ed., *Dear America: Letters Home from Vietnam* (New York: Pocket Books, 1985), 262.

10. Ibid., 51.

11. Ibid., 147.

12. Ibid., 245.

13. Ibid., 231.

14. PBS, "A Soldier's Story: The Battle for Hill 875" (2000).

15. Edelman, *Dear America*, 212.

16. Ibid., 261.

17. Ibid., 220.

18. K.J. Heineman, *Campus Wars: The Peace Movement at American State Universities in the Vietnam Era* (New York: NYU Press, 1994), 249.

19. Ken Cushner, written personal communication (October 2000).

20. Charles Fassinger, written personal communication (July 2001).

21. Alan Canfora, personal communication (July 2001) and personal web site (May4.org).

22. Maurice Isserman, *Witness to War: Vietnam* (New York: Perigree, 1995), 167.

23. According to Jeff Miller's mother, Jeff wrote this poem one month shy of his sixteenth birthday while in high school in New York. The reference to a youth dying in Ohio was purely coincidental as Jeff originally went to Michigan State, transferring to Kent State the year he was killed.

24. Larry Seeger, written personal communication (February 2001).

25. John Zutz, written personal communication (May 2001).

26. Greg Gibbons, written personal communication (February 2001).

27. Leo T. Profilet, written personal communication (May 2001).

28. Beth Marie Murphy, written personal communication (October 2000).

29. Billy C. Bryels, taped communication, transcribed by Ann Thomas (March 2001).

30. Richard Bates, written personal communication (March 2001).

31. Tran Dzoan Toi, written personal communication (March 2001).

32. Steve Hassna, written personal communication (February 2001).

33. John Lancaster, taped personal communication, transcribed by Adam Pallack (October 2000).

34. Edelman, *Dear America*, 225.

35. Elliot and Mai, "Documents," 13–14.

36. Byron James, taped personal communication, transcribed by Robert E. Vadas (March 2001).

Chapter 6

The Long Conflict Ends, Lasting Legacies Are Forged

THE SOLDIERS' WARS COME TO AN END

The Viet Nam War came to a dramatic end on April 30, 1975, when People's Army of Viet Nam (PAVN) tanks stormed the presidential palace and raised banners of the revolution in the hazy, battle smoked sky that covered downtown Saigon. That day represents liberation or independence day to most Vietnamese. To most Americans and their loyal Army of the Republic of Viet Nam (ARVN) allies, it is referred to as "the fall of Saigon." It ended the war, but not the controversy. For every person touched by the conflict, the war came to an end on different dates in different years and in different ways. The following stories illustrate this and how the legacies of the war developed and endured.

JOHN LANCASTER (LIEUTENANT, FIRST MARINE DIVISION, 1967 TO 1968)

For John Lancaster, the end of his direct involvement in the war came in the late night hours of May 5 to 6, 1968. On that night, the PAVN launched what has been since called their "mini–Tet Offensive." The assault on Lieutenant Lancaster's platoon began when a reinforced company of PAVN regulars attacked a listening post manned by two young marines near a narrow dirt road about two and one-half miles east of Hue. Here is Lieutenant Lancaster's own version of that night's events, which left him paralyzed in both legs:

We got ourselves overrun by a battalion's worth of North Vietnamese soldiers. . . . They started at about midnight; it lasted until about 5 A.M. I was hit fairly early on. . . . I saw the guy who shot me, but I didn't see him soon enough. I was running to a machine gun position that had been hit by grenades and probing mortar fire, and there was one guy dead in there and another guy severely wounded. The gun wasn't operating and we really needed that gun . . . and we needed to get to those guys who were hurt. . . . We were going out to that position to try and get the gun going again and see what I could do for the people on my platoon that were hit. . . . We saw this guy stand up out of the tall grass and open up a burst—it was an AK-47. One of the rounds got me . . . entered my left back–shoulder area, went through my chest cavity through both lungs, and clipped the inside of my spinal column. It came out over here—it went right through. Lucky it didn't hit my heart. So, needless to say, I was pretty done at that point. I was paralyzed and had two punctured lungs, so that was the end of my war. I almost died. Well, I was filling up both lungs pretty badly [with blood] and the corpsman from my platoon really didn't know what was the matter with me, and a couple of other guys dragged me back to sort of our central position. . . . One of the head corpsman in our battalion came over and figured out what was wrong with me right away. . . . He said, "Well, we gotta get him up on one side so we can keep one lung going . . . keep the drain." . . . We had to figure out which one was the best of the two. Fortunately, the left one had been hit low and the upper part of it was not filling up, just the lower lobe, or something. So he kept that lung working and sort of sacrificed the other one and just waited till about five in the morning—even later than that. Then daylight broke and they were able to get helicopters in . . . and I was in one of the first helicopters out of there with other seriously injured guys. Four guys were killed that night, twenty-something guys wounded to varying degrees; we were thirty-six strong that night, and something like thirty-two people were either dead or wounded on one level or another.
    I didn't go unconscious, totally unconscious—other than an amazing out-of-body near-death experience that I had: I could remember thinking about friends, family . . . and everything the other direction was white light . . . and it was like a choice. . . . I felt like it wasn't time to go—and the minute I made the choice, I was right back down there. . . . It was dawn . . . and I remember staying awake. Kahler was my company commander . . . and the two guys that dragged me back were Jarvis and Caratini.[1]

BILLY C. BRYELS (101ST ARMY AIRBORNE DIVISION, 1967 TO 1968)

March 21, 1968, I got wounded the second time, very severely, right at the village. We were in a very hostile territory. We were trying to rescue a marine unit that was basically pinned down and they sent in the big, bad 101st Airborne. The Vietnamese army, however, didn't give a damn about how bad we were. They hadn't heard. So early one morning, we had had some encounters the day before, and we set up for the night, and it was very noisy. You could hear things outside our perimeter. . . . It was them digging in and getting ready to kick our butts the next day. And that's exactly what happened. The next morning, as we attempted to leave our encampment, we were ambushed. It was a very close, hand to hand combat. We could see them—they could see us. We could look at each other. . . . There was a round—I'm not sure if it was their mortar or our mortar—hit a tree above me. I was in a prone position, lying on my stomach, and I get shrapnel all down the back and legs and I believe it hit a tree because there were trees and stuff falling all around us. I had a sciatic nerve in my right leg which was partially severed, so immediately I couldn't get up. I couldn't run. There was this young black kid who—in fact, the platoon started to retreat—back up a bit, and I yelled for him to help me. I can't even remember his name. . . . He was very short but built like a brick shit house. He picked me up by my belt like he would a piece of luggage and walked away with me. That's the stuff that I remember. I believe to this day that he actually saved my life. Had I been left out there, I probably would have bled to death at least.

They sent me off to Japan, Tokyo in fact. . . . The thing I remember most about that was April 4. I was a patient there, 1968. April 4 was the day Martin Luther King, Jr., was killed. I remember, I'm on this orthopedic ward and it's a really big open space of rows and rows of beds, and they announce it over the PA system, that Martin Luther King had been assassinated. Somebody said, who was behind me—I never saw this person, "It's about time somebody got that troublemaker." Talk about reality—a kind of fear came over me, to be honest.

They sent me to the hospital in San Francisco where I spent the next several months recuperating. I now have quite a bit of pain, and the nerve damage left me with a partial paralysis on the right side. My family, wife and daughter, we're here in California. . . . I didn't actually get to Little Rock until months later. Went to see my parents in August 1968. Little Rock hadn't changed significantly. It probably had changed a great deal, but my memory of America was one that was very ugly to begin with, so it wasn't like I expected anything great. . . . Particularly when just days before Martin Luther King had been assassinated. For what? I mean for eating in restaurants with dignity? That's the reality why he was—part of why he was killed.[2]

NGUYEN DUC ANH (ARMY OF THE REPUBLIC OF VIET NAM)

After 3 years of fighting in the Quang Nam Province as an officer in the 101st Battalion, I was sent to the Dalat Military Academy to help train officers for the ARVN. Soon after that, I was involved in the massive retreat from the highlands region as the northern armies crashed across Viet Nam in the early spring of 1975. Upon arriving at the coast at Phan Thiet, I boarded a navy boat, which took me and others in my unit to the coastal town of Vung Tau. It was there, in late April 1975, that my unit retreated and disbanded. I threw away my clothes to blend in with the flow of refugees fleeing the Communists. It was a chaotic time—people everywhere in the streets, in the towns and on the main roads. . . . I was stopped by the police inside of Saigon not long after April 30, 1975. I told them that I was a student and was simply heading home. . . . They believed me, as so many people were on the roads everywhere . . . and I made it to a friend's house in Saigon. There, I met up with some other former ARVN soldiers and made an attempt to make a living. Jobs were rare . . . and I was afraid of being found out by the new VC [Viet Cong] government for my actions as an ARVN officer. We had always feared that the VC would take reprisal on everyone and expected there to be many executions . . . so we were relieved to find out that that was not to be. But that early happiness turned to disillusionment as the years passed and the economy faltered. . . . Times were very hard. My friends and I lived by selling items on the black market . . . mostly medicine, which was necessary and hard to get. So I made a decent living, kind of underground sort [sic] to speak . . . but things just kept getting worse in Viet Nam. My luck was bound to run out sooner or later, and so I made the decision to leave Viet Nam—at that time, mostly for economic reasons as jobs were hard to get and only those who supported the revolution received benefits. Twelve of my friends and I, in 1981, bought a small fishing boat . . . and one night under the cover of darkness, we slipped out along the coast past the tip of Cau Mau and sailed away from Vietnam.[3]

TRINH QUANG DAI (ARMY OF THE REPUBLIC OF VIET NAM)

For two years after I was released from prison in Saigon, I resumed my duty as an ARVN sergeant in the military police in the Can Tho District area. I also spent two years on the island of Kien Giang as a guard over captured VC. There were many Vietnamese in that prison, but we usually didn't have too much contact with them. By then, I did my duty and kept quiet. I was afraid of prison again, so I did everything I was told to do. I feared for my wife and our two daughters at home in Saigon.

Things were quiet for me on the island, no combat, just daily routines . . . it was peaceful there. But then, in 1972, I was sent to Nha Trang to train further as an officer. After six months' training, I was attached to the Second Battalion and sent to the Central Highlands area where I spent most of the rest of the war. I was in and around Pleiku and Ban Me Thuot. On one occasion, my wife was able to make the trip there for a visit. She gave me news of our family and our neighbors—it made me homesick.

I had no desire to fight against my fellow Vietnamese—that is not good! And prison left me hating the South government. . . . So by late 1973, or maybe it was early 1974, I had had enough: I missed my wife and family, I missed my mother and my home. So I took a pistol and shot my right finger, my trigger finger . . . so they could not send me again into combat.

To this day I have no use of this finger, as you can see, and it took several months to heal correctly, or at least so that I could return to duty, for they sent me back to the army anyway, even with a finger like this!

I was in Nha Trang again until January of 1975. . . . My unit was sent south, toward Saigon. I spent a few months there and then on April 29, 1975, the VC were approaching the city limits of Saigon. There was much confusion and panic and we were all scared! But we had no fight left in us—mostly, the men in the ARVN units simply ran away! So I did the same, on the morning of April 30, 1975, in the early hours. I was stationed near Hoc Mon when we all decided that the war was over. We all took everything we owned, our weapons, helmets, clothes, even our shoes! We dropped everything right there on the road and scattered toward our homes the best we could. . . . There was chaos, explosions, people everywhere . . . soldiers running, everyone was very, very excited. I was also very afraid. We heard for years and years from the government radio about the Viet Cong that they would kill us all if they captured us. We heard that they would be angry and punish all of the soldiers in the South government. So, naturally, I was very afraid and hid in my home. I got all of my photographs and letters I wrote during the war and went down to the end of my street in District Three [where] . . . I threw all of those things into the river. . . . They are . . . gone now![4]

NGUYEN THI HANH (NURSE, PEOPLE'S ARMY OF VIET NAM)

On April 30, 1975, the war came to an end. Our forces were victorious over the puppet troops. Their leaders, as well as the last Americans, were forced to flee from our lands. Saigon was liberated! At the time, I was in Hanoi; everyone was ecstatic, happy beyond belief. All the suffering from the long war for reunification, a war of thirty years, was finally coming to an end. It is difficult to say what that meant: So many died, so much pain, so many years of hardship . . . now was over with us enjoying victory. Everywhere people cheered and hugged. . . . We really couldn't believe it for it happened so fast. . . . We were expecting another year or two, even three, of fighting . . . maybe even longer. . . .

Still, it was several months before I was able to make the trip south again, to the lands of my birth. The roads and railroads were destroyed so it was not until September of 1975 that I returned to the Can Tho area and saw my parents for the first time in fifteen years! It was a moment of great joy! Fate had it that my parents would both survive the long war. How can I talk about such a reunion? Fifteen years without your mother and father, of war and terrible separation. To see them again was a time of happiness for all.[5]

LEGACIES OF THE WAR

The Issue of Atrocities

Legacies about the war were forged in the conflicts that both Viet Nam and the United States endured during the years of fighting. Several key issues, such as the one dealing with atrocities, became the center of national and international debate. Since the war ended, both sides have accused the other of engaging in atrocities. Over 0.6 million Vietnamese civilians died during the war, an immense tragedy that lies at the core of the continuing debate: "Because we had to appease the Allied forces by day and were terrorized by Viet Cong at night, we slept as little as you did. We obeyed both sides and wound up pleasing neither. We were people in the middle. We were what the war was all about. . . . Children and soldiers have always known it to be terrible."[6]

The revelation in 1969 that 504 innocent Vietnamese civilians were murdered by troops of the Eleventh Division in Song My Village shocked many who had assumed that Americans were always the

The sole woman negotiator at the Paris Peace Talks was Tran Hong Anh's mother, from Can Tho. Courtesy of Southern Women's Museum, Viet Nam.

"guys in white hats." Since then, the issue of war atrocities has inundated discussions of the war in Viet Nam.

Nearly 33,000 Vietnamese civilians or government officials working for the South were assassinated by People's Liberation Army (PLA) death squads, and the Central Intelligence Agency–run Phoenix Program left another 20,000 dead.[7] Many times atrocities would occur as a result of combat tension, as soldiers would "lose it" in the heat of battle. Sometimes the brutality was politically motivated, such as when more than 200 Montagnard villagers in the Central Highlands were executed and burned with flamethrowers by PAVN troops for supporting the South. Other times, such as at My Lai, the horror was unleashed more as a random act of frustration combined with racism in which Vietnamese were seen as less-than-human "gooks." Many times after a battle, American, ARVN, or PAVN troops would kill survivors or beat prisoners for not talking. Allegations of American soldiers tossing PLA prisoners out of helicopters in flight to get the remaining prisoners to talk have circulated for years, and evidence suggests that survivors of the 173rd Brigade were executed after being overrun during a savage battle on Hill 1,338 in 1967.

Viet Nam War veteran Colonel Harry G. Summers, Jr., wrote that "contrary to the antiwar movement's charges of a 'war crimes industry,' atrocities by American forces were the exception, and those accused of such offenses were brought to trial." He added that "for the

Viet Cong and the North Vietnamese Army, however, atrocities were a deliberate, sanctioned, tactic."[8] Many Viet Nam War veterans in the United States contradicted this perception at the Winter Soldier Hearings in 1971 where dozens of vets reported atrocities committed by U.S. troops. Most Americans are inclined to believe that while many atrocities occurred, they were in the context and nature of war and the soldiers involved should not be held accountable.

Martin Bolha, the World War II veteran, held this belief in 1971 when he was asked by his local commander, H.L. Marse, to write a letter for his veterans post in Yucca Valley, California, to ask President Richard M. Nixon to pardon Lieutenant William Calley for his role at My Lai:

Veterans of Foreign Wars
Post 9431
Yucca Valley, California
April 7, 1971

The President
The White House
Washington, D.C. 20500
Sir:
I am writing in behalf of all the members of Yucca Valley V.F.W. Post 9431, concerning the recent March 30, 1971, verdict of "life imprisonment" of Lt. Calley which was handed down by a military court.

We veterans, along with our national V.F.W. Commander Rainwater, are most unhappy with this verdict.

We are sure Lt. Calley acted in the best interest of the Army and was following orders from some higher command.

Fighting an enemy under such conditions as they are in Vietnam, we are sure that "guilty of premeditated murder" while serving in combat can hardly be judged fair.

As Commander and Chief of this great country, I'm sure you are now doing all in your power to reconsider this case and make the right decision that will restore Lt. Calley in good standing and also restore future generations to have faith and want to serve in our armed services.

Respectfully,

H.L. Marse, Commander

Almost exactly thirty years later, the same sentiments rose to national prominence with the disclosure that the once-Governor and now-Senator Robert Kerrey, of Nebraska, led what has been called an execution squad in the murder of twenty-one unarmed women and children in the Mekong Delta region in 1969.[9] According to Kerrey, there was a firefight and they found the dead civilians later. In contrast, one of the men in Kerrey's squad has since told of how the twenty-one civilians were simply rounded up and, under Kerrey's orders, executed. The general response of the American nation was to shun an investigation. Pham Thi Lanh, presently a sixty-two-year-old survivor of the massacre, contradicted Kerrey's version. She, like most Vietnamese, has a different view of the role of the U.S. military during the war and refutes the impression that U.S. atrocities were aberrations in behavior.

Lieutenant Calley was eventually pardoned by President Nixon after his conviction for the murder of civilians at My Lai, an incident in which rape and mutation had also occurred on a large scale. No other soldier served time for the incident at My Lai.

In January of 2001, seventy-five-year-old Ha Thi Quy, whose children were murdered at My Lai in 1968, told a group of American students visiting the My Lai memorial that she was "happy to see Americans here to apologize for this event. Nothing can bring our loved ones back, but to see you here today makes my heart feel less sad."[10]

Here are some other voices on the issue.

RICHARD BATES (U.S. NAVY, 1971 TO 1973)

Vertical replenishments [or "vertreps," getting resupplied] involved a . . . ship (my destroyer—U.S.S. *Shelton* DD790) running alongside on an exactly parallel course with a replenishment ship. Once the parallel courses were set and the vessels' speeds were matched, thick cable lines were strewn from one ship to the other. Once secured, pallets of replenishments (food and gun ammo) were swung across to the destroyer where they were dismantled and the supplies carried to their respective storage areas. While this took place, fuel replenishment was also underway, the heavy hoses strewn between the ships by much the same process as the food and ammo rigging.

Frequently, our vertreps were challenged by Vietnamese fishing boats that lay in our path. This is not to say that they purposely opposed or confronted us—they were simply fishermen who happened to be in our direct line. . . . There was never any measure undertaken to avoid collisions with these 10- to 12-foot sampans. They were simply bowled over by our 300-foot warships if they could not scurry away in time. These men—simple fishermen—

were treated as beings something less than human. . . . Atrocities were not rare. In Vietnam, everybody was the enemy but not because they supported North Vietnam or were Viet Cong. It didn't matter. Their insignificant lives were inconsequential.[11]

JOHN LANCASTER (LIEUTENANT, FIRST MARINE DIVISION, 1967 TO 1968)

I had quite a bit of contact with the popular forces . . . and I remember they can be pretty brutal. I was involved in an interrogation of a [PLA] prisoner we had caught . . . and they were in charge of the interrogation . . . but the company commander wanted me involved. . . . They were pretty much torturing this guy . . . to get the answers out of him . . . breaking his fingers one by one. . . . We'd been operating with them and my company commander had asked me to go listen in on the interrogation. . . . I could understand a little bit of Vietnamese at the time and I had an interpreter with me, so I went and watched. . . . Finally the guy talked, they got the info out of him, but I remember walking out of this little building that they'd held the interrogation in and walking away and then hearing a gun-shot. So I went back, and they'd just killed him, after they got the info out of him. I looked around, and they just laughed at me, and said, "This is war." I turned around and walked away—what am I gonna do, arrest the guys?[12]

LARRY SEEGER (TWENTY-THIRD ARMY INFANTRY DIVISION, 1969 TO 1971)

The Vietnam War was not a conflict between morally equivalent foes. The stark contrast of the American conduct of the war to the vicious cruelty of the Viet Cong and the NVA [North Vietnamese Army] against their own people remains the major misperception of students of the conflict. They used horrific atrocities (beheadings, disembowlings) against village leaders, teachers, and children. Not randomly, but as a widespread policy to terrorize the people of South Vietnam into submission and compliance with their demands. They trained children as surrogate soldiers and kidnapped thousands of young people to serve in their army. The U.S. policy of at-tacking Viet Cong and NVA military targets, while attempting to "win the hearts and minds" of the people, was woefully inadequate in the face of such powerful actions against civilians by the forces of North Vietnam.[13]

When the South Vietnamese government collapsed in April of 1975, it fell so quickly that there was no time for the complete destruction of all of the documents concerning the torture and killings of prisoners. One such document, captured by the PLA in April 1975, is the statement made by sixteen-year-old Nguyen Thi Hiep, a supporter of the revolution living near Saigon. Hiep was arrested and, under torture, was ordered to confess her allegiance to the Communists and denounce the revolution. Instead, Hiep defied her captors and wrote the following statement:

Saigon—May 7, 1969
My name is Nguyen Thi Hiep, born 17–8–53 in Giac Thanh Commune, district Thanh Phu, Kiem Hoa Province. My father's name is Nguyen Van Cam, my mother's name is Huynh Thi Kieu. My father is a farmer, my mother, a housewife. I have 2 siblings, Nguyen Van Hoa (age 12) is my younger brother, and Nguyen Thi Anh (age 8) is currently living in the Giac Thanh Commune. I agree only to return to the revolutionary collective named: Mat Tran Giac Phuong Muis Nam (Front Commune of the Southern Revolutionaries). I determine to remain loyal to the revolutionary cause that I have chosen.
Nguyen Thi Hiep
I assert that the above statement is totally my own will. I have not been forced by any authority to state this.
Hiep
The following witnesses state that the prisoner wrote the above statement herself. . . . [14]

Hiep was executed shortly after signing this statement.

HUYEN VAN CHIA (PEOPLE'S LIBERATION ARMY)

Before I was wounded and lost my arm in 1967, I witnessed times when our comrades were captured by the Americans. We could clearly see them as we hid in our tunnels and bunkers. They would be beaten from the start and would have their hands tied behind them. We all knew what to expect if captured—torture and death. It was that simple . . . Since we knew we would die anyway, then there was no point in talking. If we talked, they would kill us and throw our bodies away and then come after our comrades. So we made pacts and talked together about this. . . . We knew that no matter what . . . we could never talk to our captors!
We also knew that sometimes the pain of torture would be too much for

any man to bear . . . so we all had false names and on units and other useful information that we prepared to state if tortured. So when the time came, we prepared in advance that we finally shout out a name or some other military information. . . . Then they would kill us, and the Americans would then go off and chase ghosts! That was Cu Chi.[15]

LEO T. PROFILET (CAPTAIN, U.S. NAVY, PRISONER OF WAR, HANOI, 1967 TO 1973)

I have no knowledge of how our side treated prisoners. I know from first-hand experience how they treated POWs [prisoners of war]. In my case (typical), I was tortured and then kept in solitary confinement with no American contact for the next twenty-seven months.

I was the commanding officer of an A6 Intruder Squadron flying from the U.S.S. *Constellation*. I was shot down by a SAM [surface-to-air missile] on the outskirts of Hanoi while attacking the railroad system. This was mission #59 for me over North Vietnam. I also fought in Korea, flying 98 missions from the U.S.S. *Philippine Sea* in AD4 Skyraiders. That war is not so much controversial as forgotten. Yet we had about the same number of KIA [killed in action] in three years in Korea as in ten in Vietnam. One of my children asked me once, "Gee, Dad, didn't you get to fight in any popular wars?!"[16]

KOREAN VETERAN

During the war, the United States gave economic aid to South Korea in exchange for Korean troops being sent to assist the United States in Viet Nam. Thousands of Koreans served in three divisions and have been accused of numerous atrocities against Vietnamese civilians.[17] An anonymous Korean veteran of the war (Third Battalion, First Regiment, Tiger Division, 1967 to 1968) said the following in an interview:

I was very sorry and pitied them, especially the children. The war was unnecessary for the Vietnamese. This war was for Americans who wanted to pursue their beliefs and foreign policies.[18]

STEVE HASSNA (101ST ARMY AIRBORNE DIVISION, 1967 TO 1968)

I captured a young man in a tunnel in the Chu Lai area . . . I find this guy in this tunnel, he gives up, I bring him out, then I have to watch the interrogators work on him. I should have left him in the tunnel, then I would not have felt like shooting the f——— interrogators while I watched them beat this guy to death!

One thing I do know: None of it worked! If anything, U.S. conduct drove more people over to the VC & NVA than not. You cannot wage free fire zones, search and destroy, search and secure, defoliation, and strategic hamlets without creating enemies. The forced relocation from ancestral homes and villages damn sure didn't help . . . and the Phoenix Program sure didn't generate recruits for our side. Plus, looking the other way at a corrupt government helped only Ho Chi Minh. Much of this I did not know at the time—none of the above was talked about.[19]

COLONEL JAMES A. HERBERT (U.S. ADVISOR, LONG AN PROVINCE, 1967 TO 1969)

I do not know any commander that takes joy in causing civilian casualties, but their mission is to knock out VC. . . . They balance out the cost in American lives versus the cost in Vietnamese lives . . . and listen to the voice of their own conscience. . . . I think they [the rules on civilian casualties] are about the most satisfactory set of rules that had been developed and are satisfactory to just about everyone.[20]

DON (FIRST INFANTRY DIVISION; LAST NAME WITHHELD)

Don was in Viet Nam as an infantryman involved in the helicopter assault on the village of Ben Suc in 1967. In a collection of his reflections found in the book *Bloody Hell*, Don wrote of the assault and his own thoughts at the time:

I remember looking down between my feet and seeing the embers of desolation not more than twenty feet below the helicopter. Smoldering cra-

An American M-41 tank lies where it was destroyed near Cu Chi, Viet Nam. This heavily defoliated area just recently has seen the return of trees. Courtesy of Robert E. Vadas.

ters, human bodies, and burning skeletons of hooches—of homes. And I remember a guilt pressing down on me so hard I could hardly breathe. I was sick of it all, sick of war, of what it was doing to us, but mostly, I was sick of myself.[21]

Viet Nam after the War

The war's end in 1975 left the nation virtually in total ruins with millions of craters and whole sections of countryside destroyed by the American chemical warfare. Bridges, roads, the national railroad all lay in ruins. Millions of displaced persons and refugees cluttered the highways, and though the industrious Vietnamese soon began the tedious job of rebuilding, political conflict continued. Reunification, a goal of thirty years, was achieved, but not without cost. Arrests of former officials of the South government began; thousands more were ordered to reeducation centers. The United States enacted an embargo on the new nation and made every effort worldwide to prevent trade with the new government.

Farmers found that their products could not be exported as governments everywhere were fearful of Agent Orange contamination. Thousands of Vietnamese babies were born with deformities attributed to the effects of Agent Orange. Thousands of children with American fathers, called "*bui poi*" (dust of the earth), were ostracized by a culture with little tolerance for any reminders of America and the war. Many were left to fend for themselves in groups of homeless that roamed city streets.

The problems facing the new government were enormous, and the new government could not effectively deal with the problems. Truong Nhu Tang, the former minister of justice for the Provisional Revolutionary Government, a supporter of the revolution his entire life, wrote in his memoirs: "As this . . . message sank in over the first year or so of independence, a deep malaise began to come over people, a malaise that showed up in their personal lives and in their working lives. . . . By 1976, paralysis was definitely in the air."[22] Tang eventually joined the thousands who left Viet Nam in the great boat exodus and now lives in Paris.

In 1976, many reforms were initiated in the South that many Southerners found intolerable. This began the exile of thousands, perhaps as many as 1 million Vietnamese, who made their way from their homeland into the South China Sea, seeking better opportunity elsewhere. Many would drown, many would be returned to face prison, but many would ultimately end up in America, Canada, Australia, or other nations where sponsors would come forward.

In addition, neighboring Kampuchea, taken over by the Khmer Rouge in 1975, began to assault Vietnamese villagers in the border region to agitate for the revival of ancient land disputes between the two countries in the Mekong Delta region. Responding to these incidents, the Vietnamese government launched a full scale invasion of Kampuchea in December 1978. Designed to end the brutal Khmer regime noted for its massacre of millions in what has been described as the "killing fields of Kampuchea," the invasion was initially successful, but rebels held out for years, involving the nation in warfare into the middle 1980s. To "punish" the Vietnamese for destabilizing its Kampuchean ally, China, the ancient enemy of Viet Nam, launched its own invasion of Viet Nam in February 1979. After nearly 50,000 people died, the Chinese retreated back to its border, claiming to have "taught" Viet Nam a lesson, although perhaps it was Viet Nam that was the teacher, as it bloodied the Chinese and brought their troops to a standstill with local militias. Either way, the Vietnamese nation found itself engaged in war on two fronts, shunned by the American-led embargo in the West and plagued by economic woes at home that brought near starvation to many of its people. In 1988, a reform movement led the Vietnamese leadership to a new policy, "Doi Moi," that initiated an "open door" to increase trade and open the nation to limited private enterprise. By 1994, President William J. Clinton had reestablished trade with Viet Nam, and in 1995, a new American Embassy was set up in Hanoi with an ex-POW, Douglas "Pete" Petersen, named as the first U.S. ambassador. Travel restrictions were lifted, and many Viet Kieu, who had risked their lives in shark- and pirate-infested waters to escape Viet Nam in the early 1980s, were returning in large numbers to reestablish relations with friends and relatives, bringing to Viet Nam much of their new wealth acquired in the United States.

The following statements from various Vietnamese individuals address and help clarify some issues concerning postwar Viet Nam. They explain what happened to many Vietnamese participants of the war and their perceptions about America:

TRINH QUANG DAI (ARMY OF THE REPUBLIC OF VIET NAM)

Dai was a military policeman in the ARVN, who had been forced to fight for the South government from 1966 to 1975. He is now a retired tailor living in a large new home in Phu Nhuan District:

In 1975, after throwing my army clothing onto the street near the Hoc Mon bridge on April 30, I went home and waited in fear for the Viet Cong to come for me. But my fears were not to be realized. Nothing happened. The soldiers went through the streets with instructions on the loudspeaker not to be afraid, that we were now all Vietnamese, and that the war was over. No one bothered us. We began to relax; we began to enjoy the reunification and the success of the revolution. Remember, I hated the South government myself, for the beatings in prison . . . so I began to be happy.

On July 12, 1975, just a couple of months after the end of the war, I received from the police a notice to report to a reeducation center; for me, it was at a school: Van Han University, on Truong Minh Giang St. in District 3, not really a camp. I reported on July 25, 1975, and went for only three days. I did not even have to stay there. . . . I just had to get there at eight in the morning and stay until around four or five in the afternoon. There we were told about the mistakes we made in fighting for the South government against the revolution. . . . Those who were high rank . . . they got up to twelve years in prisons far from Saigon. But that was for only those who were involved with the secret police and high officers in the ARVN. I felt lucky then. . . . For the first years after the war ended, life was very difficult. We always had food, but we heard of some who did not. . . . Jobs were difficult to get, and many people experienced hardship. The open door policy made life better for us. I owe this all to the revolution. I hope for better relations with America. . . . War is a terrible thing.[23]

DO HUNYL (ARMY OF THE REPUBLIC OF VIET NAM, "MIKE FORCE")

Hunyl is an ethnic B'Nai who grew up in the forests of the Central Highlands. Hunyl learned valuable knowledge in his youth, ancient wisdoms on how to survive in the dense jungle that once surrounded the town of Dak To. When war came to the highlands in the mid-1960s, he followed his father's wish and served in a "Mike Force" that had been organized in the Kontum–Pleiku region. He was a scout and reconnaissance specialist, as few knew the mountains as he did. In January 2001, Hunyl told a group of American students the following about the loss of the forests to logging:

Look at the destruction of the forests . . . much from Agent Orange . . . but much also since the end of the war. Vietnamese were brought in to populate this area and work the land as farmers. . . . We have lost something irreplaceable! It saddens me; it tears at my heart. . . . The jungles of my youth are now gone.[24]

NGUYEN DUC ANH (ARMY OF THE REPUBLIC OF VIET NAM)

When we left the coast of Viet Nam in that small boat back in 1981, it was a terrible time; we sailed for many days, and at times we believed that we would never see land again. At one point, we had to fight off some of the many pirates that sailed in those waters then. I hear that some are still out there—these pirates prey on fishermen and others. But, we finally arrived and spent 6 months in Malaysia . . . and then I got someone in the United States to sponsor me, so I boarded a plane in the early part of 1982 and flew to America. There were Vietnamese who helped new arrivals then, those who left when the Americans did back in '75. So I got some money and a

Ex–Army of the Republic of Viet Nam officer Nguyen Duc Anh (fifth from left) returns to a warm welcome in Viet Nam. Anh had fled by boat from Viet Nam and is reunited with his family after twenty-two years of separation. Courtesy of Nguyen Duc Anh.

place to stay. Our sponsor was in Houston, so I flew to Houston where I lived for many years. Today, I work at a restaurant near Williamsport, Pennsylvania, and I often think back on my experiences, my home, and my father who still lives in Saigon. My father has changed his mind on the Communists. He has called me several times and written many times telling me that things are better and that I should return home for a visit. I have been away from my homeland now for over nineteen years. I miss my childhood memories. I miss my family. I see the Communist regime as still corrupt, with the Communist leaders as the new elite.

As a United States citizen . . . I want to return to Viet Nam, though. Someday, maybe I will, but I was afraid for many years that I would be arrested if I returned. I had a sister and a brother who tried to leave Viet Nam by boat, just as I had. . . . They did not get far; in 1989 they both drowned when their boat sank in high seas just 200 yards from shore near Nha Trang. A total of 200 people drowned that night when their ship sunk. When I look back at my life, I am saddened at all the bad times, all of the deaths. . . . I can't explain it to you now . . . but something inside of me . . . is just not right. . . . Something is missing.[25]

Retired People's Army of Viet
Nam Colonel Tran Dzoan Toi
reflects on the war. Courtesy of
Robert E. Vadas.

On March 12, 2001, Anh finally flew the distance to his home in Ho
Chi Minh City, Viet Nam. It had been nearly twenty years since he
left.

TRAN DZOAN TOI (PEOPLE'S ARMY OF VIET NAM CAPTAIN)

Tran Dzoan Toi, a PAVN captain during the war, was born in
1929 just twenty kilometers from Ho Chi Minh's birthplace. The
now light haired and frail figure has taken up studying the war from
various points of view. His goal is to clarify historical "myths," as he
calls them, such as why the United States resisted the revolution in
Viet Nam and how the Vietnamese resistance forces are perceived by
the American media.

When asked about the sense of history in Vietnamese people and
the effect it had on the war, Toi reflected and responded:

We Vietnamese own the past. We respect it. It is the origin of our present reality; it is significantly important. It was our learning of our past that connected us to our heroes and past leaders—Le Loi, Tran Hung Dao, Hai Ba Trung. It was this sense of Vietnamese nationalism that gave the socialist revolution its strength against foreign rule. . . . Nothing, and I must stress, nothing, could alter that reality. The Americans, regardless of their intent, could not compete against our past for the hearts of our people. It could not be! Victory was inevitable. Our determination to win was unbreakable. This, the Americans could not understand . . . even if the war lasted another fifty years.

What upsets me is this sense that the "North" invaded the "South." This is not true in any way. It was, in fact, the fight of the entire people against foreign invasion, first from 1945 to 1954, against the French, and later, from 1955 afterwards, against the American intervention. We are all Vietnamese, from North to South. It is impossible to consider that we, as a people, accepted this temporary division in 1954, as a permanent status. But those in the South government also hoped for reunification. . . . They simply wanted reunification, at the American will, under a different government than Ho Chi Minh's ideal. So we did not see a "NVA" as you call it, . . . and a "Viet Cong," as Diem called the NLF [National Liberation Front] fighters. We were all Vietnamese resisting foreign rule. . . . It just did not matter, this preoccupation with Viet Cong and North and so on.

Us Vietnamese have always dreamed of one nation, free from foreign occupation. That is what we have now . . . so the revolution was a success. Yes, of course times have changed. We must grow with the changes in reality, we must integrate the good of socialism, with what is good in capitalism . . . for the good of the future. I have faith in this adventure.[26]

NGUYEN SON HA (VIET KIEU)

Ha, now a Canadian citizen, was very young when the war ended. He was one of thousands in the boat exodus from Viet Nam in the 1980s, who made it safely to Canada, where he lives a quiet life as a computer technician with his wife, also a boat person:

My father was a high-ranking official in the national police. So when the war ended, he was arrested and spent the full twelve years in a reeducation camp outside of Hanoi. There, he was nearly starved and suffered health problems. When he was released, he knew that he must get out of Viet Nam, so he left in 1988. He now lives in Toronto with many of our family. My father has been changed by his experience. He only will say that he "sees how he was wrong." We are not sure what they did to him in the camp, but he says only that he was wrong. Nothing more.

I had an opportunity to leave in 1983. We all got on this boat and left along the coast heading for Malaysia. But after a day or so, our engine went out. There we were, in the open sea, no land in sight, no power, with 139 people on a small boat only 14 meters long. It began to get hot, and the food ran out soon; we just drifted for days and days. I cannot remember clearly, maybe for 20–30 days. Before long, the water also ran out. We were desperate. I was only 17 years old at the time. . . . After many days the first began to die . . . usually the old ones. Maybe 4 or 6 died and we talked about even eating their flesh to survive, but we didn't. One day, a pirate ship came up alongside. . . . They usually robbed, killed, even raped, before they left you alone. But this ship, we talked into towing us to safety in return for promises to give them more riches. Some of us had rich relatives overseas, so they towed our ship to safety. I spent 1 month on the Pau La Bidong Island, then 4 months in Kuala Lumpur before a sponsor accepted me into Canada. I will never forget the boat trip and the deaths on the sea. I owe my life to those pirates. Funny, huh?

Many of us Viet Kieu continue to hate the Communists. Some want to overthrow the government there, but I do not see how. Besides, things are changing now and many of us are traveling home to visit relatives. No one is bothered by the government, except to pay bribes at the airport. That's Vietnamese life though, whether Communist or capitalist. Some things never change.[27]

NGUYEN TRAN TRAC (PEOPLE'S ARMY OF VIET NAM)

Dr. Nguyen is now director of international relations at Ho Chi Minh City University of Pedagogy. He had this to say about America's defeat in Viet Nam:

We too fought a limited war. Our allies, the Russians and Chinese, were held back for political considerations of the Cold War. Imagine if 1 million Russian or Chinese troops also fought with us during Tet of 1968. Do you still believe you would win?[28]

TRAN HONG ANH (NURSE, PEOPLE'S ARMY OF VIET NAM)

Anh is presently the director of the Southern Woman's Museum in Ho Chi Minh City. While serving as a nurse and psychologist for the PAVN during the war, she witnessed many bombings and many young men and women die in her presence. Years later, she related her thoughts on reconciliation with the Americans:

It has been many years now since the end of the war. I welcome Americans to my country. I welcome them to our museum for women in our city here. If you ask me to forgive the Americans, I can say, "yes," of course. It is our way, to look to the future, to learn from the past, to not let it control you. But we suffered so much from the Americans that now, even after all these years, do not ask me to love them—that, I cannot yet do. My best friend's father was arrested and murdered by the Americans and the Diem regime. Today, I still talk to my friend; we were reunited after the war . . . but she still now misses her father. How can she forgive? I do not know. But as long as she misses her father, the war lives on.[29]

MEL TRA (SPECIAL FORCES, ARMY OF THE REPUBLIC OF VIET NAM, 1972 TO 1975)

"Mel," the name he now goes by, was drafted into the ARVN from his home in Saigon shortly after the Easter Offensive in 1972. Growing up, he knew only the anti-Communist fight of his father, and when the war ended in 1975, Mel was retreating with his ARVN unit south of Saigon when his commanding officer addressed his men. He said that the war was lost and that those who wanted to could flee the country and go to the United States. Mel opted to flee and now owns his own electrical construction company in Pennsylvania. Years later, he put his reflections on the war in writing:

My view as an American citizen, after 26 years since my own involvement, is that looking back at the military situation, we, the United States, could never have won the war for one simple reason: The U.S. public did not support our war effort in Vietnam. In contrast, the North Vietnamese public sincerely believed that they were saving their Southern brethren from the clutches of imperialism. They were willing to give up their body and soul for their cause, even if it meant facing the most powerful army in the world. The United States was wrong to count on our superior firepower to grind the enemy down; in contrast, the North Vietnamese leadership's aim was to break the will of the American public and government to continue the conflict. Despite our military power, we misjudged the limits of such power. In war, you need two things: weapons and human beings. Ultimately, though, humans are the decisive factor.[30]

Huyen Van Chia, a People's Liberation Army fighter, who lost his arm to an American tank in 1967, outside Cu Chi. Courtesy of Robert E. Vadas.

HUYEN VAN CHIA (PEOPLE'S LIBERATION ARMY)

Chia is retired and lives a quiet life near Cu Chi. In his home, rebuilt by the government after the war, he looked out at the once-war-ravaged landscape as he told his story to a small group of Americans in January 2001:

Of course life can always be better, but in all I cannot complain. The government has met my basic needs as a disabled veteran. I live in peace now, although I have a great interest in reading about the war. The birds came back, as did the trees, and we filled in most of the craters. We have electric now, and the young schoolchildren play as they should on their way to the school. I worry about the children who suffered from the Agent Orange chemicals. What will America do about those children? Will they give us payment for the destruction? Other than that issue, I have no problems with Americans. They are always welcome here in my lands. I would like to go to America some day and visit with veterans . . . to talk to them, to talk as soldiers, to shake hands and have a drink for the future. I lost my father, my uncles, many of our relatives in the fighting here. But I am Buddhist, and that helps me go through to the future—the past is past. I hope for better relations now with my former enemies.[31]

NGUYEN THI KIEU

Kieu, now in her seventies, lost her husband and son to the war. She herself fought for the PLA and Viet Minh from the early 1950s. Her grandson was born badly deformed, a result, she feels, of his parents' exposure to Agent Orange. Kieu is now retired and living in her home built by the Vietnamese government for veterans near the village of Ben Huong, outside of Tay Ninh City. Her daughter, Thi Ran, fell in love with an American who wanted to marry her. At the time (1968), Kieu forbade the marriage. Thi Ran was very angry with her, and they did not speak for several years. "I lost my husband, and my oldest son, to the Americans, so I couldn't accept this marriage with an American," she related in an interview in 1998, "but forgiveness is part of our culture . . . so we have since made up."

Thi Ran then interjected, "His name was John, I truly loved him. . . . To this day, I think of him. I wonder where he is?"[32]

THICH MINH GIAC (BUDDHIST MONK)

In 1963, Giac witnessed the self-immolation of Quang Duc on a Saigon street corner. It was a protest by the Buddhist against the American presence and the Diem regime. Today, nearly eighty years old, Giac lives in the Hoa Khanh Pagoda and can still vividly recall the fire that consumed his mentor:

We wanted the Americans out. . . . We made a statement with the purity of fire. Today, it is Vietnamese who rule Vietnamese. We are happy that foreigners do not rule us. . . . I am old and pray for America and Viet Nam to make peace. Peace is the only way.[33]

GENERAL VO NGUYEN GIAP (PEOPLE'S ARMY OF VIET NAM)

I appreciated the fact that they [the Americans] had sophisticated weapons systems, but I must say that it was the people who made the difference, not the weapons. . . . Any mistakes were due to following the domino theory. They thought that if the theory was put into practice here, it would become the pivotal location to check the expansion of communism to the whole of Southeast Asia. And it was a mistake.[34]

The United States after the War

The deep divisions that the Viet Nam War highlighted within American society continued long after the final battle for Saigon in 1975. Americans, not used to losing, endured trying times in redefining their national identity. Many vets went through periods of anger and withdrawal. Most schools simply avoided the subject.

Incidents of post-traumatic stress were reported to affect thousands of American veterans of the war. Another aspect of the dark side of the Viet Nam War rose to national prominence in 1978 when American veteran Paul Reutersham filed a lawsuit against several chemical companies for the toxic effects of Agent Orange. Paul died of cancer before his lawsuit came to an end, claiming that "I died in Vietnam and didn't even know it."[35] Over 20,000 other veterans joined in a class action suit that eventually was settled with a $180 million payment to the veterans fund. Thousands of Vietnamese who died or were born deformed have yet to have their concerns met, although some countries, including Japan, have set up research stations in defoliated areas such as the Xac Forest in southeast Viet Nam.

In 1974, President Gerald R. Ford made a controversial effort to begin the healing over Viet Nam by offering limited amnesty for draft dodgers and military deserters. The policy failed, as most were unwilling to admit that their resistance to the war was wrong. In 1976, President Jimmy Carter offered a more extensive program in which still only 9 percent took part. These efforts proved controversial as war resisters felt this program did not allow for legitimate disagreement over the morality of the war and those on the opposite side felt it had sold out those who had actually fought in Viet Nam.

Even the design of the Viet Nam memorial, regarded by some veterans as innappropriate, was controversial until it was dedicated in

1982, in Washington, D.C. Thousands of vets paraded through the streets to make the statement that those who fought the war would not allow the nation to forget their sacrifice.

The 1980s witnessed many attempts beyond the dedication of the Wall to deal with the legacies of the war, including the passing of the 1987 Amerasian Homecoming Act, which eventually allowed nearly 25,000 children of American veterans to enter the United States legally.

The Viet Kieu communities in America were openly hostile to any reconciliation with the new Vietnamese government. Any attempt to depict Viet Nam positively or negatively was met with fierce opposition from the opposing side. Americans were unable to find ways to agree on the aftermath of the war. Even the issue of POWs was politicized as any effort to reconcile with Viet Nam was met with a tirade of protest from those who felt that Viet Nam was deliberately concealing the whereabouts of the 2,000 U.S. men missing in action. Black missing in action (MIA)/POW flags can still be seen on many buildings nearly thirty years after the end of the war. Hanoi, still bitter over the United States' retracting its promise to assist Viet Nam rebuild, was initially slow to offer assistance in the search for American MIAs. The Vietnamese denied accusations that they were not doing all they could and pointed to the fact that over 300,000 Vietnamese were also MIA and the government was overwhelmed. President Clinton's decision to reopen relations with Viet Nam was done so only after investigations confirmed that Viet Nam was doing all it could to find missing American soldiers. By November of 2000, when Clinton became the first American president ever to visit Hanoi, a total of 589 remains had been identified and returned to their families for burial in the United States.[36] In response, the United States released copies of thousands of captured documents to the Vietnamese government in an effort to provide them with clues to find their missing soldiers.

Although differences remain, the years of antagonism seem to have diminished, even though many Americans still find it hard to forget. In February 2001, Senator John McCain, Republican from Arizona, who had spent nearly five years as a POW in Hanoi, caused a stir when he referred to the Vietnamese as "gooks." "I hate the gooks," McCain had told reporters on a campaign bus. "I will hate them as long as I live."[37] McCain refused to apologize, saying he was referring to the guards that beat him during his captivity. Viet Nam demanded an apology and put out a statement that it was time for the former enemies to "set aside the past and look forward to the future and cooperate for mutual development."

Further postwar reflections from Americans follow:

KEN CUSHNER (KENT STATE UNIVERSITY STUDENT, 1970)

Ken Cushner now teaches at the same university, Kent State, that he had protested at on May 4, 1970, when four students were killed by National Guardsmen. Ken has had much to reflect on in the years since. The killings at Kent State helped direct Ken's career into teaching history and social studies. He wrote the following in reflection of the war and that terrible day at Kent State over thirty years ago:

I have seen the consequences of unwarranted violence on our campus— and this, I am sure, was nothing compared to the experiences many of my young peers had during the war in Viet Nam. But I had also seen other possibilities. I began to realize that there is a diverse world beyond my shores in which I could actively participate. Teaching was a way I could reach young people and perhaps present them with alternative experiences that would shape their lives in more positive, less violent ways. I have since devoted my life to bridging cultural gaps for young people as well as professional educators. I have . . . worked with young people from regions in conflict and have organized and led travel programs for young people and educators on all seven continents—all with the hope of demonstrating how differences can be bridged through extensive interpersonal immersion experiences.

I have also traveled to Viet Nam and have found people wonderfully warm and open to Americans. This certainly was unanticipated, and a wonderful opportunity to challenge some of my own stereotypes. . . . I had expected to meet people who resented me because I was an American. To the contrary, I found people welcoming my presence, making such statements as "Let bygones be bygones" and "The war was over a long time ago—let's get on with our lives."[38]

LARRY SEEGER (TWENTY-THIRD ARMY INFANTRY DIVISION, 1969 TO 1971)

U.S. Army veteran Larry Seeger, wounded when his helicopter was shot down over Laos in 1971, now lives in upstate New York, not far from the St. Lawrence River. A licensed land surveyor, he wrote the following reflections on the war:

What can I contribute to a discussion of the politics of United States involvement in the Vietnam War? As a junior officer, I was not the lowest peon on the battlefield, but neither was I a policymaker. I was there to carry out the mission, and virtually all of my fellow soldiers viewed our tour(s) in the Republic of Vietnam as a necessary obligation: a dusty (or muddy, depending upon the season), somewhat hazardous, sometimes arduous period away from home and family. I think the conflict has to be viewed first of all in the context of the Cold War. The validity and the practicality of tyrannical versus participatory forms of government was the issue then as it somewhat remains today. I don't think that the case for becoming involved in South Vietnam was ever properly and forcibly made to the U.S. population by JFK or LBJ [Presidents John F. Kennedy and Lyndon B. Johnson]. Our purpose of providing relative stability, a reprieve from external violence so that some form of representational government would have a chance to take hold, may have been just and consistent with American ideals, but was it ever feasible?

I don't think that the American people or their elected representatives, for that matter, understood in the 1960s where Southeast Asia was in the continuum of the development of systems of government. Vietnam's limited experience with democratic principles and their lack of trusted government structure made it easy to destabilize any fledgling attempts at representative democracy. Their emergence from under Japanese domination and French colonialism created a mind-set that perseverance would wear down any outside influence. It was easy to characterize American intervention as typical of the past, and the price for not cooperating with the Viet Cong was severe. My impression was that the Vietnamese people practice being anonymous and inconspicuous as a means of survival. They would be transparently loyal to whomever they believed was capable of influencing their lives, because there was no experience in their memory of a stable or responsive structure within which to express dissent or seek justice.

It is hard to imagine a worse way for a country to commit its military forces than that which the U.S. did in Vietnam. We never declared a war against North Vietnam, nor did we muster broad public support for our reasons for going there. We incrementally introduced units over the entire course of the conflict without ever identifying clear military goals. We failed to apply overwhelming military force to achieve whatever goals we did vaguely specify. We allowed micromanagement of the war by unqualified civilians. And we lacked the moral courage to seek a true military victory. For all the reputation of the importance to the Oriental person of not losing face, it is truly ironic that our early reluctance to withdraw without admitting failure led to repeated deceptive escalations of the war without public support. Richard Nixon was left to preside over the so-called Vietnamization of the war, a gradual withdrawal of our units, which no one truly believed would result in anything but the inevitable fall of South Vietnam.[39]

BILLY C. BRYELS (101ST ARMY AIRBORNE DIVISION, 1967 TO 1968)

Billy C. Bryels returned, in 1968, to a divided America that he feels was not much different from the one he left a year earlier. While recovering from serious wounds, he decided to find his part of the economic pie, raise his children, and live life the best he could. He remains cynical about race relations in America. He presently owns a successful business in the San Jose, California, area:

I haven't seen the "Wall" yet, but they had the moving replica of the Wall come to San Jose and I did go to that. Vets have had issues with the government, but I personally didn't experience that [mistreatment of vets upon their return], on the one hand, but I didn't go out of my way to have people know I was a vet. I tried to blend in. I don't think we have really improved relations with Viet Nam these days. I think what we're doing now we're exercising the initial thing we wanted to do: to find another market-place. [About] economics . . . at this point in time what we really want to do is sell refrigerators and air conditioners to Vietnamese and have most of them do the manufacturing at very low labor rates. That's what we're really after. We could give a damn about the Vietnamese. We don't care about folks in lower Louisiana. Why would we care about the Vietnamese? We simply don't. It's all about money. We are a capitalist society. Period. If there's no money attached to it, we're simple not interested.

No, I do not think we really learned from the war, not at all. I think it's indicative in the last election where we have this tremendous 50 percent divide. Where half of us think one way and the other half thinks another way. We are in total denial about all of the real problems going on around us. We've had a selfish kind of conditioning. There's still racism! We got folks in Appalachia who hate me and they've never seen me! So we have this division going on because we're talking primarily about economics. That's what we're really talking about. The haves and the have-nots. We've been conditioned to believe if you've got it and I don't have it, we have to be at odds with each other. Neither one of us really have it. In the United States today, a very few people have most of the wealth.[40]

STEVE HASSNA (101ST ARMY, AIRBORNE DIVISION, 1967 TO 1968)

I don't think America learned any lessons from Viet Nam. I think the powers that be just shook their heads when it was over and said, "Don't worry, we will rewrite its history in 20 years!" And that's what is happening now. What America should have learned is that you can't go in like a bully and mess with someone else's problems. Imagine 500,000 foreign troops in California tomorrow, and what do you think would happen to them? But it was the Cold War, and we were the big dog on the block. Since Nam we have had El Salvador, Nicaragua, Panama, the Persian Gulf, and now Colombia. . . . America don't learn lessons; it just ignores reality.

I have been involved with many groups and programs since 1972. . . . I have been speaking to high schools and colleges since 1974. . . . I would like to go back . . . to see through different eyes and learn about that culture. . . . We should have diplomatic relations [with Viet Nam]. Open up trade and know the Vietnamese in a different way with respect and dignity. If this had been done in 1945, things would have been a whole lot different.[41]

ALAN CANFORA (KENT STATE UNIVERSITY STUDENT, SHOT MAY 4, 1970)

I remain convinced that the U.S. government/military war in Southeast Asia was a terrible example of mistaken foreign policy. Millions of Asians and thousands of Americans—including some of my schoolmates—died for no good reason. As patriotic Americans, our antiwar movement had no choice. Our conscience demanded increasingly strong antiwar actions to stop our government and military during a serious crisis. . . . After the very unpopular, controversial war in Southeast Asia, U.S. politicians and military officials now basically admit that the war was wrong. During the Persian Gulf War in 1991, for example, U.S. military leaders said all future U.S. wars would be different than the war in Southeast Asia. They said future U.S. wars would be: A) clearly understood; B) brief; C) winnable; and D) supported by the American people. . . . Hopefully, our leaders have learned valuable history lessons after Vietnam and Kent State. Never again should young Americans be forced to fight and die in controversial foreign wars in places like Viet Nam—and never again should young American students be shot down and killed while crying out for peace.[42]

GREG GIBBONS (CORPSMAN, U.S. NAVY, 1969 TO 1970)

The sacrifices of the men in the field were real, and, in the end, the war was not worth the cost! It became clear to me that, given the restriction imposed on us by our commanders/government, the effort was futile. We simply could not win the war, although we could (and did) win the battles. It also became clear that most of the Vietnamese I met, out in the countryside, really did not care very much what government was in place. They were much more concerned about being free to raise their crops or conduct their business, raising their families without fear, and generally living their lives.

I've been to the Wall on a number of occasions. . . . On each visit, I find an appropriate place of remembrance and a place of personal catharsis. Certainly, the first time I went was by far the hardest—the most emotional— seeing those names I knew on the panels of granite and knowing of others whose names I didn't know. It again raised the question of "Why them and not me?" What has not changed in those visits, and which I find utterly amazing to this day, is the atmosphere of this place. It is almost as though it is sacred! . . . How amazing it seems that, when this memorial was designed, the design was controversial. I have not met a single Vietnam veteran who has been there that would change a thing! The place and atmosphere speak volumes!

I am not convinced that as a whole the country learned anything from the Vietnam War. Certainly, we have done a better job of supporting the troops, irregardless of our views on the actions they have been called upon to undertake, but none of those actions have come close to covering the span of time that Vietnam did. Truly I believe that the true answers to this question cannot come yet.[43]

WILLIAM C. WESTMORELAND (GENERAL, U.S. ARMY)

For years after the war, General Westmoreland attempted to rationalize his tactics and explain why the United States lost the war. A summary of his thoughts on why the United States lost the war follows:

The Vietnam War was a limited war, with limited objectives prosecuted by limited means, with limited public support. . . . The military did not lose a single battle of consequence and did not lose the war. The war was lost by congressional actions withdrawing support to the South Vietnamese government despite commitments by Nixon.[44]

DANIEL ELLSBERG

Daniel Ellsberg, a former defense department and Rand Corporation analyst, leaked the "Pentagon Papers" to the *New York Times* in 1971. Many have called him a traitor, others a national hero. The papers, once classified documents from the U.S. government concerning Viet Nam, Laos, and Cambodia, present strong evidence that the war in Viet Nam was primarily the result of a deliberate American policy of deception and influence in Vietnamese affairs. Many of the documents contradict what American presidents publicly told the American public. Ellsberg's contact with the papers changed his perspective on the war, leading him to become an antiwar advocate. Ellsberg wrote the following regarding the claim that the war was a civil war that America became entangled in:

The popular critique that we have "interfered" in what is "really a civil war"—a notion long held privately by many of my former colleagues—is as much a myth as the earlier official one of "aggression from the north." To call a conflict in which one army is financed and equipped entirely by foreigners a "civil war" simply screens a more painful reality: that the war is, after all, a foreign aggression. Our aggression.[45]

ROBERT M. SUTTER

Robert Sutter, a union elevator constructor now living outside of Columbus, Ohio, grew up with the Viet Nam generation in a working class part of Columbus and suffered the nation's agony over the war, although he never fought in Viet Nam. He came to disagree with the government's policy and still feels disenfranchised by the revelations during the war years:

Vietnam is one of the worst mistakes this country has ever made. . . . It polarized the nation's youth. . . . I know—I was one. My father fought in the Pacific during World War II, so I grew up with the patriotism that that era handed down to us. But it was all wasted by what we did to those Vietnamese. Maybe some day we can set things right again . . . and start treating people around the world with respect.[46]

Veterans, War, and Reconciliations

Psychologists refer to it as "post-traumatic stress syndrome. It is a very real emotional issue for hundreds of thousands of veterans from both sides of the conflict. With symptoms including nightmares, restlessness, flashbacks to traumatic events (especially to incidents of heavy combat for veterans) often resulting in the inability to focus, retain jobs and/or relationships, this type of post-traumatic stress lies at the core of issues relative to postwar relations between the U.S. government and the American soldiers who fought in Viet Nam.

Perhaps the final words on the tragic war in Viet Nam come from the "grave" as excerpts from President Lyndon B. Johnson's hours of secretly taped conversations in the White House have been discovered and released in the book *Reaching for Glory: Lyndon B. Johnson's Secret*, by presidential historian Michael Beschloss. According to the newly released tapes, Johnson exhibits a demeanor behind closed doors of fear, insecurity, depression, and anxiety of Viet Nam—in stark contrast to his bold and confident public appearance. After ordering the initial bombing in Viet Nam on February 26, 1965, Johnson fears that he could not win in Viet Nam without using nuclear weapons and says to then secretary of defense, Robert McNamara, that "now we are off to bombing these people, we're over that hurdle. I don't think anything is going to be as bad as losing and I don't see any way of winning."[47]

LEO T. PROFILET (CAPTAIN, U.S. NAVY, PRISONER OF WAR, HANOI, AUGUST 1967 TO 1973)

We POWs, upon repatriation in 1973, were given a tremendously warm and loving welcome home. My concern is with how, during the war, the individual GIs returning after their Vietnam tour of duty were treated with indifference bordering on contempt by the country. I believe that the trauma caused by that treatment is responsible for most of the psychological problems of some Vietnam veterans. This was the most shameful episode in the history of the country.

On Secretary of Defense Robert McNamara's comment that he knew the war was unwinnable back in 1964: By all accounts, McNamara was a very intelligent man, in the narrowest sense of intelligence. He possessed none of the leadership abilities so necessary in a secretary of defense. Did he tell the president [Johnson] what he "knew"? I doubt it, because that would have meant admitting he was wrong before 1964, something his ego would not permit.[48]

HEIDI BARACH (R.N., U.S. ARMY)

The whole stupid war was a mess, and it seemed no one cared. That's why I wanted to go back, too, because no one cared. So I had to go, and I had to care. But how stupid I was, because I do not think I knew how to care. I went back a second time because it was the only place I fit in. I was a machine. Vietnam stripped me of all emotions . . .

In triage I was told to keep Americans alive, but let the Vietnamese die. Nobody should have to make such choices. I went as a girl of 21, but I came back an old woman. I wanted to help, but I wasn't prepared to see what I saw. When you live in an environment of hate and anger, you become hate and anger. . . .

You'll have to forgive in order to heal. A lot of Vietnam vets go around feeling victimized, but have to turn it around to begin to heal. You have to start taking responsibility for what you did.[49]

BYRON JAMES (FOURTH ARMY INFANTRY DIVISION, 1970 TO 1971)

Byron returned from Viet Nam in 1971 to the Navajo reservation in the four corners region of the Southwest. Unable to go back to school or find a job, he resumed life in the traditional Navajo way, herding sheep on his grandfather's ancestral lands near Round Rock, Arizona. Thirty years later, he was found alone out in the desert near his home, looking for a lost calf:

There are a couple of things they [medicine men] usually do when a warrior returns from battles. You just do not get back from there and come into the house. The medicine man starts singing, takes you by the hand, and leads you back into the house, takes you around the hogan, shakes hands with the family—that's one thing they still do. Another thing is called the squaw dance.[50] It takes a whole weekend. . . . It involves getting a juniper stake, decorating it with yarn and ribbons, and riding by horse to another house. Then they have black day, to blacken the veteran, to scare evil spirits. They get a bone or something and take you way out there [in the mountains] and when you get back here, you shoot the bone four times, and kill the evil spirit. I haven't yet done this . . . and I believe that's when I started losing my family. There is just us right here now. . . . One of my uncles living here by this side of the trading post says it has to get done. . . . because I still get recurring bad dreams, all that stuff—all kinds of bad things started happening to me. The mind starts going in different directions. . . . It has to be done. . . . Hopefully I can finally get that out of the way, and get on with recovery . . .

What's a parade? I can do without a parade; it's no big deal. I'd go but if not, the world's not going to end. As far as protests, I hear them, and I understand why they did that, but when I got back . . . at the airport . . . there were five or six protesters in the lobby. I had my uniform on. One came over, started talking about babies being killed: "How many hooches you burn for this medal?" Finally, one of the security guys kicked them out.

Today, I think it's [reconciliation with Viet Nam] a long time coming. . . . It's a good thing; things should have been better right after the war. We need their help, to find our MIAs. I think they are still out there somewhere. I think there's some airplane crash sites with our remains. . . . We need their help. . . . I think its about time . . .

I guess, I got no hard feelings against those guys. They were soldiers like we were. . . . The only thing I regret . . . is that when I was returning home . . . I had my bag, my small duffel, stolen from a bus. . . . I do not have anything left from the war . . . just my memories. . . .

I spend most of my time now alone, out in the steppe. . . . I see my sheep, my land. . . . I get lonely. . . . I live alone, no wife, no children—most of my family is gone. Out here, so much space, so much time, I think a lot about the war, and my life out here. . . . Time heals, they say. But not yet, not quite yet.[51]

JOHN LANCASTER (LIEUTENANT, FIRST DIVISION, MARINE, 1967 TO 1968)

John Lancaster, paralyzed by an AK-47 round in May 1968, presently works for Viet Nam Assistance for the Handicapped in Hanoi, providing technical assistance to the Vietnamese government in the development of law, policy, and programs for people with disabilities.

After the war ended, much of the media presented the returning Viet Nam veteran as an angry and confused man, unemployable, easily brought to violence, a time bomb waiting to explode. Statistics since the war have shown that many vets did, in fact, suffer from anger and resentment, suicide, alcoholism, divorce, and imprisonment at a slightly higher rate than the national average (see Appendix D). But most veterans dealt with their issues over the years, and a large majority went on to live healthy and productive lives. Though John has spent his time in a wheelchair since being wounded in 1968, he was named director of the President's Committee on Employment of People with Disabilities by President Clinton and has been back to Viet Nam several times to assist disabled American and Vietnamese veterans of the war. But for the first years after the war, things did not go so well for John, as he returned to a changed and often hostile nation:

I never really answered the question of why we were there. I don't think McNamara or anybody has ever really answered that one for me. I think we just needed a good war to fight. . . .

When I got back from the war, the war really impacted me and my family in a huge way. My parents were devastated. . . . My mom didn't want me to go into the Marine Corps anyway. . . . I think while they were proud of me and I know they were, they were devastated by my disability and all . . . probably more so than I was. Mom was very angry about it for a while. . . . She never thought we should have been over there from the beginning.

. . . I was really depressed for three maybe four years. . . . I finally got out of the VA hospital in February 1969 . . . and I went into law school. It took me four years to finish . . . because I was drinking so much. . . . I basically flunked out my first year. . . . In 1974 or '75 . . . I woke up. It was amazing, stopped being depressed, I started to come to terms with the whole thing . . . stopped talking about the war . . . stopped thinking about it so much . . . and started really coming around and got into the issue of disability. . . . But a lot of other things opened up for me in that period. I was angry. . . . Here I was, a veteran, went over and did what I was asked to do . . . but now I got back and I couldn't even get on a goddamn bus! My own university was arguing about about whether or not to let me in . . . merely because I was in a wheelchair. I was really pissed: . . . Send me to fight your dirty little war, then come back and you want nothing to do with me. . . . The only place I got a job was at the Veterans Administration . . . as a staff legal advisor. . . . Then I met a man who took me to lunch and gave me a job as a legislative director up on Capitol Hill doing lobbying . . . vets issues and disabilities issues. In 1982 I was at the Wall opening in D.C. I was involved in the march the day they dedicated it. I remember that President

Beth Marie Murphy today. She was
stationed on a hospital ship off the coast
of Viet Nam during the war. Courtesy of
Beth Marie Murphy.

[Ronald] Reagan wouldn't come. . . . The Wall was very controversial at the
time. . . . It was a huge parade that day . . . but the president didn't come.

If I had to do it over again? I probably would have stayed and become a
conscientious objector. . . . Knowing what I do now . . . I would not have
participated. Nor would I have chosen a military career. I think there are
other ways to solve these issues. I'm not saying we are to a point in mankind
where there may never be a need for military, but I'd rather think we are
getting to that point. . . . I don't regret that I served; knowing what I know
now, I'm not sure that's what I would choose. I'm proud of my service and
proud of the guys that I served with.[52]

BETH MARIE MURPHY (R.N., HOSPITAL SHIP U.S.S.
SANCTUARY, 1969 TO 1970)

I think the nation as a whole has still not recovered from Viet Nam, and
I hope it never does. One can see this when the public says that it does not

want another Vietnam. . . . I am afraid the country is forgetting the lessons of Vietnam. The war has affected all of my life since that point. In the last 30 years, I have moved 20 times and had about 14 different jobs. It has been impossible for me to stay in one place doing one thing for long. I have experienced depression and anxiety most of the time. Life has been very different than when I went to Vietnam. It was not until the dedication of the women's memorial in D.C. that I realized that I could be suffering from post-traumatic stress syndrome. I went to a conference in connection with the memorial, and I thought they were telling my story. I was amazed. Since I was an Anglican priest, I was asked to lead prayer services for a number of events. . . . [As] I prepared the sermon, I did so much crying it was hard to write. I did not even know why. I had never cried over Vietnam before. It was a beginning of healing. I knew I had to do something about how Vietnam affected my life.

War is hell. . . . I am not sure America has learned this lesson at all; look at all the other places that America has stuck her nose into. I think the lesson America learned was not to get into a war you can't win, which is a far cry from learning that war is hell. No one wins in war.[53]

WILLIAM BROWN (173RD ARMY AIRBORNE BRIGADE)

In January 2001, the War Remnants Museum in Ho Chi Minh City held a one-month exhibition of hundreds of photographs of the Viet Nam War taken by more than 100 photographers from eleven different nations who died while photographing the conflict. The project, the Indochina Requiem Project, was a joint American–Vietnamese project to honor the sacrifice. In a room next to an exhibit was a small case with medals sent to the museum and a short note from Sergeant William Brown, of the 173rd Airborne Brigade, 503rd, the unit that had fought the severe and costly battle for Hill 875 in November 1967 near Dak To. All the note said was: "I am sorry, I was wrong."

HOANG VAN MY (PEOPLE'S ARMY OF VIET NAM)

My is the lone survivor of his entire unit of over 400 men who walked the Ho Chi Minh Trail in 1969 as volunteers to fight. Today, he is a history professor at the National Pedagogic University in Ho Chi Minh City. He related these thoughts in an interview in 1998:

We must forget the pain of the war—only look at it as history. We cannot let the war prevent us from having good relations with the United States. We wish to extend our hand in friendship. I wish also to visit the United States one day with some of my fellow veterans. I would like to sit down with American veterans and shake their hands. We never had hatred of the American people, only their government. Now, I enjoy my interest in art and reading. Of course, I still have bad dreams about the war, but reading helps me. Yes, reading about the war, as a historian. I want the next generation, my students, to understand how it was. But only so that we can always fight to prevent another war. It must not ever happen again. Otherwise, it's no point in hashing over the old issues.[54]

Three years later, after viewing the tragedy of the World Trade Center collapse in New York City, Hoang Van My commented that,

As a person who has survived a war, I was absolutely sad when I saw the ruins and death on TV and papers concerning the September 11th New York City event. My heart goes out to those innocents of that time, to all innocents of all wars.[55]

TRAN VIET NGAC (PEOPLE'S ARMY OF VIET NAM)

Ngac is presently a history instructor at the National Pedagogic University in Ho Chi Minh City. At a panel discussion with American students in January 2000, Ngac was asked by one of the Americans if Vietnamese veterans suffered the same problems that American vets did. He replied:

I fought in the war and saw many horrible things. Yes, of course. You ask us if we have nightmares, if we have a hard time sleeping at night because of the things we saw. I can only tell you this, that yes, as veterans we have had a hard time. But I think we all sleep well at night. It is simple. We believed in what we were doing. We had a mission to fight for our country, for our lands, for our families, and, even though it cost us dearly in lives, we succeeded. We did a good day's work, so to speak. And it is natural, is it not, that when one does a good thing in the day, that one sleeps well at night?[56]

The author, with elderly Viet Minh veterans of the war with the French, tour a museum in Ho Chi Minh City, Viet Nam. The veterans later fought against the Americans. Courtesy of Hanh Thi Ngoc Trinh-Vadas.

Many American veterans have made reconciliation journeys to Viet Nam, and some also have left mementos at Vietnamese memorials and museums. A PLA battle flag was given to the War Remnants Museum in Ho Chi Minh City in 1992. A message was printed on the flag from the American veteran from the Twenty-Fifth Infantry Division near Tay Ninh in 1968 who returned it:

March 26, 1992
In the spirit of respect and peace between Vietnam and the U.S.A. . . . I wish to return this flag to the rightful owners—the brave soldiers of the 241st NVA Infantry Regiment. May God bless their souls and peace to their families.
Stephen M. Campbell
Lt. U.S. Army

When the story of the massacre at My Lai broke in 1969, it seriously affected the national psychology in ways that still have not been resolved. The theologian Reinhold Neibuhr summarized it when he wrote: "I think there is a great deal of evidence that we thought all along that we were a redeemer nation. I think there is a lot of illusion in our national history. Now it's about to be shattered."[57]

Viet Nam did shatter many of the illusions that had developed in post–World War II America during the 1950s. This "Vietnam syndrome," as many refer to it, prospered under the unwillingness of many to listen to the other side. Thich Nhat Hanh, a Buddhist monk exiled from South Viet Nam during the war, has dedicated his life to reconciliation and forgiveness. He wrote the following:

We have to listen in a way that we understand the suffering of others. . . . Just by listening deeply, we already alleviate a great deal of pain. . . . This is the beginning of healing.[58]

NOTES

1. John Lancaster, taped personal communication, transcribed by Adam Pallack (October 2000).
2. Billy C. Bryels, taped personal communication, transcribed by Ann Thomas (March 2001).
3. Nguyen Duc Anh, personal communication (October 2000).
4. Trinh Quang Dai, taped personal communication, translated by Hanh Thi Ngoc Trinh-Vadas (January 2001).
5. Nguyen Thi Hanh, taped personal communication, translated by Hanh Thi Ngoc Trinh-Vadas (January 2001).
6. Ly Le Hayslip with Jay Wurts, *When Heaven and Earth Changed Places: A Vietnamese Woman's Journey from War to Peace* (New York: Plume, 1990), xiv–xv.
7. Harry G. Summers, Jr., *The Vietnam War Almanac* (Novato, CA: Presidio, 1999), 283.
8. Ibid., 90.
9. "Once Again, Nation Faces Ghosts of Vietnam," *USA Today*, 1 May 2001, 14a.
10. Ha Thi Quy, personal communication (January 2001).
11. Richard Bates, written personal communication (March 2001).
12. Lancaster.
13. Larry Seeger, written personal communication (February 2001).
14. Courtesy of the Southern Women's Museum, Ho Chi Minh City, Viet Nam.
15. Huyen Van Chia, taped personal communications, translated by Hanh Thi Ngoc Trinh-Vadas (January 1998 and January 2001).
16. Leo T. Profilet, written personal communication (May 2001).
17. Associated Press, "S. Korean Forces Killed Civilians in Vietnam, Report Says," *Cleveland Plain Dealer*, 12 February, 2000, 7A.
18. Anonymous Korean veteran, personal communication, 1999). (http://mcel.pacificu.edu/as/students/koreavet/home.htm).
19. Steve Hassna, written personal communication (October 2000).

20. Jeffrey Race, *War Comes to An Long* (Berkeley: University of California Press, 1972), 235.

21. Daniel Hallock, *Bloody Hell* (Farmington: Plough Publishing, 1999), 50.

22. Truong Nhu Tang, D. Channoff, and Toi Van Doan, *A Viet Cong Memoir* (New York: Vintage Books, 1985), 289.

23. Trinh. (January 2001).

24. Do. Hunyl, personal communication, Dak To (January 2001).

25. Nguyen Duc Anh.

26. Tran Dzoan Toi, personal communication (January 2001).

27. Nguyen Son Ha, written personal communication (January 2000).

28. Nguyen Tran Trac, personal communication, Ho Chi Minh City (January 1998).

29. Nguyen Thi Hanh.

30. Mel Tra, written personal communication (May 2001).

31. Huyen Van Chia.

32. Nguyen Thi Kien and Nguyen Thi Ran, personal communications, Viet Nam, translated by Hanh Thi Ngoc Trinh-Vadas (January 1998).

33. Thich Minh Giac, personal communication, Ho Chi Minh City, translated by Hanh Thi Ngoc Trinh-Vadas (January 2001).

34. CNN, "The Cold War," CNN television series (June 1996).

35. Edward Doyle and Terrence Maitland, eds., *The Vietnam Experience: The Aftermath* (Boston: Boston Publishing, 1985), 142.

36. U.S. Department of Defense, Washington Headquarters Service, 18 September 2000.

37. David Brunnstrom, "Vietnam Condemns McCain's Use of Racial Slur," Reuters News Service, 21 February 2000.

38. Ken Cushner, written personal communication (November 2000).

39. Seeger.

40. Bryels.

41. Hassna.

42. Alan Canfora, written personal communication (June 2001).

43. Greg Gibbons, written personal communication (February 2001).

44. B. McCloud, *What Should We Tell Our Children about Vietnam?* (Norman: University of Oklahoma Press, 1989), 137.

45. Daniel Ellsberg, *Papers on the War* (New York: Simon and Schuster, 1972). 33.

46. Robert M. Sutter, written personal communication (May 2001).

47. Michael Beschloss, "I Don't See Any Way of Winning" [book excerpt], *Newsweek* (November 11, 2001), pp. 58–61.

48. Profilet.

49. Hallock, *Bloody Hell*, 312.

50. The term "squaw," usually considered derogatory, is commonly used by Navajo in reference to one of several nights of a variety of "Blessing Way" ceremonies. For a returning warrior, it is called an "Enemy Way" ceremony.

51. Byron James, taped personal communication, transcribed by Robert E. Vadas (May 2001).

52. Lancaster.

53. Beth Marie Murphy, written personal communication (November 2000).

54. Huong Van My, taped personal communication (January 1998).

55. Ibid. (written personal communication, November 21, 2001).

56. Tran Viet Ngac, videotaped public speech, Ho Chi Minh City (January 2000).

57. Daniel Hallock, *Hell, Healing, and Resistance* (Farmington: Plough Publishing, 1998), 227.

58. Thich Nhat Hanh, *Love in Action: Writings on Non-Violent Social Change* (Berkeley, CA: Parallax Press, 1993), 67.

PART III

REFLECTING

Chapter 7

Ideas for Exploration

The following are suggestions for inquiry and discussion of important issues relative to the Viet Nam War. These issues are grouped within traditional areas of disagreement that have been the center of controversy about Viet Nam over the years.

- Proponents of America's initial entry into the affairs of Viet Nam in the 1940s and 1950s argued that Ho Chi Minh's revolutionary movement was part of a worldwide Communist movement and was thus a threat to the interests of the United States. Critics have argued that Ho's movement was mostly a nationalist-driven attempt to win independence for Viet Nam free of foreign rule. Consider the historical summary outlined in the early part of chapter 1, and integrate data from personal reflections in chapter 3 to discuss this controversy.

- Review the personal letters written by Americans and Vietnamese in chapters 4 and 5. What differences and commonalities can be discovered? To what degree did these differences contribute to the conflict? What historical and cultural characteristics helped create these differences?

- A brief discussion of the cruelty of war is found in chapter 6. Contrast the perception of Larry Seeger with a contrary perspective, such as the People's Liberation Army fighter from Cu Chi, Huong Van Chia, or of a fellow American, such as Richard Bates. What could be the cause of such diversity in opinion?

- Review chapter 3, which relates the initial motivations of various men who fought in Viet Nam on both sides. What commonalities exist? What differences? Contrast these initial expectations with the reality of the war that they soon discovered. Do you see any major differences between the American and Vietnamese fighters?

- Six U.S. presidents ruled over the Viet Nam War from 1947 to 1975. Discuss what realistic options each had and how they dealt with them. What should they have done at that time?

- Think of the growing rebellion and reluctance of American soldiers to wage determined war after Richard M. Nixon took office in 1969. What options did the military leadership have to deal with those issues? What role did Nixon's "peace with honor" policy have in the rise in troop rebellions?

- Debate has raged both during the war and since the war's end in 1975 over the role and impact of the antiwar movement against U.S. involvement in Viet Nam. How does a democracy deal with internal dissent during a national crisis? What options did American political leaders have? Discuss whether or not you feel that dissent is a healthy form of democratic expression or a threat to the security of a nation such as the United States.

- Compare the experiences and background of Billy C. Bryels, an African American from Arkansas, with those of Larry Seeger or Greg Gibbons. What differences or commonalities can be found in their stories? How did these differences shape their conclusions about the war?

- Review the experiences of women in the war through the eyes of the American Beth Marie Murphy and Nguyen Thi Hanh who fought with the People's Army of Viet Nam. What commonalities and differences can be found in their reflections? Imagine what it might have been like for women and men during the war. Should women be forced to fight in combat as men are in the military?

- Review the brief analogies of the Ia Drang Battle in chapter 1. Both sides claimed victory. Which side do you think could truly claim victory? How did this bode for the war as a whole?

- Review the comments from Americans in chapter 6. Discuss what lessons the United States has learned from its experience in Viet Nam. Contrast the Vietnamese postwar reflections with those of the Americans. What differences and commonalities can be found in these stories?

Suggestions for Further Reading

Of the great amount of literature to come out of the Viet Nam War, the following can be considered just a partial review, divided into several categories or issues:

Comprehensive overviews of the war: Committee of Concerned Asian Scholars, *The Indochina Story*, Bantam Books (1970); Boston Publishing Co. series *The Vietnam Experience* (1981–86), several volumes, especially *A Collision of Cultures* and *Setting the Stage*; Gloria Emerson, *Winners and Losers*, Harcourt Brace Jovanovich (1976); Stanley Karnow, *Vietnam: A History*, Viking Press (1983).

Educational: B. Lee Cooper, "The Images of Vietnam: A Popular Music Approach," *Social Education* (October 1985); W.D. Erhart, "Carrying the Darkness: The Poetry of the Vietnam War" *Social Education* (1985); John Newton, "Vietnam War Literature" *Social Education* (1982); N. Bradley Christie, "Teaching Our Longest War: Constructive Lessons from Vietnam," *English Journal* (April 1989); Joe P. Dunn, "Teaching Teachers to Teach Vietnam," *Social Education* (January 1988).

Discussion of Vietnamese culture: Edward Doyle, Samuel Lipsman, and Terrence Maitland, eds., *The Vietnam Experience: The North*, Boston Publishing (1986); Frances Fitzgerald, *Fire in the Lake*, Vintage Books (1972); Nguyen Vien Khac, *Viet Nam: A Long Story*, Gioi Publishers, Hanoi (1993); Yevgeny Koblev, *Ho Chi Minh*, Progress Publishers, Moscow (1983).

Books on specific battles: Tracey Burke and Mimi Gleason, *The Tet Offensive, January–April 1968*, Gallery Books (1988); Vo Nguyen Giap, *Dien Bien Phu*, Gioi Publishers, Hanoi (1999); Edward Murphy, *Dak To: America's Sky Soldiers in South Vietnam's Central Highlands*, Pocket Books (1993); Edward Murphy, *Semper Fi: Vietnam: Marine Corps Campaigns*

1965–1975, Presidio (1997); John Pimlott, *Vietnam: Decisive Battles*, Barnes & Nobles Books (1990).

Books on the clash of cultures during the Viet Nam War: Edward Doyle and Stephen Weiss, eds., *The Vietnam Experience: A Collision of Cultures*, Boston Publishing (1984).

Women's issues: Kathryn Marshall, *In the Combat Zone: An Oral History of American Women in Vietnam (1966–75)*, Little, Brown (1987); Ho Chi Minh City Southern Women's Museum, *Tales and Legends of the Women in Viet Nam*, Art of Publishing House, Ho Chi Minh City (1994); Karen Turner and Thanh Hoa Phan, *Even the Women Must Fight*, John Wiley & Sons (1998).

Issues of American soldiers: antiwar or resistance movements: Daniel Hallock, *Hell, Healing, and Resistance* (1998) and *Bloody Hell* (1999), Plough Publishing; Richard Moser, *The New Winter Soldiers*, Rutgers University Press (1996).

About the 1960s, civil rights, or antiwar movement: Juan Williams, *Eyes on the Prize*, Viking Press (1987); *The Vietnam Experience: Nineteen Sixty Eight*, Boston Publishing (1983); Todd Gitlin, *The Sixties: Years of Hope, Days of Rage*, Bantam Press (1987); web site: May4.org; Morris Dickstein, *The Gates of Eden*, Delta Press (1977).

Books on politics and controversies of the war: F. James Dunnigan and Albert A. Noti, *Dirty Little Secrets of the Vietnam War*, Thomas Dunne Books (1999); James W. Gibson, *The Perfect War: Technowar in Vietnam*, Atlantic Monthly Press (1986); Robert S. McNamara, *In Retrospect*, Times Books (1995); John Prados, *The Hidden History of the Vietnam War*, Elephant Paperbacks (1995).

Books with documents or archival information: Maurice Isserman, *Witness to War: Personal Narratives from the Conflict in Vietnam*, Perrigee Books (1995); Daniel Ellsberg, *Papers on the War*, Simon & Schuster (1972); Gareth Porter, *Vietnam: A History in Documents*, Meridian Books (1979); Jerrold L. Schector and Huong Tien Nguyen, *The Palace Files: Vietnam Secret Documents*, Harper & Row (1986).

Books on the Vietnamese revolution: Tang Nhu Troung; D. Channoff–and Toi Van Doan, *A Viet Cong Memoir*, Vintage Books (1985); Jeffrey Race, *War Comes to An Long*, University of California Press (1972); Ho Chi Minh, *The Prison Diary of Ho Chi Minh* (introduction by Harrison Salisbury), Bantam Books (1971); Tom Mangold and John Penycate, *The Tunnels of Cu Chi*, Berkeley Publishing Group (1985); David Channoff and Doan Van Toai, *Portrait of the Enemy*, Random House (1986).

Literature relating individual stories: A spiritual journey of a Viet Kieu who seeks his identity while bike touring Viet Nam is Andrew X. Pham's *Catfish and Mandala*, Farrar, Straus & Giroux (1999); Philip Caputo, *A Rumor of War*, Ballantine Books (1977); Bernard Edelman, ed., *Dear America: Letters Home from Vietnam*, Pocket Books (1985); Ly Le Hayslip with Jay Warts, *When Heaven and Earth Changed Places*, Plume Books (1989); Michael Herr, *Dispatches*, Picador (1977); Bao Ninh, *The Sorrow of War*, Secker & Warburg (1993); Tim Page, *Ten Years After: Vietnam Today*, Knopf (1987); Neil Sheehan, *After the War Was Over*, Random House (1991); Robert Olen Butler, *A Good Scent from a Strange Mountain*, New York: Henry Holt (1992) (a collection of stories about the war, life, love, and the Vietnamese people as told by Vietnamese relocated in U.S.A.).

Web sites: A comprehensive review of the war listing a multitude of web sites, alphabetically: http://www.lbjlib.utexas.edu.

Comprehensive web site for prisoner-of-war/missing-in-action issues: www.nampows.org.

DOCUMENTARIES/MOVIES

Hearts and Minds (1975), Peter Davis, Best Documentary at Cannes Film Festival

Coming Home (1976), Hal Ashby, precarious romance of disabled vet and wife of vet

Born on the 4th of July (1989), Oliver Stone, marine's change from patriot to dissenter

Remembering My Lai (1989), Frontline, told through stories of soldiers and Viet survivors

Indochine (1992), French-era romance set against Viet Minh revolt

Heaven and Earth (1933), Oliver Stone, Vietnamese woman's personal journey

Three Seasons (1998), Mike Bui (Viet Nam), contemporary issues in Saigon

Appendix A: Speech by Ho Chi Minh for Declaration of Independence in Hanoi

The following is the speech written by Ho Chi Minh for Viet Nam's Declaration of Independence in Hanoi.

"All men are created equal. They are endowed by their Creator with certain inalienable rights, among these are Life, Liberty, and the pursuit of Happiness."

This immortal statement was made in the Declaration of Independence of the United States of America in 1776. In a broader sense, this means: All the peoples on the earth are equal from birth, all the peoples have a right to live, to be happy and free.

The Declaration of the French Revolution made in 1791 on the Rights of Man and the Citizen also states: "All men are born free and with equal rights, and must always remain free and have equal rights." Those are undeniable truths. Nevertheless, for more than eight years, the French imperialists, abusing the standard of Liberty, Equality, and Fraternity, have violated our Fatherland and oppressed our fellow-citizens. They have acted contrary to the ideals of humanity and justice. In the field of politics, they have deprived our people of every democratic liberty. They have enforced inhuman laws; they have set up three distinct political regimes in the North, the Center, and the South of Vietnam in order to wreck our national unity and prevent our people from being united. They have built more prisons than schools. They have mercilessly slain our patriots—they have drowned our uprisings in rivers of blood. They have fettered public opinion; they have practiced obscurantism against our people. To weaken our race, they have forced us to use opium and alcohol. In the fields of economics, they have fleeced us to the backbone, impoverished our people, and dev-astated our land. They have robbed us of our rice fields, our mines, our forests, and our raw materials. They have monopolized the issuing of bank-notes and the export trade. They have invented numerous unjustifiable taxes and reduced our people, especially our peasantry, to a state of extreme pov-erty. They have hampered the prospering of our national bourgeoisie; they have mercilessly exploited our workers. In the autumn of 1940, when the Japanese Fascists violated Indochina's territory to establish new bases in their fight against the Allies, the French imperialists went down on their knees and handed over our country to them. Thus, from that date, our people were subjected to the double yoke of the French and the Japanese. Their sufferings and miseries increased. The result was that from the end of last year to the beginning of this year, from Quang Tri Province to the North of Vietnam, more than 2 million of our fellow-citizens died from starvation. On March 9, the French troops were disarmed by the Japanese. The French colonialists either fled or surrendered, showing that . . . they had twice sold our country to the Japanese. On several occasions before March 9, the Viet Minh League urged the French to ally themselves with it against the Japa-nese. Instead of agreeing to this proposal, the French . . . intensified their terrorist activities against the Viet Minh members that before fleeing they massacred a great number of our political prisoners detained at Yen Bay and Cao Bang. . . . From the autumn of 1940, our country had in fact ceased to be a French colony and had become a Japanese possession. After the Japanese had surrendered to the Allies, our whole people rose to regain our national sovereignty and to found the Democratic Republic of Vietnam. The truth is that we have wrested our independence from the Japanese and not from the French. The French have fled, the Japanese have capitulated, Em-peror Bao Dai has abdicated. Our people have broken the chains which for nearly a century have fettered them and have won independence for the Fatherland. Our people at the same time have overthrown the monarchic regime that has reigned supreme for dozens of centuries. In its place has been established the present Democratic Republic. For these reasons, we, members of the Provisional Government, representing the whole Vietnam-ese people, declare that from now on we break off all relations of a colonial character with France; we repeal all the international obligation that France has so far subscribed to on behalf of Vietnam; and we abolish all the special rights the French have unlawfully acquired in our Fatherland. The whole Vietnamese people, animated by a common purpose, are determined to fight to the bitter end against any attempt by the French colonialists to reconquer their country. We are convinced that the Allied nations which at Tehran and San Francisco have acknowledged the principles of self-determination and equality of nations will not refuse to acknowledge the independence of Vietnam. A people who have courageously opposed French domination for more than eighty years, a people who have fought side by side with the

Allies against the Fascists during these last years, such a people must be free and independent. For these reasons, we, members of the Provisional Government of the Democratic Republic of Vietnam, solemnly declare to the world that Vietnam has the right to be a free and independent country and in fact it is so already. The entire Vietnamese people are determined to mobilize all their physical and mental strength, to sacrifice their lives and property in order to safeguard their independence and liberty.

2 September 1945

Appendix B: Letter from Ho Chi Minh to President Harry S Truman

In an attempt to solicit support from the U.S. government during the late 1940s, Ho Chi Minh presented President Harry S Truman a total of seven cablegrams to explain his cause. Below is an excerpt from the first one, sent on February 16, 1946:

I avail myself of this opportunity to thank you and the people of the United States for the interest shown by your representatives at the United Nations organization in favor of the dependent peoples.

Our VIET NAM people, as early as 1941, stood by the Allies' side and fought against the Japanese and their associates, the French colonialists. . . . We request of the United States as guardians and champions of World Justice to take a decisive step in support of our independence.

What we ask has been graciously granted to the Philippines. Like the Philippines our goal is full independence and full cooperation profitable to the whole world . . .

Ho Chi Minh 16 February 1946

Press conference reply of President Dwight D. Eisenhower to a request to comment on the importance of Indochina to the free world:

First . . . you have the specific value of a locality in its production of materials that the world needs . . . you have the possibility that many human beings pass under a dictatorship that is inimical to the free world. Finally, you have broader considerations that might follow what you would call the

"falling domino" principle. You have a row of dominoes set up, you knock over the first one, and what will happen to the last one is the certainty that it will go over very quickly. So you could have a beginning of a disintegration that would have the most profound influences. . . . So, the possible consequences of the loss are just incalculable to the free world.
April 7, 1954[1]

NOTE

1. G. Porter and S. Loory, *Vietnam: The Definitive Documentation of Human Decisions* (Stanfordville: Coleman Enterprises, 1979), 6.

Appendix C: American Casualties in the Viet Nam War

		Deaths	Wounded (Seriously)
Total men served	2,750,000	58,194	153,303
Total women served	7–11,000*	8	27

Viet Nam War casualties by race or ethnicity (nonofficers only):

Group	Percentage of Population (1968)	Died in Viet Nam	Percentage of Combat Deaths
Caucasian	82.7**	42,490	80.3
African American	11.0	7,115	14.1
Native American	0.5	219	0.003
Hispanic	4.5	2,513	5.5
Asian American	1.0	343	0.006

(*Source*: U.S. Department of Defense data base computer tape released through the National Archives, 1994).

*The exact number of American women serving in Viet Nam is not known. Differences in casualty rates can be attributed to several factors. All enlisted men were given the Armed Forces Qualifications Test and scored into five categories: I and II (score 65 to 100), III and IV (score 10 to 64) and rejection for service (less than 10). Those scoring in categories I and II were given more technical assignments with reduced chance of seeing combat. A disproportionate number of nonwhites were sent to combat assignments especially in the earlier war years. The black percentage of combat deaths reached a high of 20 percent in 1966, after which President Lyndon B. Johnson ordered more equitable combat assignments. The data also reveal a slightly higher percentage of deaths for lower-income Americans: 16 percent higher rate for the lower 50 percent income than the upper 50 percent. The largest variable affecting death rate appears to be college education. College entrance exam scores as well as motivation to go to college were the largest social factor affecting combat service in Viet Nam. College students or graduates had a greater chance of avoiding combat in Viet Nam.

**Some sources include Hispanic veterans as "white," thus raising the percentage of Caucasians to 87 percent.

Military Involvement and Casualties by Year in Viet Nam (Number As of December 31):

Year*	U.S. Personnel	Total Deaths: All Causes	Other Data**
1950	35	1	Total cost to U.S.: $189 billion
1954	462	3	Draft evaders: 570,000
1960	900	8	Convicted: 8,750
1961	3,205	24	U.S. medals of honor: 237
1962	9,000	77	Defoliated land: 5.2 million acres
1963	16,500	195	Vietnamese deaths: 3 million
1964	23,300	401	
1965	184,300	2,265	
1966	385,300	8,409	
1967	485,600	19,562	
1968	536,100	36,151	
4/30/69	543,400 (peak)	—	
12/31/69	475,200	47,765	
1970	334,600	53,849	
1971	239,200	56,205	
1972	24,200	56,845	
1973	240	57,011	
1975	0	58,202	

Missing in action: A total of 1,994 Americans are still listed as missing as of September 18, 2000.

Prisoners of war: A total of 740 U.S. military personnel and civilians were known to be captured. Of those, 28 escaped, 64 were released early, 80 died in captivity, and 568 were released in 1973. Source: Mike McGrath, president, Nam–POW Corporation, http://www.nampows.org.

Source: U.S. Department of Defense official records.

**Source*: Edward Doyle, and Samuel Lipsmann, eds., *The Vietnam Experience: Setting the Stage* (Boston: Boston Publishing, 1981).

Appendix D: Post-Traumatic Stress Disorder

The estimated occurrence of post-traumatic stress disorder among American Vietnam veterans is 30.9 percent for men and 26.9 percent for women. An additional 22.5 percent of men and 21.2 percent of women have had partial post-traumatic stress disorder at some point in their lives.

Forty percent of Vietnam theater veteran men have been divorced at least once (10 percent with two or more divorces), 14.1 percent report high levels of marital problems, and 23.1 percent have high levels of parental problems. Almost half of male Vietnam theater veterans currently suffering from post-traumatic stress disorder have been arrested or in jail at least once—34.2 percent more than once—and 11.5 percent have been convicted of a felony. The estimated lifetime prevalence of alcohol abuse or dependence among male theater veterans is 39.2 percent, and the estimate for current alcohol abuse or dependence is 11.2 percent. The estimated lifetime prevalence of drug abuse or dependence among male theater veterans is 5.7 percent, and the estimate for current drug abuse or dependence is 1.8 percent.[1]

NOTE

1. Richard A. Kulka et al., *Trauma and the Vietnam War Generation: Report of Findings from the National Vietnam Veterans Readjustment Study* (New York: Brunner/Mazel, 1990); Ronald C. Kessler et al., "Post Traumatic Stress Disorder in the National Comorbidity," *Survey Archives of General Psychiatry*, 52 (December 1995): 1048–1060.

Glossary

Buddhism: A religion representing the beliefs of Siddhartha Gautama of India. Buddhism spread to Viet Nam in 189 A.D. The Vietnamese practice a type of Buddhism called Mahayana. Buddhism is a way to achieve nirvana, or a state of perpetual peace. It stresses that desire is the cause of human suffering. There are four "noble truths" that recommend a path between self-denial and self-indulgence.

Geneva Conferences: The first, held in 1954, attempted to facilitate the withdrawal of French forces after their defeat at Dien Bien Phu. The agreement led to a temporary line between French-controlled Viet Nam and those Viet Minh troops that held most of the northern part of Viet Nam. Controversy about the accords rages to this day as many members did not sign it, thus adding ambiguity to its legitimacy.

Gook: Derogatory term for Vietnamese used by Americans. Although the true origin is debated, it is probably a term originated by U.S. troops in Korea, derived from the Korean *Dong Guk*. *Dong Guk* refers to the "people of the East," and the term *Guk* is usually associated with Korean peasants or villagers.

Ho Chi Minh (1890–1969): "Bac Ho," or Uncle Ho as he is still called today, rose to leadership in the Viet Minh and later of the Democratic Republic of Viet Nam. Ho lived the life of a monk in many respects, never married, and always claimed that he was Vietnamese first and Communist second. His rule also left thousands dead in riots and revolts against his harsh economic measures in the 1950s. Ho is credited with inspiring Vietnamese resistance to the Japanese, French, and Americans.

Kampuchea: Formerly called "Cambodia," Kampuchea was a neutral country next to Viet Nam and the scene of political unrest and instability. People's Army of Viet Nam and People's Liberation Army forces routinely used Cambodia for sanctuary and for travel down the Ho Chi Minh Trail. Both sides violated Cambodian neutrality, and U.S. attempts to bomb, or cut, the trail were unsuccesful.

Khmer Rouge: The Khmer Rouge seized power in Cambodia in 1975 after years of insurrection. Thousands were executed in mass purges. The chaos finally ended as People's Army of Viet Nam forces invaded Cambodia in 1978 and destroyed most of the Khmer forces.

Montagnards: French reference to the many tribes of people inhabiting the mountainous regions of western and central Viet Nam. Their origins are different from Vietnamese, and most anthropologists consider them to be of Austroasiatic and/or Malayo–Polynesian origins. Long-standing hostility between them and the Vietnamese was manipulated by U.S. forces, and many were hired as mercenaries in the U.S. fight against the Communists.

My Lai: A hamlet in Quang Ngai Province, My Lai was the scene of the slaughter of 504 civilians by U.S. forces in 1968. "My Lai," means "beautiful fields" in Vietnamese.

Phoenix Program: A program begun in late 1968 as an attempt to identify and destroy the National Liberation Front (NLF) infrastructure. Plagued with corruption, murder, and torture, the Central Intelligence Agency–led program was eventually ended in 1972. After the war, high-ranking Vietnamese leaders claimed that the Phoenix Program had decimated NLF forces, although many innocents were murdered and tortured as well.

War Powers Act: Passed in November 1973 over the veto of then-President Richard M. Nixon, the War Powers Act attempted to resolve the issue of presidential authority in using the U.S. armed forces overseas in times of conflict. The act has been generally ignored by U.S. presidents since, and its constitutionality is sometimes questioned.

Index

About the Author

ROBERT E. VADAS is Associate Professor in the Department of Education at State University of New York, Potsdam. He started researching the Viet Nam War as a high school student in Cleveland in the 1960s. He was drafted in the early 1970s. Vadas now teaches a course on Viet Nam and every year takes his students there.